SEATTLE

THE MINI ROUGH GUIDE

D0448747

There are more than one hundred Rough
Guide travel, phrasebook, and music titles,
covering destinations from Amsterdam to
Zimbabwe, languages from Czech to Thai,
and musics from World to Opera and Jazz

Forthcoming titles include

Bangkok • Barbados • Japan
Jordan • Syria • Music USA
Country Music

Rough Guides on the Internet

Rough Guide Credits

Text editor: Andrew Rosenberg. Series editor: Mark Ellingham
Typesetting: Judy Pang, Helen Ostick
Cartography: Melissa Flack, Maxine Burke

Publishing Information

This first edition published July 1998 by
Rough Guides Ltd, 1 Mercer St, London WC2H 9QJ.

Distributed by the Penguin Group:

Penguin Books Ltd, 27 Wrights Lane, London W8 5TZ
Penguin Books USA Inc., 375 Hudson Street, New York 10014, USA
Penguin Books Australia Ltd, 487 Maroondah Highway,
PO Box 257, Ringwood, Victoria 3134, Australia
Penguin Books Canada Ltd, 10 Alcorn Avenue,
Toronto, Ontario, Canada M4V 1E4
Penguin Books (NZ) Ltd, 182–190 Wairau Road,
Auckland 10, New Zealand

Typeset in Bembo and Helvetica to an original design by Henry Iles.
Printed in Spain by Graphy Cems.

ISBN 1-85828-324-8

SEATTLE

THE MINI ROUGH GUIDE

by Richie Unterberger

We set out to do something different when the first Rough Guide was published in 1982. Mark Ellingham, just out of university, was traveling in Greece. He brought along the popular guides of the day, but found they were all lacking in some way. They were either strong on ruins and museums but went on for pages without mentioning a beach or taverna. Or they were so conscious of the need to save money that they lost sight of Greece's cultural and historical significance. Also, none of the books told him anything about Greece's contemporary life – its politics, its culture, its people, and how they lived.

So with no job in prospect, Mark decided to write his own guidebook, one which aimed to provide practical information that was second to none, detailing the best beaches and the hottest clubs and restaurants, while also giving hard-hitting accounts of every sight, both famous and obscure, and providing up-to-the-minute information on contemporary culture. It was a guide that encouraged independent travelers to find the best of Greece, and was a great success, getting shortlisted for the Thomas Cook travel guide award, and encouraging Mark, along with three friends, to expand the series.

The Rough Guide list grew rapidly and the letters flooded in, indicating a much broader readership than had been anticipated, but one which uniformly appreciated the Rough Guide mix of practical detail and humor, irreverence and enthusiasm. Things haven't changed. The same four friends who began the series are still the caretakers of the Rough Guide mission today: to provide the most reliable, up-to-date and entertaining information to independent-minded travelers of all ages, on all budgets.

We now publish more than 100 titles and have offices in London and New York. The travel guides are written and researched by a dedicated team of more than 100 authors, based in Britain, Europe, the USA and Australia. We have also created a unique series of phrasebooks to accompany the travel series, along with an acclaimed series of music guides, and a best-selling pocket guide to the Internet and World Wide Web. We also publish comprehensive travel information on our Web site: **http://www.roughguides.com**

Help Us Update

We've gone to a lot of effort to ensure that this first edition of *The Rough Guide to Seattle* is as up to date and accurate as possible. However, if you feel there are places we've underrated or over-praised, or find we've missed something good or covered something which has now gone, then please write: suggestions, comments or corrections are much appreciated.

We'll credit all contributions, and send a copy of the next edition (or any other Rough Guide if you prefer) for the best letters. Please mark letters: "Rough Guide Seattle Update" and send to:

Rough Guides, 1 Mercer St, London WC2H 9QJ, or
Rough Guides, 375 Hudson St, 9th floor, New York NY 10014.

Or send email to: mail@roughguides.co.uk
Online updates about this book can be found on
Rough Guides' Web site (see opposite)

The Author

Richie Unterberger has contributed to several Rough Guides, including the *Rough Guide to Rock*, the *Rough Guide to the Pacific Northwest*, and the *Rough Guide to the USA*. He recently wrote *Unkown Legends of Rock'n'Roll*, and he is currently working on the *Rough Guide to Music USA*, a music and travel guide to be published in 1999. During his increasingly brief respites from the road, he lives in San Francisco.

Acknowledgements

Thanks most of all to Jack Thompson and Carrie Chambers Thompson for their hospitality and helpful pointers during all my Seattle visits. Special thanks, too, to Ruth and Bob Kildall for their excellent accommodations, expert advice, and generous friendship. Also to Bill Tilland for sharing his knowledge of Vashon Island and providing general all-around assistance; Paul Mailman for the coffee and restaurant tips; Darek Mazzone for guidance through the Seattle club/dance scene; Dave Rauh and Toni Holm for their help in Olympia; Scott Jackson and VJ Beauchamp for providing lodgings and good company in Portland; Janet Rosen and Stuart Kremsky, for housesitting and valuable feedback; and Robert Shepard, agent and friend. Also, everyone at the Rough Guides who helped see this book through, particularly editor Andrew Rosenberg for his many hours of dedication to refining and improving the guide, and to Martin Dunford for helping to get the project off the ground.

CONTENTS

INTRODUCTION

Hip **Seattle**, commercial and cultural star of the Pacific Northwest, is one of America's most liveable cities – and looking around it's not hard to see why. Surrounded by water, densely packed with scenic hills and tree-lined streets, and with snow-capped mountains visible in almost every direction, it's a rare urban environment, in which outdoor-style living has not been sacrificed for cosmopolitan culture. Its central core, narrowly saved from the wrecking ball by popular outcry, has been converted to colorful historic districts that also happen to hold the best in the city's arts, shopping and nightlife. Unfortunately for its long-time residents, who value the tight-knit communities and sensible urban planning that have made this possible, the secret is out, and the subsequent increases in tourism, development, and population have begun to cause trouble in paradise.

Indeed until recently Seattle was seen as something of a cultural backwater by the rest of the country, tucked into a remote corner of the continental United States, nearly a thousand miles from the closest major American city. Its years as a thriving port, relying on the timber industry for its well-being, did little for its national image; neither did its role as home to the enormous University of Washington, or hosting a world's fair – even one which left Seattle with its most prominent icon, the **Space Needle**. The city did not hit the big time until the 1980s and early 1990s, when a few key companies, and the subcultures they generated, made it a household name. It was then that Seattle turned coffee consumption into an art form, and with it, a local purveyor, **Starbucks**, became a national phenomenon; and the success of computer giant **Microsoft** has made the metropolitan area a breeding ground for high-tech communications outfits. Perhaps equally important, at least in public perception, was the advent of **grunge music**, with Seattle as its nominal birthplace, which led to the meteoric rise of bands such as Nirvana and Pearl Jam.

For all its new status, though, Seattle is not a large, nor incredibly happening, city, and those expecting the throbbing pulse of New York or Tokyo will definitely be underwhelmed. While its **museums** are reasonable, its **theater scene** vibrant, and its **café culture** unmatchable, at least in the US, offering social centers where coffee drinking, avant-garde arts, and lively performance meld in one unpretentious pot, the overall mood is decidedly low-key, and Seattle, more than most places, takes time to fully appreciate. In fact, it's best experienced on an itinerary that puts as much emphasis on nature hikes, neighborhood strolls and ferry rides as it does sightseeing and nightlife – the city is the departure point for ferries to the wooded islands of the **Puget Sound** and the more remote (and more beguiling) **San Juan Islands**.

There is, of course, a downside to the city. Seattle has a reputation as the teenage runaway capital, along with a correspondingly high level of homelessness. Meanwhile, the recent influx of people has brought commuter traffic to a standstill in some places, and civic ambitions have spurred far-reaching development projects that threaten to tear at the very fabric of Seattle's inherent small-town nature. In a way, that's part of the excitement of Seattle – which, perhaps more than any other US metropolis, is still in the process of defining itself.

When to visit

Seattle tourist authorities proudly note that the town ranks 44th among US cities as far as **rainfall** goes, somewhat belying its reputation as the cloud capital of the US. Still, the reputation is mostly deserved: it's not the quantity of the rain, but its regularity – in the fall, winter, sometimes even spring, drizzly days can pile upon one another endlessly, and when it's not raining, it's often overcast.

Despite this, Seattle's never really that cold, even in the middle of winter. **Summers** are lovely – the average monthly rainfall in July and August hovers around just one inch, the skies often sunny, but almost never scorching. For this reason, you should consider defying conventional traveler wisdom about peak season. Mid-summer may be the most crowded time of year, but it's also undeniably the best, both for the weather and the numerous fine festivals. Accommodations can get tight, but with enough advance planning you should be fine. If you want a bit more breathing space, May, June and September are all recommended, although the weather won't be quite as warm, or as dry. Any time outside of those parameters, you risk one of the city's wet spells, though even in the coldest months there's still plenty going on to keep you occupied.

Seattle's climate

	°F Average daily		°C Average daily		Rainfall Average monthly	
	max	min	max	min	in	mm
Jan	46	37	8	3	5.4	137
Feb	49	38	9	3	4.0	101
March	53	40	12	4	3.8	96
April	59	44	15	7	2.5	63
May	66	49	19	9	1.9	48
June	70	53	21	12	1.7	43
July	75	56	24	13	0.9	23
Aug	74	56	23	13	1.2	30
Sept	69	53	21	12	2.0	51
Oct	60	48	16	9	3.2	81
Nov	52	42	11	6	5.6	142
Dec	48	40	9	4	6.0	152

THE GUIDE

INTRODUCING THE CITY

Roughly speaking, Seattle has an hourglass shape, quite skinny in its central section and widening to the north and south, with water pretty much all around. To the west of the city is the **Puget Sound**, a finger-shaped inland waterway that extends about a hundred miles from its northern entrance to its southern tip; downtown lies on the **Elliott Bay** portion of the sound. Seattle is separated from its eastern suburbs by **Lake Washington**, which is connected to the Puget Sound by the **Lake Washington Ship Canal**, a narrow waterway that, at various points, widens into Portage Bay, Union Bay, and Lake Union. Boats – and salmon – can exit the canal into the Puget Sound through the **Hiram M. Chittenden Locks** in Ballard, at the western edge of **Salmon Bay.**

  Downtown contains many of the city's top attractions, particularly **Pike Place Market**, the best open-air urban market in the US; **Pioneer Square**, Seattle's oldest district; the

waterfront, where ferries depart for destinations throughout the Sound; and the **Seattle Art Museum.** Just south of downtown is the **International District**, aka Chinatown, none too lively and falling short of most other US Chinatowns in terms of allure. A mile or so north of downtown is the **Seattle Center**, a large complex of theaters, sports arenas, and leftovers from the 1962 World's Fair, like the **Space Needle**. Between downtown and Seattle Center is **Belltown**, one of the city's several hip, youthful neighborhoods.

The I-5 highway divides downtown from **Capitol Hill**, the neighborhood with the best combination of residential streets, shopping, and nightlife; it's also home to much of the city's gay population. North of here, bridges across the ship canal lead to the **University District** ("U District"), dominated by the campus of the **University of Washington** and its main thoroughfare of student life, **University Way**. Just west of here, **Fremont** is the city's most unpretentiously bohemian corner; north of Fremont, the **Woodland Park Zoo** is an excellent family outing, as is nearby landlocked **Green Lake**. Less affluent **Ballard** is known for its previously mentioned Locks; across the canal from Ballard, **Magnolia** contains Seattle's best open space, **Discovery Park.**

The western border of **Lake Washington** runs through some of Seattle's prettiest areas; on its eastern side are a few suburbs, the most interesting of which is **Bellevue**. In Seattle's southern industrial section is the first-rate **Museum of Flight**, while **Alki Beach**, in West Seattle, is separated from downtown by the industrial area of Elliott Bay's Harbor Island.

To get the most out of a visit to Seattle, it's necessary to get on a ferry and explore some of the Puget Sound; any of its islands make for a good excursion. **Vashon Island**, **Bainbridge Island**, and **Whidbey Island** are the closest, while to their north, the **San Juan Islands** – actually in the strait of San Juan de Fuca – are justly renowned as some of the most scenic spots in the Northwest. Landlocked options include the cities of **Tacoma** and **Olympia**, neither too much to look at, though 25 miles east of the city, **Snoqualmie Falls** offers spectacular natural scenery.

The telephone code for Seattle is ©206.

Arrival

All points of arrival into Seattle, whether by **air**, **bus**, or **train**, are fairly convenient to the city center – the airport is a bit outside of town, but there are plenty of cheap and easy ways to make it in from there. If you're coming by **car**, be prepared for traffic and a tough time parking.

By air

The **Sea-Tac Airport** (©431-4444 or 1-800/544-1965), fourteen miles south of downtown, is compact and easy to navigate. Four large concourses and two satellite terminals are connected to the main terminal via swift underground trains. Baggage claim is on the lower level of the main terminal, and there's a small **visitor's information kiosk** in front of baggage carousel 8. If you're using public parking in the garage across from the main terminal, rates are $2 per forty minutes.

Several **car rental** firms have counters in the baggage claim area, with pickup and dropoff on the first floor of the garage across from the main terminal; other companies have branches elsewhere in the airport and operate shuttles to their pickup points. **Buses** to Seattle leave from the north end of the baggage claim area. The cheapest option is the local Metro bus #194 ($1.10, $1.60 during peak hours). The Gray Line Airport Express bus drops off at major

ARRIVAL

hotels downtown (6am–11.30pm every 20min; $7.50), while Shuttle Express has door-to-door service downtown (©622-1424 or 1-800/487-RIDE; $18, $6 for second guest, $4 for each additional guest). **Taxis** charge about $25 for the downtown–airport route.

By train

Trains from all around arrive at the **Amtrak** station, at 3rd Avenue and Jackson Street near the International District (©382-4125 or 1-800/872-7245). It's about a dozen blocks from here to the city center; just to the east along Jackson Street, the International District Station is a hub for frequent Metro buses going downtown.

By bus

Greyhound is at 8th Avenue and Stewart Street (©628-5526 or 1-800/231-2222), on the eastern edge of downtown, just a fifteen- or twenty-minute walk from most downtown accommodation; Seattle is a fairly big hub of bus activity in the Northwest. Green Tortoise does two runs per week along the Seattle–San Francisco route, with stops in most sizable towns along the way; it drops off and picks up at 9th Avenue and Stewart Street (©1-800/867-8647).

By car

If you're driving, you'll most likely arrive on I-5, the main north–south highway connecting Northern California and Canada; from the east you'll probably arrive via I-90, which runs from Seattle to central Washington. The downtown exits (164-167) come fast and furious; keep alert for off-ramps onto Stewart or Union streets for downtown.

ARRIVAL

Information and maps

The **Seattle-King County Visitor's Bureau**, inside the Washington State Convention Center at 7th Avenue and Pike Street (Mon–Fri 8.30am–5pm, Sat & Sun 10am–4pm), has hundreds of free brochures on Seattle and Washington state, plus copies of free basic maps and alternative weekly papers, and complimentary magazines geared toward the tourist trade. There's a wallful of free bus maps in the hall outside the bureau, opposite the Gray Line counter. The staff is friendly, though most suggestions are fairly mainstream; it can also help with accommodations, though it's best to arrange for the first night or two in advance instead of just turning up here.

The free official travelers' guide, *Washington State Lodging and Travel Guide* (call ©1-800/544-1800 for a copy), has a comprehensive list of the state's accommodations. If you're going to be here for an extended length of time, Theresa Morrow's *Seattle Survival Guide* (Sasquatch) can't be beat for insider information.

Seattle's sometimes confusing street layout makes detailed maps highly advisable; the color ones at the back of this guide will suffice for city areas, but if you're venturing into the more remote edges, look into comprehensive maps, such as the free American Automobile Association (AAA; or the British AA or RC), only available to members; pick up a copy at the AAA office near Seattle Center at 330 6th Ave N (Mon–Fri 9am–5pm). Otherwise, Rand-McNally's Seattle-Bellevue map is a good option ($2.95). Specialized **hiking** and **trail** guides, very useful in the mountainous and scenic Puget Sound region, are carried by most bookstores and camping/outdoors shops.

The **Seattle CityPass** ($23.75) covers admission to the Seattle Art Museum, Seattle Aquarium, Pacific Science Center, Space Needle, Museum of Flight, and Woodland Park Zoo Public, and costs half of what it would to visit all six places at regular prices. It can be purchased at the first participating attraction visited.

Newspapers and magazines

Seattle's daily papers mostly pale in comparison with the best ones in the east; fortunately, the city is awash in alternative tabloids and arts magazines, most of them free. The city's two daily **newspapers** are the *Seattle Post-Intelligencer* (50¢), which comes out in the morning and is simply called "the *P-I*" by locals, and the *Seattle Times* (50¢), published in the afternoons; the pair are combined for a single large Sunday edition ($2), and both have worked under a joint operating agreement since 1983. Each puts out weekly entertainment supplements (Thursday's *Datebook* in the *Times*; Friday's *What's Happening* in the *P-I*) that include comprehensive listings, though better are the free alternative weeklies *The Stranger* and the *Seattle Weekly*, both available throughout the city in cafés, bookstores, and newspaper boxes.

Seattle cafés and bookstores are also stacked with local neighborhood and arts publications: some of the better ones include the *Seattle Press*, a biweekly covering many overlooked neighborhood issues, and *Seattle Gay News* (25¢), with good features and events listings. There's also *The Rocket*, a biweekly covering the Northwest music scene; *Resonance*, an alternative music bimonthly with some coverage of other art forms; *Aorta*, a bimonthly on the local arts scene; and *Voltage*, a bimonthly dedicated to extremely underground music and apocalypse culture.

The Internet

Seattle, home to Microsoft and many other telecommunications powers, is one of the most **Internet**-savvy places in the world. Many businesses in the Seattle area now have their own Web pages, and the number of such establishments is growing quickly. If you have the time and access,

SEATTLE ON THE INTERNET

Art Access
www.artaccess.com
Artist profiles, exhibit reviews, and local venues.

City of Seattle
www.ci.seattle.wa.us
Comprehensive visitor information site, sponsored by the city, with links to most everything you need.

Pandemonium
www.seattlesquare.com/pandemonium
Band biographies and complete concert listings for local alternative music.

Riderlink
www.riderlink.gen.wa.us
Information on every type of transportation option in the greater Seattle area.

Sidewalk Seattle
www.seattle.sidewalk.com
As brought to you by Microsoft, a good place to find nightlife and entertainment listings.

Speakeasy
www.speakeasy.org
This café's Web site serves up local jazz, literary happenings, and a list of specialty indie bookstores.

The Stranger
www.thestranger.com
Alternative weekly with a good online events calendar, from avant-garde theater to dance clubs.

you can do plenty of prep work before your trip. Some good starting points are described in the box on p.9, while a number of Internet addresses are included throughout the text of this guide.

If you want to get online during your stay for either business or pleasure purposes, it won't be hard, even if you don't have your laptop along. There are plenty of **cybercafés**, not to mention regular cafés that happen to have a terminal or two; see listings on p.162 for some of your better options.

City transport

Seattle's downtown is easy to cover by **walking**, the **buses** are frequent and well run by US standards, and most of the more interesting neighborhoods are pretty close to one another. There are, however, substantial drawbacks: steep hills challenge weak knees both downtown and elsewhere, traffic is surprisingly horrendous at peak hours, and some areas are not well served by public transportation, especially at night.

A street guide

Whatever your mode of transportation, it's essential to familiarize yourself with a few basics of Seattle's confusing streetplan, whereby most addresses are preceded or followed by a direction (ie 13th Ave E, or NW 67th St). The location of something on 2nd Avenue W, for instance, could be a good five miles or so from an address on 2nd Avenue S. Furthermore, some streets, particularly in central Seattle, are not tagged with a direction at all.

Thoroughfares running east–west are usually designated as Streets, with the direction at the beginning of the address (ie 77 N 18th St), while those running north–south are usually designated Avenues, with the direction following the address (ie 304 6th Ave SE); there are also streets that are Ways, Places, or what have you: the direction affixed varies according to whether it runs east–west or north–south.

Metro

Seattle's mass transit system is the **Metro** (℡553-3000), which runs bus routes throughout the city and King County, extending into the Eastside suburbs across Lake Washington, and south to the airport. In general it's efficient and pleasurable, with frequent service between downtown and Capitol Hill and the University District, and (to a lesser extent) downtown and Fremont/Ballard.

Metro's best feature is its **downtown ride-free area**, bounded by Battery Street, S Jackson Street, 6th Avenue, and the waterfront. From 6am to 7pm daily, rides beginning and ending within this zone are free. (The free scheme does *not* apply, however, to the waterfront streetcars running from Pier 70 to the International District.) If you're taking advantage of the free rides, you'll save time by using the 1.3-mile **Metro Tunnel**, which runs buses on underground streets, thus avoiding traffic lights and the sudden lurches and stops that define the inner-city bus-riding experience. The tunnel has five stations, all in busy downtown areas (Convention Place, Westlake Center, University Street, Pioneer Square, and the International District), and is open weekdays 6am to 7pm, Saturdays from 10am to 6pm; when it's closed, tunnel routes operate on 3rd Avenue.

Fares are 85¢ off-peak, $1.10 peak (Mon–Fri 6–9am & 3–6pm); if you're taking a "two-zone" ride that takes you outside the city limits (for instance, from downtown to the airport), the prices rise to $1.10 off-peak and $1.60 peak. If you board within the downtown ride-free area and get off outside of the free zone boundaries, you pay when

CITY TRANSPORT

USEFUL BUS ROUTES

#2, **3**, and **4** From downtown to Seattle Center and Queen Anne.

#10 From downtown to Capitol Hill, along Pine St and 19th Ave E.

#12 From downtown to Capitol Hill, along Madison and 19th Ave E.

#17 From downtown to Ballard and the Hiram M. Chittenden Locks.

#19 From downtown to Magnolia and Discovery Park.

#26, **28**, and **29** From downtown to Fremont.

#27 From downtown to Lake Washington Blvd, Leschi Park, and Colman Park.

#37 From downtown to Alki Beach via Harbor Ave and Alki Ave, then through West Seattle along Beach Drive to Lincoln Park.

#43 From downtown to University District, via E John St, 23rd Ave E, and 24th Ave E in Capitol Hill.

#71, **72**, and **73** From downtown to University District, including frequent express buses from about 7am to 7pm weekdays.

#99 Waterfront streetcar, from the International District through Pioneer Square to Pier 70.

#174 and **194** From Sea-Tac Airport to downtown.

you get *off*, not when you get *on*. (Bus operators routinely drive in the ride-free area with their hand covering the collection box to prevent accidental payment.) That means fare collection works on an honor system of sorts when you travel from the ride-free area to other neighborhoods. If you board outside of the free zone, however, you simply pay as you get on, whether or not downtown is your final destination. Transfers are valid for about one hour after they're issued. Day passes for $1.70 are available for weekends and holidays only; buy them from the driver.

Pick up a map or a schedule at the visitors' bureau, libraries, shopping centers, and Metro Tunnel stations. The customer service offices also dispense free copies of the large *Metro Transit System Map*, although this is such a densely packed grid that you're better off picking up the pocket-sized schedules of the routes you plan to travel frequently.

If you'll be in town for a while, you may want to pick up a **pass** or **ticketbook**. Passes are available in one-month, three-month, and twelve-month varieties; the monthly pass costs $39.50 (one-zone peak), $57.50 (two-zone peak), $30.50 (one-zone off-peak), or $39.50 (two-zone off-peak). You can get a book of ten or twenty tickets, but it doesn't save you anything except time. Passes and ticketbooks are sold at Metro customer service offices and most *Bartell Drug* stores.

The monorail

Built for the World's Fair in the early 1960s, the **monorail** that connects Seattle Center with the Westlake Center shopping mall downtown isn't of much use unless you need to get from downtown to Seattle Center in a flash. Then it's *very* useful, though you shouldn't gear up for a thrilling or particularly scenic hi-tech ride: with no stops on the route, the journey takes just two minutes or so from start to finish. Trains run every 15 minutes from 9am to 11pm daily, and cost $1 each way.

Incidentally, a light rail system running throughout Seattle and much of the Puget Sound region, *Link*, projected to cost nearly $2 billion, is scheduled for completion in 2004, though fears of cost overruns and the environmental impact of a tunnel in Capitol Hill may change some of the plans.

Taxis

It's been reported that one of the biggest cab companies in Seattle has 190 **taxis** on duty, and delivers nearly three mil-

CITY TRANSPORT

lion passengers a year, though visitors will have a hard time believing it. Taxis are usually hard to find here, and have comparatively high fares. Nonetheless, there are times when you'll want to use them, particularly if you're out clubbing in downtown areas that can get a bit dubious after midnight, or in a neighborhood where bus service becomes infrequent or nonexistent after the early evening. The more reliable companies include Broadway Cab (℡622-4800), Graytop Cab (℡282-8222), and Yellow Cab (℡622-6500). Fares for the big outfits have standardized at $1.80 for the meter drop, and $1.80 for each mile. Be wary of unmarked, unregulated private cabs, which can rip you off badly.

Driving

A **car** isn't vital to reach most of Seattle's worthwhile sections; traffic is a nightmare; and sometimes streets become one-way or lanes become right-turn-only with practically no warning. Still, if you're going to do a lot of hopping around, having a vehicle is quite convenient.

Parking downtown is tough, with virtually all of the spaces metered ($1/hr) from 8am to 6pm, and $20 tickets routinely imposed after your time runs out. Capitol Hill and the University District are not as heavily metered, but space is still at a premium. If you're going to park in a lot, downtown rates start at about $5 for the first hour, and can rise to as high as $15/day. For late afternoon/evening times, the Public Market Parking Garage under Pike Place Market, 1531 Western Ave, has an evening rate of $1 per hour after 4pm, and remains open until 11pm every day but Sunday. In residential neighborhood blocks, things get a lot more manageable, but even there weekday restrictions apply on how long you can leave the vehicle in one spot (usually two hours).

Ferries

If you do any traveling outside of the city during your visit, particularly into the Puget Sound, you'll likely be using **ferries** quite often. Most routes are run by Washington

MAJOR PUGET SOUND FERRY ROUTES

Seattle–Bainbridge Island Departs from Pier 52 at least hourly from 6.20am to 11.15pm, also boats at 12.50am and 2.10am; 35min; foot passengers $3.50 round-trip, vehicle and driver $11.80 round-trip, $14.20 peak season.

Downtown Seattle–Vashon Departs from Pier 50 (passenger-only); eight per day Mon–Fri 6am–8.15pm, six Sat 9.30am–11.30pm; no Sunday service; 25min; $3.50 round-trip.

Fauntleroy, West Seattle–Vashon Around every half-hour 5.30am–1.55am; 15min; foot passengers $2.30 round-trip, vehicle and driver $7.95 round-trip, $9.55 peak season.

Point Defiance–Tahlequah, Vashon Island 21 daily; 15min; foot passengers $2.30 round-trip, vehicle and driver $7.95 round-trip, $9.55 peak season.

Mukilteo–Clinton, Whidbey Island Departs Mukilteo, about thirty miles north of Seattle, and arrives on Whidbey Island 5am to 2am every half-hour; 20min; foot passengers $2.30 round-trip, vehicle and driver $8 round-trip, $9.60 peak season.

Anacortes–San Juan Islands To Lopez (45–55 min); Orcas (1hr 5min–1hr 25min); Friday Harbor (1hr 5min–2hr 10min). Fares are $4.95 for foot passengers regardless of destination; with car, $14.75 to Lopez from the peak season of mid-May to mid-Oct ($12.30 off-season), $17.65 to Orcas ($14.70 off-season), and $20.30 to Friday Harbor in San Juan Island peak season ($16.80 off-season). There's a $2.75 surcharge for bicycles, and fares are free for eastbound trips of any sort.

State Ferries (✆464-6400 or 1-800/84-FERRY; *www.wsdot.wa.gov/ferries*); schedules are available on the piers, and at many places throughout town, usually at the same locations that carry racks of Metro bus schedules. Timetables and fares do vary by the season, so it's best to pick up sailing/fare schedules before making plans.

Seattle tours

There are dozens of walking, boat, plane, and bike **tours** in Seattle. Before taking to the water for an organized cruise, though, consider that much the same view of the Seattle skyline and Puget Sound can be had for much less money on the local ferries.

Bus, biking, and walking tours

Chinatown Discovery Tours ✆236-0657. These take in lesser-known parts of the International District, such as a fortune cookie factory; also with customized tours for topics such as acupuncture or herbs.

Gray Line ✆626-5208 or 1-800/426-7532. Three-hour narrated tours of Seattle's most well-known attractions ($24); also a six-hour Grand City Tour ($33) is on offer daily at 10am from April 1 to October 15.

Terrene Tours ✆325-5569. Bike tours covering the Seattle region, from neighborhoods to island tours ($69–119). These are only offered from late spring through the early fall, but they do have customized and self-guided tours throughout the year.

Viewpoints ✆667-9186. Walking tours through the architectural highlights of several Seattle neighborhoods on selected Wednesday lunch hours and Saturday mornings (April–Oct; $7 Wed tours, $18 Sat tours).

Cruises and ferries

Argosy Cruises ℂ623-4252, *www.seattleonline.com/argosy*. They offer tours through most local waters, including a Harbor Cruise of Elliott Bay (1hr; $13.40), the Lake Cruise in Lake Washington and Lake Union (2 hr; $17.10), and the Locks Cruise (2hr 30min; $21.70).

Emerald City Charters ℂ624-3931. Sailboat trips from Pier 56 ($20–35), including sunset departures.

Specialty tours

Galvin Flying Service ℂ763-9706. Open cockpit biplane tours of various lengths, departing from Boeing Field in the south part of town: it ranges from a ten-minute whoosh over Capitol Hill to a 45-minute jaunt over Snoqualmie Falls ($49–225).

Private Eye on Seattle ℂ622-0590. Van tours through scenes-of-the-crime given by semi-retired private investigator Windsor Oldson (90min; $20).

DOWNTOWN SEATTLE

Downtown Seattle is undoubtedly the densest and busiest district of the American Northwest, its infrastructure barely able to accommodate the flow of land and sea traffic. Its borders are most easily defined as the **ride-free bus zone** from Jackson Street (bordering the Kingdome and the International District) to Battery Street (several blocks south of the Space Needle), and 6th Avenue in the east, where I-5 divides the city center from residential neighborhoods – quite a small area on the whole, though with a few towers, visible from miles around, that lend a touch of cosmopolitan drama.

Downtown is not, however, Seattle's most exciting quarter. Much is functional and drab, with the same proliferation of national chain department stores that afflicts every large US city. Less drab, but still depressing, is the high concentration of tawdry sex joints; there's also, somewhat predictably, the city's biggest homeless population, particularly toward the waterfront. Indeed, downtown is probably best appreciated from the water: the

skyline, taking in the landmarks of the Space Needle and Kingdome, may be the city's best feature and is certainly less impressive once you're in the midst of it all. But the cityscape is softened everywhere by views of Puget Sound, with its steady traffic of passenger ferries, pleasure boats and commercial vessels.

Still, downtown holds most of Seattle's mainstream tourist sights. **Pioneer Square** is the city's oldest and most historic district, as well as its most architecturally impressive, and it's a hotspot for nightlife. The large, recently constructed **Museum of Modern Art** has bolstered Seattle's cultural clout considerably, and the city's best galleries also dot the area. **Pike Place Market** is a great place to eat and shop, at least during daylight hours. Even the stiff **business district** holds sporadic appeal, principally the architecturally imposing structures of the 76-story **Columbia Seafirst Center** (the highest US building west of the Mississippi River), the **Smith Tower**, and the **Rainier Center**, one of the most oddly shaped skyscrapers to be found anywhere.

Whether you want to or not, you'll probably spend a fair amount of time here, as it's where much of the city's accommodations are based. Fortunately, a medium-sized walk – or short bus ride – away are the more happening neighborhoods of Belltown and Capitol Hill, as well as the Seattle Center. Downtown itself is compact and easily covered on foot too, though going east from the waterfront it can be quite hilly. If you get weary, you can always hop on any passing bus for free, as long as you observe the limits of the ride-free zone.

The area covered by this chapter is shown in detail on color map 3.

PIKE PLACE MARKET

Map 3, B3.

The best place to start your tour of downtown is **Pike Place Market**, ground zero of central Seattle's pedestrian life; any Seattle bus that passes through downtown will let you off within just a few blocks of the market, whose entrance is at 1st Avenue and Pike Street. Pike Place Market is a rarity in America, a thriving city-center market run and patronized by locals; indeed, if it weren't so busy, it might seem an anachronism. It's also huge, its dozen or so buildings covering several square blocks and encompassing some 250 produce and fish vendors, bakeries, craft stalls, and small retailers, many of whom grow or make what they sell (in fact, it's a requirement in the Main Arcade). There are numerous options for some of Seattle's cheapest ethnic eats, and you can also take in a meal at several restaurants offering views of Puget Sound, if you're prepared to both lay out a bit more cash and accept that the scenery will be considerably more impressive than the food.

Most of the customers buying produce and poultry are locals, attracted by the high-quality goods, affordable prices, and the rare experience of personal service. As a traveler you may be unlikely to fry up some fresh fish back at your hotel, but there's still plenty of produce and baked goods to choose from. And for every tacky souvenir-laden hole-in-the-wall in the bowels of the market, there's a genuinely interesting one as well, including Seattle's most prominent left-wing bookstore, a retailer of exotic musical instruments, and an outfit stocking condoms of all colors, designs, and flavors.

For the best shops in Pike Place Market – and elsewhere – see "Shopping," p.249.

The chief draw of Pike Place Market, however, lies more in its ambience: you come here not so much to buy as to browse and enjoy the buskers in the Main Arcade. It can get almost unbearably crowded on weekends and warm days, and parking can be difficult, making early morning the best time to come. With the exception of some restaurants, the market largely shuts down by 6pm, and it's best not to linger after dark. If you can stand the crowds and you're in town around Memorial Day, check out the market's annual **street fair**.

It's actually a miracle Pike Place Market exists at all. Established in 1907 as a way for local farmers to sell their products directly to the city's consumers, it was slated for demolition before noted local architect **Victor Steinbrueck** headed a campaign in the 1960s to save it, both for its turn-of-the-century buildings and to ensure that lower-income Seattleites had a place to buy affordable groceries. A "Keep the Market" initiative was approved by voters in 1971, paving the way for its restoration with the establishment of a Market Historical District in 1974.

No one's talking about tearing down the market today, but political intrigue continues to hover around its seven acres. There have been accusations that anti-Asian racism has been behind the eviction of some tenants, and speculation that some of the less commercial enterprises will find it difficult to keep their spaces. It's certainly true that the authorities would no doubt be pleased if the X-rated businesses near the market's entrances also packed up their tents, and some of those establishments have indeed left after their leases were not renewed.

Inside the market

There's an **information booth** on the traffic island at the 1st Avenue entrance; stacks of the free monthly *Pike Place*

Market News, which includes a map, are piled liberally throughout the buildings. A favorite meeting place is the **brass pig** in front of the Public Market Center sign at the very foot of Pike Street – not a sculpture but an actual piggy bank, with receipts going to various charities. Directly behind the pig, the **Pike Place Fish Company** is a prime spectator attraction, its workers raucously chanting signals like football quarterbacks and heaving fish ten to twenty feet through the air behind the counter for wrapping.

On the south side of the traffic island, the aisle of **Economy Row** has the Italian and Mediterranean delicacies of *DeLaurenti's* store and deli, plus an enormous international newsstand. Across the street in the **Corner Market**, the collectively run *Left Bank Books* is Pike Place's least commercial establishment and proud of it, stocking a wealth of political and feminist tracts, most of the left-wing variety. This area and nearby **Sanitary Market** have most of the top bakeries and food stalls.

The best action centers around the ground level of the **Main Arcade** (just to the right of the brass pig as you're facing the waterfront), with its dozens of produce stalls. Every Wednesday is Organic Farmers Day, when you can buy organic produce under canopies that are set up on the cobblestones of Pike Place itself. The crowds can get particularly claustrophobic as you proceed to the narrower, crafts-dominated **North Arcade**, clogged with stalls of jewelry, silkscreened shirts, and wooden carvings. Persevere for a minute or two and you emerge to reach **Victor Steinbrueck Park**, whose pleasantly modest, hilly patches overlooking Puget Sound are jammed on sunny days with a melange of tourists, lunching office workers, and downtrodden transients.

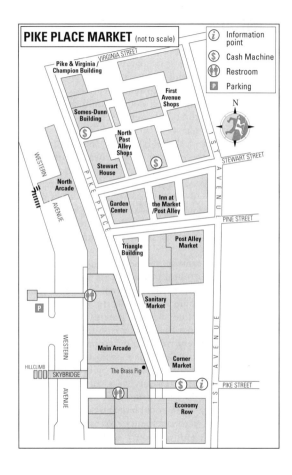

PIKE PLACE MARKET (not to scale)

(i)	Information point
(S)	Cash Machine
(restroom)	Restroom
P	Parking

VIRGINIA STREET

Pike & Virginia / Champion Building

First Avenue Shops

Somes-Dunn Building

North Post Alley Shops

1ST AVENUE

STEWART STREET

WESTERN

North Arcade

PIKE PLACE

Stewart House

Garden Center

Inn at the Market / Post Alley

PINE STREET

AVENUE

Triangle Building

Post Alley Market

P

Sanitary Market

Main Arcade

Corner Market

HILLCRIMB   SKYBRIDGE

The Brass Pig

1ST AVENUE

PIKE STREET

WESTERN

AVENUE

Economy Row

N

THE WATERFRONT

Map 3, A4–C6; Map 4, A4–F9.

Heading west from the brass pig, descend the **Hillclimb**, a long staircase that leads down past several levels of cafés and shops to the **waterfront**, a busy stretch of ferry landings, souvenir stalls, and hotels. You'll see plenty of vessels on the water down here, but not the bigtime ships, as Seattle's harbor is no longer deep enough to accommodate them; the port's major commercial business now sails to the north and south. **Waterfront Park**, the area around Pier 57 and Pier 59, is pleasant enough, although aside from its decent aquarium, there's not much of interest. In good weather, the stretch from the ferry docks to **Myrtle Edwards Park** in the north makes for a nice stroll, though the din of traffic from Alaskan Way and overhead freeways diminishes the pleasure somewhat.

One of the best ways to see the waterfront is to use the **streetcar** (85¢, $1.10 peak), which starts at Jackson Street in the International District, proceeds through Pioneer Square and then runs up Alaskan Way from Pier 48 to Pier 70/Broad Street. (Note that the waterfront route is *not* considered part of the downtown ride-free zone; every passenger pays for every ride, and tickets permit you to get on and off at any of the nine stations for ninety minutes.) Streetcars from Melbourne, Australia, built in 1927, were imported especially for this service when the line began operation in the early 1980s. You don't take the streetcars if you're in a hurry – you could probably walk the distance just as fast – but like San Francisco's cable cars, it's an indulgence worth enjoying once or twice. The blocks passing before you as you rattle along might be undergoing some serious changes in the near future. One recent plan calls for the current Waterfront Park, Aquarium, and Piers 62 and 63 to be combined into a single park, with the Aquarium tripling in size to 200,000 square feet, with new exhibit pavilions that will form part of an ambitious "Portal to the Pacific" experience. As in so many ambitious Seattle development projects, it's already a source of considerable controversy, due mostly to its projected cost of around $135 million.

Seattle Aquarium

Map 3, A4. Daily: Memorial Day–Labor Day 10am–7pm; rest of year 10am–5pm; $7.50.

The main reason for heading down this way is the **Seattle Aquarium** on Pier 59, just across the street from the Hillclimb, with over 400 species of fish, birds, plants, and marine mammals in a reasonably spacious, easily navigable layout (a small part of which is actually outdoors near the waterfront shore). Highlights include black tip Pacific Coral Reef sharks and electric eels; a 400,000 gallon underwater dome that recreates life in Puget Sound; a functional salmon hatchery and fish ladder displaying the life cycle of Pacific salmon; and a hands-on Discovery Lab allowing visitors to fondle tidepool specimens. The **sea otters** are the true show-stealers, though, with their goofball, poker-faced expressions as they ceaselessly backpaddle to and fro. In fact, this was the first aquarium in the world in which sea otters were successfully conceived, born, and raised to adulthood.

Tickets for the Aquarium and one IMAX film at the Omnidome in the same building are $12.75; the aquarium and two films cost $15.75.

SEATTLE AQUARIUM

The Omnidome

Map 3, A4. Daily starting at 10am; $6.95, $3 for each additional film; call ©622-1868 for current films and show times.

Pier 59 also houses the **Omnidome**, just opposite the Aquarium, an IMAX theater that boasts a 180-degree, 100-foot curved domed screen and six-channel sound system, often alternating the *Eruption of Mount St. Helens* documentary with other short features having similar themes. Usually clocking in at a mere half hour or so, it's not great value considering the high admission fee, though if you're also planning to visit the Aquarium, you can save a bit of money with a combined ticket.

South to Colman Dock

The area between Pier 59 and the ferry terminals to the south is largely populated by indifferent tourist-oriented souvenir shops and restaurants, an exception being **Ivar's Acres of Clams** (Map 3, C6), perhaps the waterfront's best restaurant, which has its own "Clam Central Station" stop on the waterfront streetcar. It's actually the main branch (and not necessarily the best) of a citywide chain, and Seattleites say it's declined somewhat, at least in atmosphere, since the death of owner-founder Ivar Haglund, a jovial fellow who posted "seagulls welcome" signs on the pier where his patrons dined. If you want some seafood for lunch at the waterfront, this is the place to stop. A few yards to the south is Pier 52, where **Colman Dock** (Map 3, C6) is the terminal for the Washington State Ferries; Pier 50, just to its south, handles foot passengers between the

Places to eat on the waterfront and the rest of downtown are reviewed starting on p.170.

city and Vashon Island. There are proposed improvements for renovating the dock with a tower which will serve as the highest observation point on the waterfront. For now the best position for watching the boats is on the elevated platforms that run along the side of the terminal.

Myrtle Edwards Park and Pier 86

North of Pier 59, not too much goes on along the waterfront, at least until you hit **Myrtle Edwards Park** (Map 4, A4), where bike and pedestrian paths wind along the shore for a couple of miles and continue through the adjoining Elliott Bay Park before terminating near the **Magnolia Bridge**. It's an excellent place to watch the Sound and the downtown skyscrapers from a distance, especially at sunset. Shadowing the paths are the dubious landmarks of the rotating globe atop the **Seattle Post-Intelligencer** building (with its "It's in the P-I" inscription) and the grain terminal at **Pier 86**, whose mammoth tubes load ships at the rate of 3000 tons per hour, and whose awkward bulk and incessant hum detract considerably from the atmosphere down here.

PIONEER SQUARE

Map 3, D6–D7.

Less than a mile south of Pike Place Market, the **Pioneer Square** is the city's most historic district, seen in the brick structures and ornate facades of its late nineteenth- and early twentieth-century buildings that have been carefully renovated and preserved, both with an eye for the tourist trade and downtown commerce. They're pleasant enough to admire from the exterior, but do not, with the exception of a few structures such as the **Smith Tower** and the **Pioneer Square Building**, merit detailed inspection unless you're big on architecture; their interiors are now largely taken up by offices and retailers. The free *Discovering Pioneer Square Map & Guide*, which covers basic highlights of the neighborhood's history and architecture, can be picked up at the entrance to **Elliott Bay Book Company**, at 1st and Main, the best place to hang out on the Square.

Nightlife is one of the Square's big draws, its restaurants and taverns drawing a diverse clientele of yuppies, sports fans stopping in before or after events at the nearby Kingdome, and partygoers of all ages. There's lots of live music here as well, and although much of it is generic R&B bar bands, there are some of the city's most adventurous clubs here too (see p.207). Highbrow culture and hedonism find a welcome middle ground on the first Thursday evening of every month, when dozens of Pioneer Square art galleries hold simultaneous openings (with, sometimes, free wine) between 6 and 8pm for **Gallery Walk**. Gentrification is more in evidence in Pioneer Square than it is in most of Seattle, but few people actually *live* here, and the small parks in the area are a magnet for the city's indigent and homeless. As in Pike Place Market, the slightly seedy air to the neighborhood that purportedly gave birth to the term "Skid Row" (p.34) in the early twentieth century is still very much evident.

When Seattle was settled by white pioneers in the middle of the 1800s, the twenty or so square blocks of the Pioneer Square neighborhood were a tidal mud flat at the bottom of steep, tree-laden cliffs. It nonetheless offered much more shelter from the elements than the site that Seattle's founders had originally hoped to call home, Alki Beach (p.100). By the end of the 1880s, Seattle's population – most of whom lived in or near Pioneer Square – had increased to over 40,000, despite the conflicting street plans of feuding founders Arthur Denny and Doc Maynard. This resulted in thoroughfares north and south of Skid Road,

The Great Seattle Fire

The **Great Seattle Fire** of 1889, which caused more than $15 million worth of damage and devastated downtown, was in many ways a blessing in disguise: the city was compelled to rebuild the area with a safer infrastructure, paving the way for the modernization of its business district and the construction of many of the buildings that give Pioneer Square its historic flavor today.

The fire occurred June 6, 1889, when one **John Back** was melting glue on a stove in a basement carpentry shop. The gluepot overheated, starting a blaze that quickly spread to the streets, a situation made worse when the flames ignited about fifty tons of ammunition in some hardware stores. More than ninety percent of the buildings in the central business district were wooden, with both streets and buildings on stilts to be out of mud's reach, and (though no lives were lost) much of Seattle was wiped out overnight.

When Mayor Robert Moran addressed several hundred businessmen the next day, citizen Jacob Furth presciently remarked: "The time is not distant when we shall look upon the fire as an actual benefit. I say we shall have a finer city than before . . . in eighteen months." Indeed, while businesses operated from makeshift tents, the wooden structures were replaced by brick ones, and streets were straightened and widened to make them more conducive for commerce. Seattle actually gained 17,000 residents over the next year. The city also gained the underground passages now seen in **Bill Speidel's Seattle Underground Tour**, created when the area's streets were elevated a full story – done to construct a new sewer system – a process that took about thirty years to complete. Storefronts at the original level continued to do business for years, with customers actually descending by ladder to conduct transactions.

now Yesler Way, that didn't quite connect – one reason why Pioneer Place Park, which marks the heart of the neighborhood, is a triangle, not a square.

The Seattle fire of 1889, the site of which is marked by a small plaque on the side of the post office at the corner of 1st and Madison, decimated Pioneer Square's wooden buildings, but within five years brick structures, many designed by noted local architect Elmer Fisher, had risen to take their place, and many of them still stand. Their survival was hardly assured, as the neighborhood was in decline through much of this century, leading to an urban renewal plan in the late 1960s to raze the district and create parking for downtown. The grim, gray parking structure (disparaged by locals as "the sinking ship") opposite the Pioneer Square Building at James and Yesler – a site formerly occupied by the elegant Hotel Seattle – is just a taste of the horror that might have been visited upon the area.

Citizen and community efforts, however, resulted in Pioneer Square becoming a historic preservation district in 1970, with many of its sites granted landmark status, though it's really only recently that the area has begun to thrive. This is most in evidence along 1st Avenue between Yesler and Jackson, lined with street lamps, a median strip of tall trees, and a steady flow of pedestrian activity. Businesses have also settled into the area in considerable force, and it's not just galleries, bookstores, antique shops, and the like – the Heritage Building on Jackson Street is home to NBBJ, the second biggest architectural firm in the US.

The highest of the area's old buildings – and one of the few worth a quick visit – is the **Smith Tower**, 506 2nd Ave (at Yesler Way). Distinguished by its bright white color, terracotta trim, and pyramid-shaped peak, it ranked as the highest building west of the Mississippi when it was built in 1914, though it's long been superseded by the Columbia

PIONEER SQUARE

Center and other Seattle skyscrapers with less character. There's also an **observation deck** at the top ($5), though this is often – and unpredictably – closed to the public. Even if you can't get to the top, step inside to look at the carved Indian heads in the lobby and to take a ride on the old-fashioned elevators, complete with metal gates and obsequious operators asking what floor you want.

Pioneer Square Park

Map 3, D7.

A triangular sliver of open space marks **Pioneer Square Park** at James and 1st, dominated by Fisher's **Pioneer Square Building**. Designed in the Victorian Romanesque Revival style, it's worth a quick peek inside to admire the atrium-like interior, constructed to give the impression of a streetscape facade. Also check out the 1914-vintage gated elevators and the wall safe on the second floor, another early-1900s relic. Back outside, the restored iron **Pergola Shelter**, at James and 1st, originally led to gigantic restrooms, although nowadays it usually gives cover to weary transients or bike messengers wolfing down their lunch between deliveries. The nearby **totem pole** was originally installed in 1890, stolen booty from a drunken foray into a nearby Tlingit Indian village. When an arsonist burned the pole in the 1930s, the city commissioned the Tlingits to carve a replacement – no free ride this time, with the bill running to $10,000.

Bill Speidel's Underground Tour

Map 3, D6. Daily, starting at 10am or 11am, schedules varying according to season and day of the week, $6.50; call ©682-4646 for exact times.

Physical reminders of Pioneer Square's strange evolution

can be best viewed on **Bill Speidel's Underground Tour**, which departs from *Doc Maynard's* pub at 610 1st Ave, an amusing look at the underground passages that were once this neighborhood's streets. The streets originally ran well below their present location, but when rising tides backed up the sewers and caused floods, the street levels had to be elevated by an entire story. The original storefronts became underground businesses in more ways than one. Although the underground was legally closed in 1907, some establishments – including speakeasies, burlesque joints, and other viceful enterprises – were accessible via subterranean passages well into the twentieth century.

The ninety-minute walking tour is well worth the time, not so much for the decaying, musty interconnected underground chambers as for the chance to ingest the most colorful and corrupt aspects of Seattle's early history. The guides, many of whom are off-duty comedians, keep up a witty, informative patter while herding groups around the rotting pipes, remnants of the houses of sin, and the occasional rat. The tour actually only covers parts of three blocks that were reopened to the public in the 1960s, just a small fraction of the 33 that comprised the entire underground; some of the remaining space is now occupied by the basement galleries and antique stores in the underground arcades along 1st Avenue.

Klondike Gold Rush National Historical Park

Map 3, D7. Daily 9am–5pm; free.

A few blocks south of *Doc Maynard's* is the Square's other main tourist establishment, the **Klondike Gold Rush National Historical Park**, at 117 South Main St, really just a small indoor museum housing a few exhibits on the

1897 stampede to find gold in the Klondike in northwestern Canada. Though far from Seattle itself, Klondike had a considerable impact on the city's development, as thousands of eager prospectors – including the mayor of Seattle, who resigned to organize an unsuccessful mining exhibition – passed through the city on their way up north. The ensuing business ended the economic depression that had gripped the city since the Panic of 1893, and played a big role in changing Seattle from a small lumber and sawmill town into a manufacturing and shipping center. The tools, photos, and newspaper reprints on display testify to the hard life of the goldseekers, many of whom had been lured into expeditions by fabulous tales of fortunes in the Yukon, and very few of whom struck it rich. The museum staff will run a few short documentary films on request, the best overview being the half-hour *Days of Adventure, Dreams of Gold*. Also, Charlie Chaplin's silent classic *The Gold Rush* is shown for free at 3pm on the first Sunday of the month, while between mid-June and the first week of September, the park rangers give free tours of Pioneer Square daily at 10am.

Occidental Park and Occidental Avenue

Map 3, D7.

Right across the street from the museum is **Occidental Park**, a ragged cobblestoned space uncomfortable to pass through day or night. Despite the proliferation of nearby businesses, it's home to some of the city's most unfortunate, and occasionally belligerent, down-and-outers and substance abusers. The park is presided over by four of Duane Pasco's **totem poles**, carved with grotesque images from Northwest Native American legends. A block east on Main, at the building marked with a plaque as the birthplace of the United Parcel Service, is the blink-and-you'll-

Skid Road

Was "Skid Road" the first "Skid Row"? There seems to be no certain answer as to whether the term originated with the street in Seattle that was once called **Skid Road**. When Henry Yesler built his steam-powered lumber mill in Pioneer Square in the 1850s, Skid Road was the route on which cattle dragged timber down to the mill from the forest above town, the logs skidding down the road. It was renamed Mill Street, and then renamed again as Yesler Way, its current tag. The road also marked the division of property between feuding founding fathers Arthur Denny and Doc Maynard, resulting in contrarily plotted properties and streets that still twist around Yesler Way like so many mismatched jigsaw pieces.

When Klondike Gold Rush fever hit in the 1890s, single men invaded Pioneer Square in force; gambling, drinking, and prostitution thrived here. The Gold Rush didn't last for long, however, and made very few people a fortune; when it was over, many of the men remained, but Seattle's commercial center moved north, leaving the square to decay and giving rise to a population of generally destitute and out-of-work folk, and many alcoholics. Though the original Skid Road was long gone, the term "Skid Road" came to refer to the area in general, by then a haven for men on the skids; the altered "Skid Row" has now become common parlance for any such down-and-out area in the States.

miss-it **Waterfall Garden**, whose 22-foot waterfall dominates this tiny refuge in one of Seattle's most congested areas.

Back a block, the contrast between Occidental Park and the pedestrianized zone of **Occidental Avenue** just south of it could hardly be greater. This block holds the greatest concentration of Seattle's **galleries**, the best of which are the **Foster/White Gallery** at 311 1/2 Occidental Ave S, which has quality modern glasswork and interesting pieces by contemporary Northwest artists, and **Meyerson & Nowinski** at 123 S Jackson St (corner of Occidental and Jackson), which also showcases contemporary artists from the Northwest working in a variety of media, as well as past notables.

For more gallery listings, see p.265.

SEATTLE ART MUSEUM

Map 3, C4. Tues–Sun 10am–5pm, Thurs until 9pm; $6, free first Thurs of the month.

The stretch of 1st Avenue between Pike Place Market and Pioneer Square is an odd jumble of galleries, pawn shops, and commercial sex establishments, with nothing much but a fading black-and-white mural of **Jimi Hendrix** above *Freedman's* at 1208 1st Ave. Also in the midst of this is the striking **Seattle Art Museum**, 100 University St, designed by Robert Venturi and constructed to the tune of $62 million. The museum, completed in 1991, served notice that Seattle was determined to elevate itself in the international arts community, and it's certainly impossible to ignore, with Jonathan Borofsky's 48-foot *Hammering Man* flailing away in front of the entrance. Inside, however, while solidly assembled and presented, it doesn't quite rate as one of the nation's top modern art museums, due in part to the relatively limited space; indeed, what you see in the twentieth-century galleries represents only selected highlights.

From the lobby, an imposing staircase winds to the second floor, which presents temporary exhibitions. The third floor is given over to displays of both traditional and modern works from Japan, China, Korea, Indonesia, the Andes, and the near East, with especially large sections of African and, most interestingly, Northwest Coast Native American art. Especially good are the African masks and the Native American totem poles, rattles, and canoes. Contemporary African art is on display as well, with the *Mercedes Benz Shaped Coffin* by Ghana's Kane Kwei taking first place for originality: its description reads, "This representation was a resounding success in Ghana and led to many commissions for coffins that allude to the lifetime trades of their occupants." Japanese tea ceremonies are periodically conducted at the full-size replica of the Japanese teahouse; $10 ticket covers access to such a ritual and also covers regular museum admission.

Northwest modern art gets the biggest section of the top floor, with frequently rotating exhibits yielding exposure to regional talents who may not yet have established themselves as household names. There are small, unimpressive sections for eighteenth- and nineteenth-century works, as well as corners for Baroque, medieval, Renaissance, and ancient mediterranean. But the main attractions are the twentieth-century pieces: there's Warhol's famous double Elvis exposure, *Double Elvis*, the sixteen photographic tunnels of Gilbert & George's *Coloured Shouting*, Jacob Lawrence's *Study for the Munich Olympic Games Poster*, and Bruce Nauman's witty Three-Stooges-gag-as-neon-tube wall piece *Double Poke in the Eye II*, as well as Robert Arneson's instantly provocative *John With Art* – a toilet stuffed with bodily excretions that leaves nothing to the imagination.

The museum also holds a full schedule of concerts, films, lectures, and other special programs, detailed in the quarterly program guides available in the lobby; there's a fine art bookstore just inside the entrance as well. Remember, too, that tickets are also good for the Seattle Asian Art Museum (p.60) if used within two days.

THE BUSINESS DISTRICT

Map 3.

Most of downtown is given over to the massive steel and glass office buildings between 2nd and 7th avenues – Seattle's **business district**. Despite a constant pulse during business hours, and the presence of a few good restaurants, there's not much reason to spend time here, especially at weekends. Indeed, the two most celebrated economic powerhouses of the region, **Boeing** and **Microsoft**, are not even here: both are based out in the suburbs, and many of the county's thriving concerns are headquartered not in Seattle itself, but in Bellevue, on the eastern shores of Lake Washington. Some large Seattle-founded enterprises do have their flagship stores downtown, including Eddie Bauer and Nordstrom, and there are department stores and shopping complexes aplenty, though not many you couldn't find in any other American city.

If you're using mass transit, it's almost inevitable that you'll cross through here at some point, as many lines have hubs on the avenues or the Metro Tunnel that runs underneath them. The heart of the district, inasmuch as there is one, is the diagonal **Westlake Park** on 4th Avenue between Pike and Pine, which hosts occasional lunchtime concerts and, more rarely, political rallies near its water-wall fountain.

A few blocks south on 4th Avenue, your gaze will inevitably be drawn to Seattle's highest building, the darkly glowering **Columbia Seafirst Center** skyscraper of offices and lower-level shopping floors at 4th Avenue and Columbia (locally nicknamed "the Darth Vader building"). The 76-story structure is made more striking by its combination of exteriors that curve both outwards and inwards. Inside it's ordinary, but you can get a good panoramic view of the surrounding area on the **observa-**

tion deck on the 73rd floor (Mon–Fri 8.30am–4.30pm; $5). Only slightly less ominous is the **Rainier Tower**, at 5th Avenue and University, the bulk of which is connected uneasily to a relatively tiny pedestal with a thin curved block of concrete. The impression is of a building upside down and in danger of toppling over at any moment, notwithstanding the fact that thousands of people work here every day. Between these giants, on 4th Avenue between Columbia and Marion, is the **Rainier Club**, the only downtown Seattle building that exudes top-drawer old-style European grandeur. The meticulous brickwork can only be admired from the outside, as the unmarked structure – easily mistaken for an elite hotel or apartment complex – is a private club, with a select membership that until recently was all-male.

Commercial development at its most garish hits you on 6th Avenue and Pike at the **Meridian**, Seattle's newest retail complex, which houses a huge *Niketown* sporting goods store with cinema-sized video screens and *Gameworks*, a *Star Wars*-ish video arcade that can hold 900 enthusiasts at a time – a joint venture between Japanese electronics manufacturer Sega and movie mogul Steven Spielberg that draws an average of 20,000 visitors a weekend. The Meridian – and a new neighboring branch of the *Planet Hollywood* restaurant chain next door to *Niketown* – are favorite whipping boys of Seattleites opposed to commercial development in the city center. In spite of this, the complex has been instrumental in drawing crowds to the mostly deserted business area during weekend nights.

Of the other downtown shopping centers, only two merit a visit, but not for the stores. **City Centre**, at 5th and Pike, has displays of glass art by artists affiliated with Washington's **Pilchuck School**, the most renowned generator of talented glassblowers. **Rainier Square**, 4th Avenue and Union, houses the Seattle Architectural Foundation's relatively little-known gallery/exhibit on Level 3, *Blueprints: 100 Years of Seattle Architecture* (Mon–Fri 10am–4pm; free). Employing detailed text and numerous vintage Seattle photos, it's a fairly exhaustive display – *too* detailed, perhaps, for most people – but the foundation does offer architectural walking tours during the warmer months (see p.16).

THE BUSINESS DISTRICT

THE
INTERNATIONAL
DISTRICT

Just south of Pioneer Square, the ragtag **International District** has long housed the newest of the city's ongoing waves of Asian immigrants. As you might expect, some of Seattle's best and most affordable ethnic restaurants are here, but unless you're in the area to buy or eat food, there's no getting around the fact that there just isn't much to do. Bordered by 2nd and 12th avenues west-east and Washington and Weller streets north–south, the dozen or so blocks that comprise the district can be covered by foot in an hour or two and are rarely too lively, except during events at the nearby **Kingdome**, home to Seattle's baseball and football teams. The hulking stadium is

See p.176 for eateries in the International District.

on the district's edge near the waterfront, but its days are numbered: schemes are underway to build two new outdoor stadiums close by, with the Kingdome slated for demolition by 2000.

Originally known as Chinatown, the neighborhood has been renamed recently in an effort to keep pace with its changing demographics; it's now populated by Vietnamese, Laotian, Japanese, Korean, and Filipino immigrants as well as the original Chinese, who have had a strong presence here dating back to the 1800s – if not one always welcomed with open arms. Thousands of Chinese immigrants, many of whom had been brought to the West Coast to help build transcontinental railroads, came to the Seattle area in the late nineteenth century to earn money in the city's canneries and mills; however, economic depression fueled anti-Chinese riots in the Northwest in the 1880s. Many were expelled from nearby Tacoma in late 1885; a few months later in Seattle, an anti-Chinese committee forcibly delivered Chinese residents and their possessions to a dock, where a steamer was about to depart for San Francisco. The ship refused to accept them as passengers unless their fares were paid; a surrounding mob quickly coughed up the dough. The Chinese were belatedly offered protection from an armed guard, but many of them chose to leave town anyway.

Today the district – where the Chinese settled when they began to return to the area in the early 1900s – is dominated by eateries, groceries, and other small businesses catering to its community, with most of the action between 5th and 8th avenues on Jackson and King streets. Seattle residents from everywhere come to its restaurants and shops for

---

The area covered by this chapter is shown in detail on color map 3.

---

specialty ethnic fare; a great place to get a flavor for this is at the huge Asian supermarket-cum-variety store *Uwajimaya* at 519 6th Ave.

WING LUKE MUSEUM

Map 3, G7. Tues–Fri 11am–4.30 pm, Sat–Sun noon–4pm; $2.50, free Thursdays.

The cultural highlight of the area is the **Wing Luke Museum**, 407 7th Ave S, whose namesake became the first Asian-American elected official in the Northwest when he won a seat on the Seattle City Council in 1962. The lone museum in the US devoted to Asian Pacific American culture, its permanent exhibit portrays two hundred years of Asian and Pacific Island immigration to Washington, from the first Hawaiian settlers to the most recent waves from Southeast Asia. Its several small rooms are easily covered within an hour or two, encompassing photos and artifacts, the most eye-catching of which are the hand-painted kites that hang from the rafters. Better are the text-heavy displays that trace the changing immigration patterns and demographics of the Seattle area, as well as the sometimes brutal discrimination faced by these minorities until quite recently. The internment of Japanese-Americans during World War II is merely the most notorious of these; a miniature model simulates the assembly center in Puyallup, Washington, where thousands of American-born Japanese from Seattle were incarcerated.

HING HAY PARK AND KOBE TERRACE PARK

Map 3, F3.

Hing Hay Park, at the corner of King and Maynard streets, is the nominal center of the International District, with its ornate pagoda and large, rather faded dragon mural, although the park is usually fairly devoid of human activity. Take a steep hike up to the top of Washington to enter the far greener **Kobe Terrace Park**, named after Seattle's Japanese sister city, where an 8000-pound stone lantern graces the entrance. Narrow paths wind down through community gardens built into the park's slope, though any hope of tranquility is dashed by the rush of traffic on nearby I-5. The park, too, seems to be as much of a haven for unsavory layabouts as local gardeners.

JACKSON STREET

Map 3, C7–G7.

You'd never suspect it these days, but the strip of **Jackson Street** that runs through the International District and down to the waterfront was the crucible of both vice and afterhours jazz clubs during the swing era. In the days when Seattle's musician union was segregated, this was the place for its African-American jazzers to find work. Teenagers Quincy Jones (later to produce Frank Sinatra and Michael Jackson, among many others) and Ray Charles (who moved here briefly after growing up in the South) cut their teeth here in the late 1940s, although neither truly got on the path to stardom until they left town shortly afterwards. These days it's just another stretch of dingy industrial-type buildings, leading past the fading brick **train station**, whose clock tower projects a far greater sense of grandeur than its rundown interior.

THE KINGDOME

Map 3, E8. Tours April–Sept; ©296-3148 for times; $5.

Directly south of Pioneer Square stands the generally loathed **Kingdome**, the cast-iron industrial wedding cake structure where the Seattle **Mariners** baseball squad and **Seahawks** football team play, though both are in the process of finding new homes. The construction of these new facilities, along with the ultimate fate of the Kingdome, has in recent years been the biggest political hot potato in the state of Washington.

For ticket information to Seattle Mariner and Seattle Seahawk games, see "Sports," p.236.

Home to the Mariners since 1977, the dark and cavernous Kingdome is hardly a prime space to watch baseball, a game best enjoyed outdoors anyways. The reasoning behind the structure was solid enough: to prevent the notoriously inclement weather from canceling too many games, or making it too unpleasant to endure even on rainless days and nights. Still, the dome itself wasn't the only problem. The Mariners were perennial losers, with ownership often rumored to be leaving town, and the franchise here before them, the Pilots, lasted but one season in 1969.

In mid-summer 1994, falling tiles raised doubts about the structure's safety and forced the Mariners to play on the road for the rest of the 1994 season (curtailed in mid-August by a players' strike). Though the Kingdome reopened after four months of costly repairs, a 1995 proposal to fund an open-air baseball park went before the voters of King County. Its failure seemed inevitable, before a funny thing started to happen: the Mariners began to win. Indeed, they came back from a thirteen-game deficit to tie with the California Angels at the end of the season, then won the American League West championship in a one-game playoff. The ballot measure, voted upon in mid-September, still failed, but narrowly, forcing another look by the authorities, and within about a month the county

THE KINGDOME

passed a bill to fund a new open-air baseball facility – with natural grass and a retractable roof – through the combined financial efforts of the Mariners, King County, and the state of Washington. Though it's due to open by 1999, construction – within a stone's throw of the Kingdome – has only proceeded in a limited capacity, thanks to a pending lawsuit from the anti-stadium group "Citizens For More Important Things."

The Kingdome's fate was further sealed by billionaire and Microsoft co-founder **Paul Allen**, who purchased the city's football team, the Seahawks, with the stipulation that a new open-air facility – though separate from the new baseball stadium, with the $425 million expense mostly funded by taxpayers – be built. Allen, amid opposition from citizen groups, paid the $4.2 million cost of conducting the referendum on the issue, and outspent his opponents by nearly $5 million. The referendum barely passed, in June 1997, and the Kingdome is to be razed in the fall of 1999, after which the Seahawks will play in Husky Stadium, at the University of Washington, until their facility is ready in 2002.

BELLTOWN AND THE SEATTLE CENTER

Just above the city center – and only a short walk or bus ride away from it – is **Belltown** (also referred to as the **Denny Regrade**), which has a number of bohemian cafés and some of the city's best budget shopping and eating, as well as a distinctly lived-in, community vibe that's almost entirely absent from downtown. The progression of activity continues across Denny Way, as Belltown gives way to the **Seattle Center**, not so much a neighborhood as a large entertainment/cultural complex that offers a wealth of things to investigate, including state-of-the-art technology museums and venues for some of the city's best

The area covered by this chapter is shown in detail on color map 4.

cultural and sports events. Towering over the grounds here is the **Space Needle**, for better or worse the visual symbol of Seattle.

BELLTOWN

Belltown, which starts just to the north of Pike Place Market and extends a mile in the same direction toward Seattle Center, is one of the city's more up-and-coming neighborhoods and the one that best embodies Seattle's casual blend of chic and avant-garde. Its renaissance in the last fifteen years or so from decaying inner-city district has been remarkable – and now, predictably, it's having to deal with planning struggles and overdevelopment. It's by far the most interesting part of the **Denny Regrade**, created when the site once occupied by Denny Hill was flattened in the early 1900s to allow the downtown business district to expand north. Shiny new condos stand shoulder-to-shoulder with funky brick flophouses; thrift stores and art galleries coexist with bars and pool halls that mostly cater to the locals. It's also stomping grounds for a large transient population, which adds to the grittiness, a flavor unlikely to go away despite gentrification. Like its sister neighborhoods across the US, such as the East Village and the Haight-Ashbury, it's an enclave that rises late and often doesn't shut down until after midnight.

2nd Avenue and around

Map 4, D5–F6.

The core of Belltown is the five-block area of **2nd Avenue** between Stewart and Battery, choked with cafés, vintage clothing outlets, used record stores, and offbeat galleries that cater to Seattle's large student and artist communities. Many of the customers (and even proprietors) affect a slacker pose that belies the hard work they've put into reviving the neighborhood. As recently as the mid-1980s, some of the hip storefronts currently lining the sidewalks were boarded up, neglected by both business and city developers. A decade or so later, it's one of the city's more vibrant sections, conducive to idle budget browsing by day and partying by night in the numerous restaurants and alternative clubs.

Belltown's restaurants are listed starting on p.178; club listings begin on p.207.

Belltown has been a focal point of Seattle's music and arts scene since the 1980s, offering local bands places to play original material (and local audiences affordable places to see them). **Sub Pop Records**, famous for its promotion of the grunge scene with early releases by Nirvana, Mudhoney, and Soundgarden, began its operations on the edge of Belltown, where it still remains, occupying several floors of the Terminal Sales Building. Near its offices, the company has opened a tiny retail store, the ironically named **Sub Pop Mega Mart**, at 1928 2nd Ave, which mostly sells Sub Pop (and Sub Pop-distributed) records and memorabilia. Though you shouldn't expect to see Dave Grohl or Chris Cornell here, you can find snapshots of such heroes – taken while the musicians were browsing through the store – on the "Wall of Fame" display to the side of the counter.

Also in Belltown, the "slam poetry" movement tapped into the energy of the punk underground, upping the ante with staged competitions in which poets were graded for their work like Olympic divers (see p.222). The focus of Seattle slams is now downtown at the *O.K. Hotel*, but lots of literary events – as well as other media – can be found at

2ND AVENUE AND AROUND

the **Speakeasy Cafe**, at 2304 2nd Ave. This is as close as Belltown gets to a community center, offering Seattle's most eclectic bill of readings, music, neighborhood meetings, avant-garde films, and more. It can also be a pleasant place to while away an hour or so with tea, espresso, or snacks, and there are computers with Internet connections if you're so inclined. Other establishments mixing the usual victuals with hip entertainment and diverse crowds are found nearby, the most renowned of which is the **Two Bells Tavern**, at 2313 4th Ave. **Crocodile Cafe**, back on 2200 2nd Ave, is probably the hottest alternative rock joint in Belltown these days, presenting both unknowns and underground rock royalty in its cramped back rooms.

Integrating Belltown's underclass into the art world is the unusual **Streetlife Art Gallery** at 2301 2nd Ave (daily 11am–8pm), across the street from the *Speakeasy*, a sort of gallery-cum-social program. All the artists here are homeless, or have been homeless, and the space provides them with supplies and a venue for their art. What's on display is uneven, but at least it's an innovative approach, encouraging visitors to both browse and talk with the artists, who are usually working in the space itself.

The streets in the immediate vicinity of 2nd Avenue, although less densely populated by commercial ventures, also offer some interesting spots for milling around. Mixed-media establishments combining art, food, music, and more in the same locale are a bit of a trademark here. Unconventional sculpture and 1950s furniture decorate many of the bars and eateries; underground rock and techno pound out of the clothing stores and galleries; and mild-mannered cafés turn into lively music venues at night. The most ingenious meld of different media can be found at **Sit & Spin**, 2219 4th Ave, a combination laundromat-café-performance space easily identifiable by the Saturnesque globe above the entrance. Here you can do your wash, down some chow, view some local art, and catch some music on the same trip, all in the shadow of its large found-object sculptures and vintage electrical coils running from the ceiling right down to the tables. It's well worth a look even if you're not a party animal; indeed, during the day it's not uncommon to see senior citizens sitting on the very used-looking chairs and benches outside, patiently waiting for their laundry to complete its final cycle.

Center on Contemporary Art

Map 4, C5. Tues–Sat 11am–6pm, Sun noon–4pm; $2.

Art of a more conventional sort – barely – is on view down the street at the **Center on Contemporary Art**, 65 Cedar St, whose small space is given over to constantly rotating exhibits of work that's more risqué than what you'll see in the Seattle Art Museum's contemporary galleries. Nam June Paik, Survival Research Laboratories, and Lydia Lunch are some of the artists who received their first major exposure in the Northwest via CoCA exhibits. It's not a stodgy venue at all; in 1997, for instance, it held an exhibit of UFO-related work, in conjunction with the fiftieth anniversary of the first flying saucer sighting.

Near CoCA, a lot at the southeastern corner of Western and Wall marks the former site of "**The Jell-O Mold Building**," which was decorated with a mosaic of vintage 1950s and 1960s Jell-O molds collected by friends from thrift stores throughout the country. Long an artsy location – Jack Kerouac lived here while writing *The Dharma Bums* – it was also the center of one of Seattle's most bitter planning battles. The building was used primarily by artists as live/work spaces, and also contained the popular, bohemian *Cyclops* restaurant, but in 1997 the tenants were served with eviction notices by the property owners. The structure was demolished and there are plans to erect a much bigger one in its place, much to the consternation of some Belltown citizens, who petitioned city authorities to save the building without success.

CoCA is also just down the road from an underpass embellished by one of Seattle's few bilingual English/Spanish signs warning against loitering, primarily directed toward illegal aliens who have used the spot to solicit low-paying manual day labor. It's a somber reminder that not all folks in Belltown can afford to spend their time and money on art and shopping.

Tilikum Place

Map 4, D4.

As you approach the monorail and Seattle Center, Belltown begins to peter out, most dispiritingly at the unattractive, usually deserted **Tilikum Place**, near where 5th Avenue, Cedar, and Denny intersect. Here you'll find the forlorn statue of **Chief Sealth**, the Native American leader who befriended the white founding fathers of the city and managed to keep his people out of the Indian Wars in the region in the mid-1850s. The settlers decided to name their new home in the chief's honor, though with a bit of twist, finding "Seattle" easier to pronounce. Today his likeness presides over a litter-strewn pool – an unfortunate tribute to a man who has an important place in the city's history.

SEATTLE CENTER

Spreading north of Denny Way, **Seattle Center** grew out of 1962's World's Fair and has since been able to transform itself into an active cultural center, containing, among other things, the Pacific Science Center, Children's Museum, and stages for opera, ballet, and theater. There's also the **Key Arena**, home of the city's pro basketball team (the Supersonics, or more commonly, "Sonics") and minor-league hockey franchise (the Thunderbirds), a **monorail**, a small **amusement park**, even a free **skateboard park**. Seattle Center also hosts some of the Northwest's largest festivals, most notably the free Northwest Folklife Festival, around Memorial Day, which presents hundreds of performances; the more pop-oriented Bumbershoot Festival occurs around Labor Day, and is even bigger, though unfortunately not free. First-time visitors, however, will probably be initially drawn to Seattle's most recognizable icon, the Space Needle.

The Space Needle

Map 4, D3. Observation deck open daily 8am–midnight; $8.50.

The most prominent relic of the World's Fair is the **Space Needle**. Rising 607 feet to support saucer-shaped floors near the summit, it was built to symbolize the future, though now it looks like nothing more than a refugee from the set of a vintage sci-fi film. Whether it's high on your agenda or not, you're bound to see it throughout your stay in Seattle, peeking through the skyline for miles around in all directions, and serving as a useful orientation beacon of sorts when struggling against the traffic on the surrounding streets.

The 43-second elevator ride to the panoramic **observation deck** is a pricey but obligatory experience for the first-time visitor to Seattle, much like a trip to the top of the Washington Monument or Statue of Liberty. Cynicism tends to melt upon arrival at the top, as the panoramic view of the surrounding region is indeed impressive, taking in Lake Washington, Lake Union, the downtown skyline, Puget Sound, the radio towers on top of the elegant Queen Anne neighborhood just to the north, and the more distant mountain chains, including Mt. Rainier – if visibility is good, of course. To maximize your experience, timing is crucial; if you're in town during one of the city's frequent rainy and overcast spells, it's worth rearranging your plans to ascend the Needle on short notice if the skies clear.

Below the observation deck, the elevator also stops at two fairly mediocre revolving restaurants. A better, though still rather overpriced alternative is the modest, non-rotating bar/lounge on the observation deck. Repeat visitors might consider coming here at night to gaze at a dramatically different vista, though of course it's missing the most interesting nighttime feature of the Seattle skyline: the Needle itself, which lights up after dark. Whichever you choose, solitude is not an option, with more than 4000 visitors passing through daily. And don't even think about ringing in the Millennium here: New Year's Eve 1999 at the Space Needle has been sold out since 1991.

The Pacific Science Center

Map 4, C3. Mid-June–Labor Day daily 10am–6pm; rest of year Mon–Fri 10am–5pm, Sat–Sun 10am–6pm; $7.50, $9.50 for museum plus IMAX film or laser matinee.

The Puget Sound abounds in good family-oriented attractions, but none combines entertainment and education as effectively as the **Pacific Science Center**, southwest of the foot of the Needle. Comprising five large interconnected buildings, its emphasis is firmly upon hands-on interactive exhibits, some computer-oriented, but most requiring no technogeek know-how. Much of this is quite innovative

THE PACIFIC SCIENCE CENTER

and a great deal more fun than the standard science museum, allowing you to play tic-tac-toe against a ten-foot robot, ride a "gravity bicycle," or move a two-ton granite ball suspended on water in the courtyard's large water works space. As is appropriate in the land that spawned Microsoft, the Tech Zone offers up-to-the-minute computer activities that, for example, allow you to create your own animations or musical compositions. The virtual reality exhibits are the most exciting, like the basketball court that has you going one-on-one with an on-screen opponent (and real-life bleachers for spectators to cheer you on), or the virtual reality helmet that simulates hang gliding through a city, though you can expect long lines at these. Kids will be especially drawn to the outsize exhibits, like the 22-foot starship with a circular slide.

The range of activities here is impossible to exhaust within one visit – and unless you're accompanied by children under 13, you likely won't want to stay the whole day. Low-energy types may want to try the health-oriented Body Works exhibits in building 1, which let you measure your grip strength, peripheral vision, sense of smell, and other traits in a highly tactile manner that's more akin to operating pinball machines than getting tested at the doctor's office.

The Monorail, Center House, and the rest of Seattle Center

Also near the Space Needle is the **monorail** (Map 4, D3–G6), which provides convenient transportation to and from downtown for $1 between 9am and 11pm (with trains running every 15 minutes or so). If you're riding it for the novelty, one trip is all you'll need. The journey lasts a mere two minutes before it deposits you in the middle of the

Westlake shopping center. Near the monorail is the modest **Fun Forest** amusement park, offering a few standard whirly rides, bumper cars, and the like.

Just west of the monorail is the **Center House** (Map 4, C3), a good place to gather maps and information for the rest of the Center. There's an information booth on the ground floor and a small ethnic food court too, plus lots of open space designed for kids to burn off excess energy. A better alternative is to take them to the fine **Seattle Children's Museum** (Mon–Fri 10am–5pm, Sat–Sun 10am–6pm; $4, children $5.50) in the same building. The emphasis is again on activities that encourage direct participation, including global cultural villages and a wilderness exhibit, all scaled down to make things easy for those under four feet tall; expansion in late 1995 more than tripled its space. Most children gravitate toward the **artificial mountain** area that lets them crawl through logs or simulate a rock climb. Those herding a group could try the "If I Had a Hammer" construction zone, which has kids collaborate on building an eight-by-eleven-foot home, and for which reservations are recommended (℡441-1768).

Between the Space Needle and the Pacific Science Center, ground was broken in mid-1997 for the **Experience Music Project**, due to open in mid-1999. Largely funded by Microsoft co-founder/billionaire Paul Allen, this was originally intended as a museum for Seattle native Jimi Hendrix before Allen and the Hendrix estate had a falling out about unspecified matters. The final product will still include a fair amount of Hendrix memorabilia, but the whole thing is now envisioned as more of an interactive music museum focusing on rock and pop in general, with sections devoted to musicians of the Northwest. The exhibits are also supposed to be geared toward tracing musical developments and styles, with more audio and less

THE MONORAIL, CENTER HOUSE, AND THE REST OF SEATTLE CENTER

emphasis on superstar celebrities than Cleveland's Rock and Roll Hall of Fame.

....

**To keep up with the museum's progress,
check out its Web site at *www.experience.org*.**

....

While there's a lot to do in Seattle Center if you have a specific event or destination in mind, it's not a prime hangout spot. The lone exception is the **International Fountain** near Center House (Map 4, C2), which folks splash through to cool off on hot days while pop tunes from around the world blare through its sound system; African drummers pound out rhythms in the surrounding grassy area on weekends. In April 1994, thousands of fans gathered in the open spaces near the fountain and the Space Needle to hold candlelight vigils for local icon Kurt Cobain, shortly after the Nirvana leader committed suicide in his Seattle home. It was here that Cobain's widow, Hole singer Courtney Love, read (on a taped message) some of Cobain's suicide note, before inciting the crowd to chant "Asshole!" – surely one of the strangest moments in pop culture's recent history.

QUEEN ANNE

Seattle Center is at the foot of the steep hill that marks **Queen Anne**, one of Seattle's leafiest and most desirable residential neighborhoods. The elegant homes built here by affluent Seattleites when the area was first settled in the late nineteenth century are pretty much gone, though the architecture now still stands out for its somewhat English feel. There's not much to explore, save for a small commercial strip along **Queen Anne Avenue** between West Galer and West McGraw streets, but a walk up to the peak of Queen

Anne Hill, just a dozen blocks or so blocks north from Seattle Center, rewards you with some great downtown views, especially from the tiny park that marks **Kerry Viewpoint**, at 2nd Avenue West and Highland Drive, one of Seattle's prime spots for sunset watching. At the crest of the hill are the 500-foot television towers that make this neighborhood easy to locate from miles around.

QUEEN ANNE

CAPITOL HILL

Capitol Hill, at the top of a steep incline leading east from downtown, is one of Seattle's most desirable residential neighborhoods, both for its proximity to the city center and its liberal atmosphere. Its vague boundaries – about 20th Avenue to the east, Volunteer Park to the north, and the First Hill neighborhood a few blocks south of Pike Street – contain few standard tourist sights besides those in Volunteer Park itself, a must for its **Asian Art Museum** and first-rate **conservatory**. The real action, however, lies on **Broadway**, a ten-block stretch of stores, cinemas, and eateries that, although more commercialized in recent years, is still Seattle's best bet for offbeat shopping or just people-watching. At the southwest corner of Capitol Hill, **First Hill** contains one of the city's more notable art collections at the **Frye Art Museum**, as well as **Freeway Park**, one of the oddest municipal landscape projects in the US. On the other side of Capitol Hill, just south of Union Bay and Montlake Bridge, are the unimpressive **Museum of History and Industry**, untamed **Foster Island**, and the **Washington Arboretum**, one of Seattle's finest parks.

The Hill has been a desirable place to live since the early twentieth century, when some of Seattle's most affluent citizens built mansions in the area. Though a few of these still stand, the area is fairly mixed – the well-preserved homes share space with apartment buildings both smart and funky, if not quite seedy. It has also, since the Sixties, been a center for the city's more left-leaning political and cultural elements, an influence apparent in the area's alternative-minded shops and nightlife, the political canvassers who hawk petitions on the busiest street corners, and the fact that it remains the undisputed center of the gay and lesbian community.

The area covered by this chapter is shown in detail on color maps 5 and 6.

VOLUNTEER PARK

Map 5, C4–C5.

In Capitol Hill's quiet northern end is one of the city's most accessible open spaces, **Volunteer Park**, named for the Seattle fighters in the 1898 Spanish-American War. Enter at Prospect and 14th Avenue to ascend the 106-step winding staircase of the nearby **water tower**. At the top is the budget alternative to the Space Needle's observation deck: a free panoramic view of Seattle, although the wire mesh covering the small windows may well remind you why it's free. There's also an exhibit about the Olmsted Brothers, designers of much of Seattle's park system, though it's nothing more than half a dozen text-heavy display boards with a few illustrations.

In good weather, the **bandstand**, across the reservoir to the north, hosts music and theater performances. Also at the northern end of the park is an excellent **conservatory** (daily 10am–4pm, in summer till 7pm; free), built in

1912 and modeled after London's Crystal Palace, now cultivating a compact but often stunning array of botanical colors and fragrances. Divided into five glass houses that simulate various different climates, it's especially noted for its orchid collection just inside the entrance. There's also a wealth of ferns and cacti, along with bromeliads that crawl over rocks, shrubs, and trees; the fiddleleaf fig tree in the Palm House extends into the building's 35-foot tall dome roof.

Aside from its modest sights, such as the **Seattle Asian Art Museum**, east of the reservoir, the park is best appreciated as a place to laze alongside the frisbee players, hackysackers, and African drummers that share the grounds on warm days, especially on weekends. Pause in front of the reservoir for a look at Isamu Noguchi's stark, circular *Black Sun* sculpture, which also serves as a favorite target for camera-toting visitors, due in part to the Space Needle looming in the background.

Seattle Asian Art Museum

Map 5, D4. Tues–Wed & Fri–Sun 10am–5pm, Thurs 10am–9pm; $6, free first Thurs of month. Admission also good for one free visit to the Seattle Art Museum if used within two days.

The building that held the Seattle Art Museum from 1933 to 1991 has now been converted into the **Seattle Asian Art Museum**, at 1400 E Prospect St, Volunteer Park's top draw, which holds one of the most extensive collections of Asian art outside of Asia. Its floor of exhibits encompasses Japanese, Korean, Vietnamese, Chinese, and Southeast Asian art, spread across many centuries and dynasties. Among the more interesting pieces are the meticulously crafted Japanese landscape scrolls and the theatrically grim statues of tomb guardians, court attendants, and warriors in the early Chinese art wing. The uplifting yet humble sculpture of *Monk at the Moment of Enlightenment* in the Chinese Buddhist art room, dating from the Yuan dynasty circa the thirteenth century, presents Chinese sculpture of a more spiritual nature. Best of all is the wildly ornate array of Chinese jade and snuff bottles from the eighteenth through twentieth centuries. Adorned with miniature portraits, animals, and rural landscapes, these are crafted with as much idiosyncratic care as any fine art pieces. Tea drinkers should check out the *KADO TeaGarden* in the basement (Thurs 11am–5.30pm, Fri–Sun 11am–4.30pm), which stocks 45-plus teas from Asia.

LAKE VIEW CEMETERY

Map 5, C3–D3. Daily 9am–8pm.

Just north of Volunteer Park is the entrance to **Lake View Cemetery**, 15th Avenue E and E Garfield Street, neither atmospheric nor especially lovely. Indeed the large, rolling grounds are only really noteworthy as the resting place of kung fu film star **Bruce Lee**, the former Seattle resident who died mysteriously in 1973, and his son, actor **Brandon Lee**, who died in 1993 also under suspicious circumstances. Their graves are a bit out of the way, on the crest of the hill toward the rear of the cemetery. Look for a small marble bench facing two large tombstones, one (Bruce's) red, one (Brandon's) black; both are usually covered in flowers and notes by fans. Other bigs buried in Lake View include early Seattleites Doc Maynard and Princess Angeline, daughter of Chief Sealth. Afterwards stroll to **Louisa Boren View Park** across from the entrance to the cemetery – a small plot, virtually undiscovered by tourists, that yields some of the best views of Lake Washington to be found in Seattle.

Like father, like son

Bruce Lee remains unsurpassed as the most famous martial arts film star of all time; his son **Brandon**, also an actor, has a devoted following as well. Unfortunately, neither gained such notoriety until after their respective deaths – either of which could pass for the next plot of *The X-Files*.

Born in San Francisco in 1940, the elder Lee grew up in Hong Kong, moving back to the US in the late 1950s and enrolling in the University of Washington in the early 1960s. A boxing champion famed for his "one-inch punch" – with his arm straight out, he could knock down his opponent with a shrug of his shoulder – he developed a style of martial arts that incorporated elements from karate, boxing, and many other types of combat. Lee landed a supporting role in the *Green Hornet* TV series in the mid-1960s, but it was in Hong Kong that his career took off, via several action films. On the verge of a breakthrough in the US, he told his sister in early 1973 that he expected to die soon, a prophecy fulfilled in July of that year – while resting in bed after taking a prescription pain killer for his recurring headaches, declared by doctors as a "death by misadventure." A month later, his *Enter the Dragon* film premiered in the US to great acclaim.

Brandon Lee, born in 1965, was determined to be known as an actor on his own accord, though his first role was in a TV movie playing the son of David Carradine's character from the *Kung Fu* series. He was on the brink of making it as an action star a few years later when, during filming of *The Crow* in 1993, Lee was shot to death in a freak accident. A bullet tip had lodged in a gun barrel that was supposed to be empty, but was not properly checked when loaded with a blank shell; the tip struck Lee's spine, and he died the same day. *The Crow*, like *Enter the Dragon* twenty years earlier, was a would-be starmaking success.

MILLIONAIRES' ROW AND THE HARVARD-BELMONT HISTORIC DISTRICT

Map 5, D4–D5.

Downhill from Volunteer Park toward Broadway, you can walk by some of Seattle's grandest mansions, though none, unfortunately, is open to the public. **Millionaires' Row** holds the most celebrated cluster of these, extending south along 14th Avenue E from the park entrance to E Roy Street. Note especially the sprawling brick of the **Shafer-Baillie Mansion** at 907 14th Ave E, whose large, mostly hidden yard often hosts weddings and receptions, and the large white house facing the park on the southeast corner of **14th and Prospect**, with four huge pillars and dragon statues guarding the entrance. At 626 13th Ave E, **The Maryland** apartment building draws attention for its curved exterior and covered balconies. Just to the west of Broadway and Roy, the **Harvard–Belmont Historic District** has slightly more ostentatious properties, particularly the gated structures along Harvard between Highland and Aloha, with their half-moon driveways.

BROADWAY

Map 5, C5–C7.

Ask anyone who's lived in Seattle for more than five years, and they'll insist that **Broadway** is declining. They were saying the same thing, naturally, fifteen years ago, when the ten-block drag, between Roy and Pike streets, began to really develop. Nevertheless, expect to see these same folks patronizing Broadway's espresso carts or pounding the pavement in search of that new import disc or exotic fabric, because for all its commercialization,

Broadway remains the place to hang in Capitol Hill. It's a good one, too, whether you're browsing for knick-knacks, popping in and out of the numerous boutiques, or sitting at one of several sidewalk cafés for some excellent crowd-watching.

See p.155 for listings of the best cafés.

Broadway Market, which takes up a whole block between Republican and Harrison, is the most visible business center, a multistory hodgepodge of vaguely trendy shops, fast-food joints, and fitness/beauty centers that houses one of the best health food restaurants in town (*Gravity Bar*, see p.172) and a day-of-show half-price ticket outlet on the second floor. There's also a cinema, although the art houses on either side of Capitol Hill's north–south boundaries – *Harvard Exit* near Broadway and Roy, and the *Egyptian Theater*, a Masonic temple at 805 E Pine St – offer better films, in more characterful buildings.

The best destinations in Capitol Hill cluster not on Broadway itself, but just a block or two away on some of the adjoining streets; check especially the part of **Olive Way** near Denny Way a few blocks west of Broadway. Things get edgier, and more interesting, the further south you go in the area, particularly around **Pike** and **Pine streets**, with funkier coffeehouses and record stores, tattoo and piercing parlors, and *Beyond the Closet*, at 1501 Belmont Ave E, the city's best gay and lesbian bookstore. The south end of Capitol Hill also has the district's busiest nightlife. On Broadway proper, things peter out when you approach Pine, although that particular stretch should be walked just to see the odd life-size, unlabeled statue of **Jimi Hendrix**, north of Pine, modeled on his famous kneeling-down-to-burn-the-guitar-at-Monterey pose.

FRYE ART MUSEUM

Map 5, B5. Tues–Wed & Fri–Sat 10am–5pm, Thurs 10am–9pm, Sun noon–5pm; free.

Southeast of Capitol Hill, **First Hill** is much less interesting, although it too was home to some of Seattle's most impressive mansions in the early twentieth century. Dominated by medical centers and listless modern housing developments, it merits a visit solely for the **Frye Art Museum**, 704 Terry Ave, the most traditional of Seattle's major art museums, devoted to representational painting of nineteenth- and twentieth-century American and European artists. Though the permanent collection is mostly ordinary, often even outshone by the temporary exhibits in the Greathouse Galleries, it carries out the mission of Charles and Emma Frye – prosperous Seattleites who built their collection in the late nineteenth and early twentieth century with proceeds from Charles's meat-packing business – with style. Its spacious, low-light galleries display works by the likes of Winslow Homer, John Singer Sargent, Thomas Eakins, and a few modern artists like Andrew Wyeth, although none are among the painters' most exciting or recognizable pieces. Look for Homer's *The Wheat Gatherer*, a painting of a European farm laborer that's an anomaly in his output, as the artist is most famed for his studies of American seas.

The building also holds one of the most important concentrations of the Munich school of painting in the US, focusing on the years between 1870 and 1900, when Munich rivaled Paris as a center of arts activity. Heavy on portraits and landscapes, it's somewhat of a folksy genre that won't have wide appeal for most visitors. Most interesting are a handful of paintings from the more progressive

FRYE ART MUSEUM

65

Munich Secession movement of the late nineteenth and early twentieth centuries, particularly Franz von Stuck's *Sin*, regarded as scandalous for obvious reasons. Perhaps because of this, there was so much demand for the work that he produced eight copies; the Frye version is a late one, from 1906.

FREEWAY PARK

Map 5, A8.

The city's most valiant (if failed) attempt to ameliorate the constant drone of Interstate 5, **Freeway Park** sits right on top of the highway, linking the edge of downtown with the foot of First Hill. There are indeed trees, foliage, and flowers on this large patch of the overpass, but don't head over with a blanket and deck chair just yet. It's not so much a park as a series of grey, concrete walkways and stairways that seem to have been designed with the specific purpose of separating pedestrians from the greenery. There's hardly any lawn space, and as such, it's of little use for recreational purposes, serving more as a resting spot for the down-and-out or a shortcut for harried office workers. The only real treat is in its southern portion, where a **waterfall**, dubbed "Canyon," mimics an Escher drawing in its multileveled jumble and circulates 27,000 gallons of water per minute, though even that's not enough to mute the noise of the traffic below the overpass.

EASTLAKE

Map 5, A1–C1.

Seattle's large houseboat population congregates at various points on Lake Union, especially on the shores of

Eastlake, a small neighborhood northwest of Capitol Hill on the other side of I-5. The houseboats, and the boardwalks on which they lie, are considered the domain of the residents and their guests, and the entrances to most of these homes have signs explaining this policy in no uncertain terms. You can glance at them from a few yards away by walking along Fairview Avenue E (or get closer by taking an organized cruise; see p.17), or content yourself with a look at Lake Union from **Lynn Street Park**, a space barely able to accommodate its few picnic tables, at Fairview Avenue E and E Lynn Street. Just to the east, **Eastlake Avenue E** is the neighborhood's small commercial strip, with a couple of decent cafés and the popular, earthy *Eastlake Zoo* bar (see p.195).

THE MUSEUM OF HISTORY AND INDUSTRY

Map 6, E8. Daily 10am–5pm; $5.50. Bus #43 from downtown.

Across Montlake Bridge from the university, the **Museum of History and Industry**, 2700 24th Ave E, is one of Seattle's least impressive high-profile attractions, holding mostly lackluster content on local history. Aside from a decent simulation of a glassblowing shop, a replica of a Seattle street from the 1880s, and the corny but fun video monitors in the "Seattle Hits" section, most of the costumes, toys, and such on display are only passing diversions. The Great Seattle Fire exhibit in the basement is well done, with an interactive terminal featuring snazzy graphics that allow you to see how the fire started and spread. If you have a serious interest in Seattle history, augment your visit with a browse through the museum's immense photo library, which has more than half a million images of the Pacific Northwest from 1859 to the present (by appointment; call ☏324-1126 for reservation).

WATERFRONT TRAIL AND FOSTER ISLAND

Map 6, E8–G8.

Near the northeastern corner of the Museum of History and Industry parking lot begins the **Arboretum Waterfront Trail**, which leads through the largest remaining wetland in Seattle and over a narrow floating walkway to **Foster Island**, an undervisited wildlife habitat whose marshes are crowded with birch, oak, and pine trees, as well as dragonflies, marsh wren, and redwing blackbirds. In summer occasional clusters of water lilies can also be seen from the bark-surfaced footpath, and periodic observation platforms let you pause and take in the views of Union Bay.

Numerous varieties of fowl, plants, and birds can be detected from the trail with a little patience; pick up a self-guided trail pamphlet for 50¢ (available at the Museum of History and Industry) for assistance. As is too frequently the case in Seattle's parks, the otherwise stellar experience is disturbed by high-decibel traffic and unsightly underpasses, in this case from nearby Highway 520. After a half-mile, however, the path leaves Foster Island; take a right turn onto Foster Point Trail and continue for ten minutes to get to the edge of the Washington Park Arboretum.

WASHINGTON PARK ARBORETUM

Map 5, G1–G4; Map 6, E6–G6. Daily 7am–dusk.

With two hundred acres and more than five thousand kinds of plants, the **Washington Park Arboretum** is a lush showcase for the landscape vegetation grown in the Puget Sound region. Despite the impressive statistics – plants from about 75 countries are represented – it's come under its share of criticism in recent years. Its wetlands have suffered damage from erosion, its most popular walking path,

Azalea Way, is not draining, and the trails are arranged somewhat haphazardly. Still, for most visitors, it remains a beautiful place to stroll – best on uncrowded weekdays – and observe the magnolias, witch hazels, and more exotic specimens. It's especially radiant in the early days of spring, when Seattleites from all over the city emerge from the hibernation imposed by endless rainy days to turn the wide, grassy Azalea Way into a promenade and soak up their first sunny rays in months.

The **visitor center**, at the north end of Arboretum Drive near Foster Island Road (daily 10am–4pm), has a free trail map and can also tell you about the numerous walks and activities held on the grounds, such as the free tours that leave from the center every Saturday and Sunday at 1pm. It's best just to pick up a trail map and wander around the ponds, glens, and rock gardens. The most popular destination is the **Japanese Garden**, just off the large parking lot on Lake Washington Boulevard near the Madison Street entrance (March–Nov daily opens 10am, closes varying with season, call ⓒ684-4725 for information; $2.50). Constructed with the aid of more than five hundred granite boulders from the Cascade Mountains, it's a lovely, immaculately landscaped spot, particularly at the bridges near Emperor's Gate, where exotically colored carp swim back and forth in the pond and turtles sun themselves on nearby Turtle Island. The teahouse can only be viewed from the exterior, but demonstrations of Chadō tea rituals are offered free with admission at 1.30pm on the third Saturday of the month from April to October.

THE UNIVERSITY DISTRICT

A cross Lake Union from Capitol Hill sits the **University District** (U District), centered on the **University of Washington**, whose 639 acres buzz with 35,000 or so students, making it one of the largest universities on the west coast. The campus houses the **Henry Art Gallery**, one of the finest art museums in the city, and the **Burke Memorial Museum**, rich in its exhibits on Northwest Native Americans. But as in Capitol Hill, the U District's chief draw is its main drag, **University Way**, with its dozen or so blocks of student-oriented establishments. It lacks the flair of Capitol Hill and the underground hipness of Belltown, due in part to its transitory population and the functional drabness of some of its residential and commercial architecture, but there are still enough diversions to fill up a day or so, with the school campus as the logical starting point.

The area covered by this chapter is shown in detail on color map 6.

70

THE UNIVERSITY OF WASHINGTON

The **University of Washington** – or UW (pronounced U-dub), as it's called by locals – is the leading educational institution in the Northwest, with sixteen schools and colleges. Indeed, it's one of the leading universities in the country, receiving more federal support for research since the mid-1970s than any other. Outside of checking out its museums, there's not much to do here if you're not a student, though a casual walk through the green lawns and a glance at the architecture, with its mix of early twentieth-century brick buildings and less attractive modern additions, is nice enough.

Originally founded on a small downtown hill in 1861, UW relocated to its present site in 1895, expanding greatly with the Alaska-Yukon-Pacific Exposition of 1909. The surrounding neighborhood, still lacking sewers, lights, and paved streets at the time, also benefited substantially, with an ensuing real-estate boom and, finally, modernization.

Begin your wanderings at the **Visitors Information Center**, 4014 University Way NE (Mon–Fri 8am–5pm), to pick up the free *Campus Walk* booklet, a self-guided tour of campus highlights. Worth a look is the **medicinal herb garden** near Benson Hall, one of the largest of its kind in the US. The **Allen Library**, one of several large projects in Seattle funded by Microsoft magnate Paul Allen, holds good temporary exhibits; it's attached to the **Suzzallo Library**, which faces **Central Plaza**, dubbed "Red Square" for its red bricks. This is the hotspot for hanging out, despite being surrounded by some of the university's least visually appealing structures, excepting the Suzzallo Library itself, with its neo-Gothic facade. South of here is **Drumheller Fountain**, another popular hangout, whose center jet blasts water 100ft high. A ten-minute walk from Central Plaza,

Husky Stadium hosts the school's football team and will serve as the temporary home of the Seattle Seahawks while their new stadium is built. Legend has it that "The Wave" – the fad in which spectators create a ripple effect by standing and sitting one after the other – originated here in the early 1980s; if not, the blame is still up for grabs. At the edge of Union Bay, the **Waterfront Activities Center** (Feb–Oct daily 10am–dusk) rents rowboats or canoes for $5 an hour, a great way to take in the nearby lakes.

The most unusual sight at UW is conspicuously absent from the official literature, the **Wall of Death** skateboard park, at the University Bridge underpass on Lincoln Way, next to the Burke-Gilman bike trail. The dark, sunken concrete patch is jammed with ankle-wrenching wall jumps and obstacles to test skaters' acrobatic skills. Even if gravity-defying teen daredevils aren't skating its steep ramps, go to see the large orange ring emblazoned "The Wall of Death," supported by conic structures raising the slogan well above the heads of passersby on the bike trail.

Henry Art Gallery

Map 6, B5. Tues & Fri–Sun 11am–5pm, Wed–Thurs 11am–8pm; $5, students and children under 13 free.

Until recently a minor campus attraction, the **Henry Art Gallery**, west of Central Plaza at 15th Ave NE and NE 41st St, leaped to big-league status in 1997 with the completion of an overhaul that increased its space fourfold. The new galleries are well-suited for the type of large contemporary exhibits, especially multimedia installations, that the museum has focused much of its energy on since its reopening. Even with the expansion, however, the Henry remains a small facility, and its constant rotation of exhibits means that what you see may be totally different one visit to the next.

Selections from the Henry's permanent collection are on view in the small **North Galleries** on the Plaza Level and include late nineteenth- and early-twentieth century landscape paintings by Winslow Homer and Ralph Blakelock; a smattering of modern works, including Jacob Lawrence's *The Builders, No. 1*, with his trademark animation-like, boldly etched African-American figures; prints by Rembrandt and Whistler; and largely unimpressive Northwest art. Should it be on display, the photography section is by far the best corner, with shots by Ansel Adams and Imogen Cunningham, and Margaret Bourke-White's *The Living Dead*, an image of just-freed concentration camp victims behind barbed wire.

The **Lower Level**, devoted to changing contemporary exhibitions, holds erratic but risk-taking fare in its new **Media Gallery**, given over to multiscreen projection pieces and technology-based art, and the 6500-square-foot **South Gallery**, often with barn-size installations combining sculpture, sound, and building design. The Henry has permanently acquired Gary Hill's eerie *Tall Ships* (though this piece is often out on loan), a dark corridor in which twelve black-and-white video monitors project silent filmed images of people to the visitors, who creep along in near-total darkness as the projections appear to approach viewers until they reach life-size proportions. The images vary according to the number of people walking through the exhibit, lending the space a *Twilight Zone* quality. Return to the light at the small outdoor **sculpture court** on the middle level, which also has seating for the museum's small café.

The Burke Museum

Map 6, B4. Daily 10am–5pm; $3.

A few blocks north of the Henry Art Gallery, the **Burke Museum**, at 17th Ave NE and NE 45th St, is UW's other cultural attraction, focusing mostly on the natural and cultural history of Washington, the Pacific Northwest, and the Pacific Rim. Holding the fifth-biggest collection of Native American art and artifacts in the US, namely masks, totem poles, and baskets, the Burke is still a borderline stop, with its earnest but unscintillating presentation. The most striking of these objects are the huge feast bowls at the rear, decorated with various animal carvings. Among the fossils and minerals lies "Peggy Sue," a stegosaurus that's the only dinosaur on public view in the Northwest. A 1997 remodeling added two large permanent exhibitions: "Life and Times of Washington State," a walking timeline of geological history, highlighted by volcanic crystals and a skeleton of a giant sloth that was found during construction of a runway at Sea-Tac airport; and "Pacific Voices," displays of various Pacific communities that run from videos of ceremonies to a lode of Hawaiian musical instruments.

UNIVERSITY WAY

Map 6, B2–B5.

Off campus, the heart of the U District is the dozen or so blocks of **University Way**, known as "The Ave," that stretch northwards from NE 41st Street. It's always crowded with students and shoppers, wall-to-wall as it is with cheap restaurants (particularly Asian ones) and youth-oriented stores. Once the center of Seattle's counterculture – Seattle's underground newspaper, *The Helix*, set up shop a few blocks away on Roosevelt Way in 1967 – it's not so characterful today, with plenty of fast-food joints, chain stores, vagrants, and panhandlers.

There are a number of used **bookstores** along the strip, though slicker stuff is available at the excellent *Bulldog News*, at no. 4208, and the huge *University Book Store*, a block up at no. 4326, which despite its institutional atmosphere holds an impressive inventory and frequent interesting author readings. A grittier literary hangout is the **Blue Moon Tavern**, near I-5 at 712 NE 45th St, for the last several decades a bohemian hole for the likes of poet Theodore Roethke, among others. The half-dozen blocks between University Way and I-5 to the west also host a few nifty nooks, though browsing on foot is not so pleasant amid the busy traffic. Best are *Scarecrow Video*, 5030 Roosevelt Way NE, an unbelievably exhaustive independent video outlet; *Seven Gables Theater*, one of the city's best movie houses, at the corner of 50th and Roosevelt; and *The Black Cat Cafe*, at 4110 Roosevelt, an endearingly ramshackle, collectively run vegetarian café in a disused-looking building.

When you tire of the traffic, head north to 58th and University to enter **Ravenna Park**, one of Seattle's best neighborhood parks, its creeks and deep ravines ideal for solitary strolls. On Saturdays, you can catch the **farmers' market** on the way, on the lot at the northwest corner of 50th and University (May–Nov 9am–2pm).

MAGNOLIA, BALLARD, AND FREMONT

T he largely residential neighborhoods on the banks of the Salmon Bay Waterway and Lake Washington Ship Canal, five miles or so north of downtown – **Magnolia**, **Ballard**, and **Fremont** – see relatively few out-of-town visitors, an unsurprising fact considering that outside of the **Woodland Park Zoo** and the **Hiram M. Chittenden Locks**, these areas are quite low on tourist attractions. Instead they are fairly well-to-do, conservative enclaves, excepting parts of Fremont, known for its more free-spirited vibe and its displays of public art.

The areas covered by this chapter are shown in detail on color maps 7 and 8.

MAGNOLIA

Map 8.

Magnolia, jutting out to the northwest of downtown and the Port of Seattle, is the most affluent of these districts – and the least interesting, though it does have the glorious **Discovery Park**. Though it's only a few miles up the curve of Elliott Bay from downtown, it feels much further away, with its pleasant tree-lined slopes and aura of genteel affluence. The area was actually a breeding ground for madronas, not magnolias, when it was first sighted by explorers; legend has it that a seaman misidentified the foliage in a ship's log, leading to the name that has stuck. Mockingly nicknamed "Mongolia" by some locals for its quasi-suburban isolation, it's a far more suitable place to live in than to visit, its most exclusive homes clustering around the bluffs at its western edge – though occasional mudslides here have caused severe damage to some of the residences. There's little commercial activity bar the three blocks or so around W McGraw Street and 32nd Avenue W; head instead for **Magnolia Boulevard**, hugging the bluffs overlooking the Puget Sound as it rises toward Discovery Park.

Discovery Park

Map 8, A5–C7. Daily dawn–dusk. Bus #19.

Discovery Park is Seattle's hidden jewel, some 500 acres of rustic fields, woods, and walking/jogging trails – as well as dramatic seaside vistas, clean breezy air, and an abundance of wildlife – that feel like a true slice of wilderness. Even on the most beautiful of spring days it remains uncrowded, and on weekdays and weekend mornings it's a nearly deserted paradise for hardy hikers, runners, and dog-walkers with its empty trails and lush topography. This is

MAGNOLIA

77

also when you're most likely to spot the bald eagles and rabbits that pass through the grounds.

The park, oddly, came within a hair's breadth of becoming a linchpin of the military-industrial complex. In the early 1900s, **Fort Lawton** stood guard over Magnolia Bluff here, although it never became a truly major army installation. In the mid-1930s, the Army even offered it to the city for a mere dollar; the city declined, fearing that the cost of maintenance would be too great in the middle of the Depression. The onset of World War II put the issue on hold, as the fort served as a major processor of enlisted personnel. In the mid-1960s, the Department of Defense announced plans to turn the fort into an anti-ballistic missile site, which led to an outcry for the grounds to be converted into a park instead. It was only through the personal intervention of Washington senator Henry Jackson that plans for the base were abandoned; Jackson also helped block the acquisition of more than 150 acres by the Navy and Coast Guard.

There are still vestiges of a military presence today in the old fort buildings in the park's southwestern corner, along with a few bland modern homes used by military personnel in the park's interior. The park's visitor center has occasional Fort Lawton history tours that take you inside the **guard house**, a bit to the northwest of the flagpole, where drunk or misbehaving soldiers were jailed in three solitary confinement cells, each measuring just four feet by eight feet. Near the park's east entrance is another reminder, **Fort Lawton Military Cemetery**, with the gravesites of two notable prisoners-of-war, one a German pharmacist who killed himself by drinking lacquer thinner rather than return to his native land, the other Gluglieamo Olivotto, murdered in a racially motivated incident (see opposite).

The substantial majority of park land, however, is for public use, with a tiny parcel granted to the United Indians of

All Tribes for **Daybreak Star Indian Cultural Center** (follow signs from the north parking lot). The center has small exhibits featuring Native American artists, and an Art Market on the second Saturday of each month with a

An incident in Discovery Park

On August 14, 1944, 32-year-old Italian prisoner of war **Gluglieamo Olivotto** was lynched by American servicemen in Discovery Park, a fairly obscure historical event even to long-time Seattle residents. Olivotto's death was instigated by tension on Fort Lawton between Italian POWs and American black soldiers. Although Italy had ended its involvement in World War II in September 1943, about 3000 Italians were still based at Fort Lawton and other locations in the Seattle area doing defense-related work for the US. Somewhat perversely, the Italians had far laxer restrictions than the blacks at Fort Lawton – who were readying to fight for the US – being allowed to roam pretty much freely off the base.

Angered by the unfair treatment, the soldiers reportedly stormed the Italian barracks that August night with axes, stones, bottles, and shovels, injuring dozens; Olivotto's body was later found hanging from the neck by a steel support cable, more than ten feet off the ground. Forty-two black servicemen were charged in the lynching, three of whom were directly charged with manslaughter; twenty-six of these men were convicted, resulting in dishonorable discharges from the army and sentences totaling more than two hundred years. The trial judge advocate in the courts-martial was none other than Lt. Col. Leon Jaworski – the same Leon Jaworski who, three decades later, would become famous as the government's special prosecutor in the Watergate scandal.

salmon bake and arts and crafts for sale. The **visitor center** (daily 8.30am–5pm; ✆386-4236), just inside the east entrance at 36th Avenue W and W Government Way, organizes weekend walks spotlighting the park's abundant bird and plant life. A 2.8-mile loop trail can be entered here that winds among much of the park's most densely forested regions. It's better to head for the south entrance on W Emerson Street near Magnolia Boulevard, however, and take a trail across the windswept meadows between the parking lot and the nearby **bluffs**, where the view – taking in Puget Sound ships, Bainbridge Island, and on a clear day the snow-capped Olympic Mountains – is one of the city's grandest, especially at sunset. Follow the path at the edge of the bluff north until you reach the **South Beach trail**. A long set of wooden stairs winds down to the narrow, rocky, unswimmable beach, with its majestic bluff faces to the south, lighthouse to the north – and sewage treatment plant near the lighthouse.

Fishermen's Terminal

Map 8, F7.

About a mile east of Discovery Park, **Fishermen's Terminal**, on the south banks of the Lake Washington Ship Canal, is the leading homeport for commercial fishing on the West Coast, providing moorage for about 700 vessels. Ranging in length from a few dozen feet to a few hundred feet, many of these ships are on view at the dock by the parking lot; during weekdays, you may catch their operators unloading their crab and salmon hauls. After you've poked around the fleet for a few minutes, there's nothing else to detain you unless you're looking to eat some of that freshly caught fish, in which case you can hit the terminal's small daytime indoor **markets** or have a proper sit-down meal at *Chinook's*, rightly one of the city's most celebrated seafood restaurants, both for its menu and its dockside view. If your next stop is the Ballard Locks and you want to avoid crossing the Ballard Bridge, you can park at the small lot about a mile west in minuscule **Commodore Park**, from which footbridges lead you over Salmon Bay to the locks.

BALLARD

Map 8.

Positioned at the mouth of Seattle's main commercial waterway, the blue-collar neighborhood of **Ballard** is one of the city's most industrial areas, though some gentrification is beginning to threaten its low-key atmosphere. Scandinavians dominated the population when it was settled in the late nineteenth century, and their cultural presence remains strong in the district, evidenced by its **Nordic Heritage Museum** and annual May 17 parade in honor of **Norwegian Constitution Day**. An economic power in its own right in its early days, Ballard wasn't even part of the city until the early twentieth century; however, its demographics have begun to fall in line with Seattle's mainstream, due to the influx of middle-class families and young people attracted by relatively low rents. There's a tiny bit of **nightlife** near NW Market Street and 22nd Avenue NW, though most folks just come here to see the Hiram M. Chittenden Locks, one of Seattle's most visited attractions.

The Hiram M. Chittenden Locks

Map 8, D6. Daily 7am–9pm.

The **Hiram M. Chittenden Locks** (aka the Ballard Locks), on the north side of Salmon Bay, were designed by

BALLARD

81

a US Army Corps engineer of the same name in the early twentieth century to help keep the freshwater lakes uncontaminated by salt. These gateways herd commercial vessels and pleasure boats around the clock every day of the year; the ships, rising and sinking like slow-motion elevators as the locks are drained and filled, can be seen from overlooking platforms, a free show that draws over a million viewers a year – though many will probably wonder what all the fuss is about.

The two concrete locks – one designed for vessels up to 80 feet wide and 825 feet long, the other (measuring 30 by 150 feet) for much smaller craft – allow boats of all kinds to pass from the freshwater lakes to saltwater Puget Sound and vice versa, gating them into chambers that drain one type of water before allowing them to proceed to the next. The parade varies from tiny private affairs out for a brief weekend cruise to massive ships hauling tons of cargo into the Pacific. It's impossible to predict what might be going on at any given hour, and you might find yourself lingering for twenty or thirty more minutes before any action comes along. It's best to come on the weekends, when many amateur sailors take to the water and often chatter with spectators as their boats are guided through the portals at agonizingly slow speeds. Better still are holidays such as Labor Day, when the heavy traffic can cause backups of more than a hundred boats, which have no alternative but to wait their turns.

A footbridge alongside the canal's dam leads south from the observation platforms to the **fish ladder** on the other side of the water, a more entertaining diversion than the locks if you're here in the right season. The ladder was built to allow salmon to pass around the locks and dam, and is one of the few fish ladders in the world to be located where salt water and fresh water meet. In the larger scheme of

The Salmon Wars

Salmon fishing is big industry in the Pacific Northwest, with a harvest valued at around $300 million annually. Salmon are born and reared in fresh water before migrating to the ocean for a few years, after which they return to fresh water to spawn; human-made innovations such as the Ballard Locks are necessary to allow the salmon to thrive.

In the waterways leading to Seattle, however, salmon travel so widely that both the US and Canada cannot help but catch a good deal of fish that spawn within each other's borders. A 1985 Canada–US Pacific Salmon Treaty was established both to conserve salmon by preventing overfishing and to ensure equity between Canadian and American harvests, though with the idea that some terms be renegotiated yearly due to the variable fish population. The delicate balance was disrupted in 1997, when Canadian fishermen claimed that Americans were catching three times their share of British Columbia-bound sockeye.

In May 1997, Canada seized four US fishing vessels and fined their skippers for failing to comply with a law requiring foreign boats to notify authorities when entering Canadian waters. In July, Canadian fishermen even blockaded a popular Alaskan state ferry, *Alaska Marine Highway*, for three days to make their point. Talks of a compromise, whereby Americans would catch fewer sockeye bound for British Columbia, in exchange for the Canadians catching less coho salmon off Vancouver Island – allowing more coho to enter the Puget Sound – collapsed, and the US was unwilling to go along with Canada's request for third-party arbitration on treaty disputes, none of which had been resolved entering 1998.

THE HIRAM M. CHITTENDEN LOCKS

things, the ladder enables the fish to lay and fertilize their eggs, tasks that must be completed in fresh water. The ladder's 21 "steps," or weirs, are best viewed between July and September, when chinook, sockeye, and coho salmon jump around the ladder at the peak of their upstream migration. Mid-winter is when steelhead salmon appear, but be warned that if you get here in April or May, you'll most likely see nothing but green muck through the observation windows (which provide views of the ladder's eighteenth "step"), with migration at such a low point in the cycle that it's virtually nonexistent.

The **visitor center**, between the parking lot and the platforms (June–Sept daily 10am–7.30pm, Oct–May Thurs–Mon 11am–5pm), screens an overenthusiastic fourteen-minute slide show every half hour. Upstairs are interesting exhibits about the history of the canal and the locks' construction, with interactive displays that allow you to operate a model-size replica of the locks via remote control, or try to navigate a near-impossible maze that simulates the journey of salmon through their life cycle, in which fewer than one egg in a thousand may survive to spawn as an adult. You can also come here for the free guided tours of the locks (daily at 1pm and 3pm in summer, weekends at 2pm rest of year), necessary to get the most out of your visit, with explanations and anecdotes in plain-talk rather than engineering-speak. The **Carl S. English Botanical Garden**, across from the visitor center, has steep hillsides that are also good vantage points for watching the ships.

Golden Gardens

Map 8, C1.

Beach culture – what little of it there is here – is on display at **Golden Gardens**, a park about a mile and a half north of the locks. Its small beach is far less known than West Seattle's Alki Beach, the very same reason it makes for more pleasant beachcombing – although it does get fairly crowded in warm weather. You won't do too much swimming here, as the water is usually too cold for comfort, but there are some dunes and wetlands in the northern part that make for good, if limited, wandering.

Nordic Heritage Museum

Map 8, D4. Tues–Sat 10am–4pm, Sun noon–4pm; $5.

More than half a million Washingtonians identify themselves as Scandinavian, and their history is celebrated in the **Nordic Heritage Museum**, 3014 NW 67th St, with three floors of earnest, often mundane exhibits housed in a former elementary school. The ground floor is the most informative, with a large Dream of America exhibit that takes you through the immigrant experience from 1840 to 1920, spotlighting the Scandinavian-American communities in particular. While Scandinavians did not endure the worst sorts of discrimination inflicted upon nineteenth-century immigrants, there was still plenty of hardship to endure, many of them escaping from rural poverty in their native lands to struggle against the elements in the rugged West. In the Seattle area, many Scandinavians settled in Ballard; the Ballard Story display recreates the streetlife of the community's early years.

On the second floor, your attention is momentarily held by the world's longest tapestry, measuring 295ft and stretched across several rooms, while the top floor, with separate wings devoted to the folk art and Northwest immigrant communities of Norway, Iceland, Denmark, Finland, and Sweden, is only worth a lengthy browse if you're particularly enamored of Scandinavian artifacts and pictures of

NORDIC HERITAGE MUSEUM

Scandinavian-American organizations from the early 1900s. Judging from the large number of visitors from these countries registered in the guest books, it's a big draw for vacationing Scandinavians, including Icelandic president Vigdis Finnbogadottir, who dedicated the Iceland Room in 1990.

FREMONT

Map 7.

As you cross into **Fremont** from Ballard along Leary Way NW, or from Queen Anne Hill via the Fremont Bridge over the Lake Washington Canal, signs proclaim "Welcome to Fremont, Center of the Universe. Turn your watch back 5 minutes." Another reads, "Welcome to Fremont, Center of the Universe. Throw your watch away." Both are fair warning that Fremont is not for those who take themselves too seriously. This up-and-coming, mostly white middle-class area has more than a touch of bohemia and is far more consciously hip than either Ballard or Magnolia. Lacking any tourist draws, unless you count Woodland Park Zoo on its northern border, its true asset is a friendly, funky charm that makes its small center a great place to kill a couple of hours.

That hub is the stretch of **Fremont Avenue N** that runs from the Fremont Bridge at N 34th Street to N 37th Street, a mish-mash of cafés, chic restaurants, used bookstores, and thrift shops, most with an artsy, countercultural bent. Establishments with more commercial clout have also set up digs in Fremont, including some microbreweries, Adobe Systems software (right by the bridge), and, on its western fringe, a music studio built by Stone Gossard of Pearl Jam. Old-timers may complain about all the yuppies, but it's hard to believe that a community that proudly directs visitors to a larger-than-life statue of Lenin will soon be co-opted by the establishment.

Fremont's public art

Fremont's **public art** embodies its playful, left-wing sense of surrealism. Start your tour of it by picking up the free *Walking Guide to Fremont* at the kiosk of the **Rocket at the Center of the Universe**, in itself the beginning. This 53-foot monument at the corner of N 35th Street and Evanston Avenue looks more like a genetically accelerated toy model than any center of the cosmos. As the "Story of the Rocket" placard at the bottom deadpans, this was originally intended as a monument to commemorate the discovery of the center of the universe in Fremont in 1991.

Around the corner on N 34th Street, just east of Fremont Bridge, is Richard Beyer's brilliant late-1970s sculpture *Waiting for the Interurban*, life-like statues of five dour commuters waiting for the bus – supplemented by small child and dog – regularly adorned with football helmets, Hawaiian leis, and other accoutrements by locals. It's much harder to decorate the giant Cyclopsish **Fremont Troll** that sits underneath Aurora Bridge, a five-minute walk away at N 36th Street and Aurora Avenue N. Note the left hand of the eighteen-foot, ferroconcrete ghoul, crushing a real Volkswagen Bug; the troll also serves as an inspiration for Fremont's **Luminary Procession** on October 31, dubbed "Trolloween." Unbelievably, more troll culture is available on the Troll Control's walking tours of Fremont, conducted by a troll, given by Ladybug Books (✆632-3170; $5).

On the west side of Fremont Avenue is the huge statue of **Lenin** at the triangular corner of N 36th Street and Fremont Place. This sculpture from Poprad, Slovakia, by Slavic artist Emil Venkov, is said to be the only representation of Lenin "surrounded by guns and flames instead of holding a book or waving a hat." The late Lewis Carpenter found it after it was toppled in the 1989 revolution, and mortgaged his home to acquire it and bring it back to

Issaquah, a small town near Seattle. It's sited temporarily at this busy corner, on sale for a mere $150,000 – hence likely to stay in place for some time yet.

Fremont Art About (first Sat of each month 4–7pm), a walking tour of the area's galleries and studios, is a good way to take in the area's more conventionally situated art (maps available at the *Martin Oliver Gallery* on the corner of Fremont Avenue N and Fremont Place). The **Fremont Fine Arts Foundry**, at 154 N 35th St, is the best of these spaces, its striking modern design upstaging the dreary industrial buildings that dominate much of the neighborhood west of Fremont Avenue near the ship canal. The 17,000-square-foot building houses studios for about ten artists working in sculpture, flameworked glass, and mixed media, as well as a gallery, often featuring Foundry founder Peter Bevis's "roadkill molds."

See p.265 for listings of the best galleries in Seattle.

Redhook Brewery and the rest of Fremont Avenue

The **Redhook Brewery**, at 3400 Phinney Ave N (Map 7, C7), is the big attraction in Fremont's industrial section, just west of Fremont Avenue. Redhook, whose output is large enough to qualify it as a craft brewery, not a microbrewery, is perhaps the best beer that the Pacific Northwest has to offer, especially esteemed for its ESB ("Extra Special Bitter"). Redhook offers **brewery tours** (Mon–Thurs 2pm & 5pm, Fri 2pm, 5pm, & 6pm, Sat 1–6pm hourly, Sun 1–5pm hourly; $1), meeting at the brewery's *Trollyman Pub*, that mostly serve as an opportunity to down three or four samples.

Back near Fremont Avenue, on Sundays the **Fremont Sunday Market** (Map 7, D8; April–Nov 10am–5pm), fills up a parking lot just west of the Fremont Bridge with produce stalls and a flea market. The lot doubles as Seattle's most unusual movie venue in the summer, when the **Fremont Outdoor Cinema** projects classics against a building wall (complete with fake painted-on curtains) on Saturdays at dusk, with live music and entertainment before all shows, as well as prizes for best costume.

If you're here at the outset of summer, don't miss the annual **Fremont Fair & Solstice Parade** in late June, which allows only human-powered floats and costumes – the ideal opportunity for the city to indulge its taste for lunatic public art.

Gas Works Park

Map 7, G8.

Heading east along the water's edge from Fremont Bridge leads you through a dowdy area of industrial buildings and boating centers before **Gas Works Park** provides a relief from the concrete. It's not Seattle's most attractive park by any means, but it's certainly one of its most peculiar. Until the mid-1950s, the grounds were occupied by the Seattle Gas Company, a plant that converted coal and oil into gas. Several gigantic, ugly brown oxygen gas generator towers still remain, the clash between the rotting structures and the surrounding green hills lending the site an atmospheric dissonance – although the fences enclosing these relics haven't been able to prevent locals from splattering the monoliths with all sorts of imaginative graffiti. Remodeled into a park, its small hills and windy location on the banks of Lake Union make it a favorite spot for kite flyers. It's also Seattle's prime vantage point for the Fourth of July

GAS WORKS PARK

fireworks, with downtown and the Space Needle hovering in the east.

There's still some contamination in the soil and ground water, and posted warnings advise users not to dig in the dirt or wade or swim in Lake Union. Children should be supervised or herded into the picnic area and **playbarn**, with its large, gaudily painted industrial pipes, engines, and wheels, alongside a more conventional playground. Gas Works Park is also the best place to hop onto the 12.5 mile **Burke–Gilman Trail**, Seattle's most popular biking route (also open to walkers and joggers), which runs along the lake before swinging northward through the University of Washington and beyond.

WALLINGFORD

Between Fremont and the University District is **Wallingford**, a solidly middle-class area that's just as desirable a place to live as Fremont or Ballard with its blocks of pleasant midsized homes. It offers little in the way of exciting destinations, though the main artery from I-5 to Fremont, **N 45th Street**, has a few interesting shops and restaurants, some of which have been converted from old houses. Fearsome rush-hour traffic jams along this strip make it an avenue to avoid if you're heading to the **Woodland Park Zoo**, fifteen blocks or so north of the Fremont Bridge.

Woodland Park Zoo

Map 7, D4. Daily: mid-March–Oct 9.30am–6pm; Nov–mid-March 9.30am–4pm; $8. Bus #5 from downtown.

More than 250 species reside in the **Woodland Park Zoo**, at N 55th Street and Phinney Avenue N, a state-of-the-art facility a mile or so north of central Fremont, whose spacious layout, humane exhibits, and botanical garden-quantity of trees and plants should make it attractive to any visitor. The large plots of open space might cause some to yearn for more animals and less park, but it's far less cramped than the typical zoo for its animals, whose natural habitats are simulated with as much space and accuracy as possible. All of the exhibits – often thematically arranged to reflect different climates and geography (Tropical Asia, Northern Trail, Temperate Forest, Australasia) – can be covered in a few hours.

Though not as large as some other US zoos, the diversity is impressive, including such exotic species as lion-tailed macaques, pygmy marmoset (the smallest type of monkey in the world), porcupine, and a Malayan sun bear (the smallest type of bear in the world). While most of the exhibits are imaginative, make a special effort to check out the indoor "Day and Night" section, where you creep along in near-darkness so as not to disturb an assortment of nocturnal birds and reptiles that slither in and out of sight. Just outside are gorillas almost close enough to touch, and more than close enough to examine their puzzled facial expressions (don't worry, their habitat is safely separated from visitors by glass). You can also get within a few feet of the elephants in the Tropical Asia section, best for their daily 10am baths.

You'll have to be content to see the zebras and giraffes from a much greater distance: they're allowed to roam uncaged through the large field in the **African Savanna** section – not quite like going to African plains, but about as good a zoo facsimile as you'll get. Don't leave before taking a peek at the tiny, burrowing prairie dog, tucked into an easily missed corner (behind the Pony Ring).

Climbing the low rocks that provide a viewing platform for the African Savanna, be on the lookout for a tiny gold, bursting sun-shaped memorial to **Jimi Hendrix**.

According to the inscription, it was "funded by worldwide donations to KZOK radio in the memory of Jimi Hendrix and his music." Presumably the fundraising drive was not a massive success, as the space covered by the design is small enough to be obscured by a few birds.

GREEN LAKE

Map 7, F2.

A few blocks northeast of the zoo – just a fifteen-minute walk away through **Woodland Park** – landlocked **Green Lake** is a popular recreational retreat for neighboring Seattleites, circled by a three-mile path popular with joggers. The lake was well on its way toward becoming a swamp in the 1880s, when the creeks that fed and drained the lake were eliminated; it now hosts more than 150 species of birds, and the lake's tiny **Duck Island** is designated as a wildlife reserve to help ensure the area's biodiversity. **Green Lake Rentals**, at the northeastern corner of the lake (April–Sept, hours vary; ℂ527-0171), rents paddleboats, rowboats, canoes, and kayaks for $8/hr, sailboats for $12/hr.

There's not much to see in the quiet, well-off districts of **Green Lake** and **Greenwood** that border the lake, though there are some fair restaurants and thrift shops along Greenwood Avenue N between N 70th and N 75th streets, and the *Honey Bear Bakery*, down at 2106 N 55th St, draws a clientele from all over the city for its freshly baked breads and vegetarian snacks. Also near this stretch is the time-warp *Twin Teepees* diner and lounge, at 7201 Aurora Ave N, whose tacky pair of connected faux teepee buildings – a landmark for drivers of Highway 99 since the 1930s – would be more at home in southern California.

LAKE WASHINGTON AND OUTLYING NEIGHBORHOODS

Much of Seattle is dominated by scenic residential districts that don't offer much in the way of sights, though the extra effort needed to see **Lake Washington** and the best parts of the **outlying neighborhoods** – which includes areas outside the city proper – is easily justified. Given their geographical dispersion, having a vehicle helps: though crosstown traffic is often exasperating, cruising around conveys a sense of the diverse topography that makes Seattle such an appealing place to live. Public transportation does run to most of these places, though the routes are more sporadic than those serving more central districts.

A bike ride or car cruise along **Lake Washington Boulevard** – the eastern boundary for much of the city – takes you through some of Seattle's prettiest portions; **Warren G. Magnuson Park** and **Seward Park** have attractive, isolated walks by the water's edge. The eastern side of Lake Washington is the headquarters for Microsoft and other major technology companies, with suburban **Bellevue** the biggest of its towns.

South of downtown, Seattle becomes more industrial, although West Seattle does have **Alki Beach**, the most popular of the city's few beaches. In the heart of the industrial area, the cavernous **Museum of Flight** is one of the better museums in the Northwest; the **Rainier Brewery**, also located in the southern industrial section, is recommended for beer-lovers. The only reason to visit Renton, south of the city limits, is to pay your respects at **Jimi Hendrix's grave** in Greenwood Cemetery.

LAKE WASHINGTON

Map 2, G1–G9.

Eighteen miles from its northernmost to southernmost points and about three-and-a-half miles at its widest, **Lake Washington** is a formidable buffer between Seattle and its eastern suburbs, collectively known as the **Eastside**. In the early 1900s, tradespeople lugged ferries full of produce across the lake into the city, though the city was far more interested in the commerce generated by large vessels coming down Puget Sound into Elliott Bay. Interaction between the Eastside and Seattle took off with the construction of the 1.4-mile **Hwy-520/Evergreen Point Floating Bridge** (the longest floating bridge in the world) and the bridge sections of I-90 that run through Mercer Island, in the 1940s and

1960s respectively. These roadways facilitated the development of bedroom communities on the Eastside, and today are constantly backed up with traffic during rush hour – though the flow is in both directions now that thriving companies have become established in Bellevue, Redmond, and other suburbs.

The lakeshore is partially occupied by plush, exclusive estates, but much of it remains dedicated to public use by bicyclists and joggers – even swimmers, ever since a 1960s cleanup mostly rid the lake of pollution, though the water is too cold for pleasant swimming most of the time. If you want to get out on the water without getting *in* the water, **boat rentals** are available at the University of Washington's Waterfront Activities Center (see p.242).

Warren G. Magnuson Park

Map 2, G2. Bus #74.

A couple miles northeast of the UW campus, **Warren G. Magnuson Park** is a pleasant lakeside batch of fields and walking paths, especially at its northeastern tip, where sunbathers at **Sand Point** enjoy near-isolation. Cut off from the traffic of Sand Point Way by the large property belonging to the National Oceanic and Atmospheric Administration (NOAA), it's not convenient to public transportation, at least forty minutes by bus from downtown, but it's worth the hike if you want to experience one of Seattle's best public artworks, or if you're a particularly devoted fan of local grunge superstars Soundgarden, who named themselves after Douglas Hollis's **Sound Garden** near Sand Point. The metal rails at the small gate in the fence at the park's northeastern section mark the entrance to the NOAA grounds; to the left, a curving path leads along eleven spindly towers of futuristic metallicism.

Hollow pipes dangle to the side of the towers, helping to produce low hums that can be mistaken for horns from distant ships in the water. A windy environment is needed for maximum effect; that's usually not a problem, but the odd calm day will find the Sound Garden soundless.

Lake Washington Boulevard

From the mouth of the Washington Park Arboretum, **Lake Washington Boulevard** meanders through the wealthy Madison Park district for a mile or so before reaching the shores of the lake, where it hugs the water's edge for about five more miles. It's Seattle's most scenic drive, whether you're glancing at ritzy, high-walled properties on the narrow twisting part of the road near the arboretum, or looking out across Lake Washington toward the Eastside on a horizon dotted with boat traffic. The road passes the posh neighborhoods of **Madison Park** and **Madrona** in the north, and then through the **Mt. Baker** and **Rainier Valley** districts before terminating at Seward Park to the south. It's best on the occasional weekend days (the second Saturday and third Sunday of summer months) when the stretch from Mt. Baker to Seward Park is closed to traffic and the tree-lined thoroughfare fills with cyclists and joggers.

The northern end of this route, in Madrona near Denny Blaine Park, was the setting for one of rock music's greatest tragedies. Nirvana singer/guitarist **Kurt Cobain** was living in one of the mansions on Lake Washington Boulevard overlooking the water when he shot and killed himself in April 1994, in an apartment above the property's garage. The carriage house where he died has since been torn down, and Cobain's widow, Hole singer and actress Courtney Love, moved out and put the home on the market in 1997, though diehards still make pilgrimages there.

Kurt Cobain and Nirvana

When **Kurt Cobain** committed suicide on April 5, 1994, Nirvana was one of the best-selling and most critically acclaimed rock bands in the world. They had gone, in a few quick years, from just another unknown group on the Sub Pop label to the leaders of a perceived movement – grunge, alternative rock, whatever – though Cobain was never comfortable in the rock idol role. The secret to their success lay in the band's strong pop sensibilities, notable on their signature song "Smells Like Teen Spirit," off the album *Nevermind*, mingled with his tormented lyrics – a mixture of self-pity, bitter irony, and humor.

Though their sudden success was a shock, his death, unfortunately, was not, as he had spent much of his last few years battling drug and medical problems. Rumors of his instability had gone into overdrive just a month before, when he nearly died from an overdose of tranquilizers in Rome. Although this was reported as an accident, Cobain – who used heroin, in part to alleviate chronic stomach pain – was clearly in bad shape. A few days before the overdose, several dates on Nirvana's European tour had already been postponed due to Cobain's voice trouble, and the musician returned to his Seattle home to recuperate.

Just a couple of weeks later, Cobain's wife, singer (and, since the mid-1990s, actress) Courtney Love, reported a suicide threat by her husband to the Seattle police, who confiscated a gun and drugs when they arrived at his house. A week later, Cobain was confronted with an "intervention" from his bandmates, friends, and record company representatives; he was convinced, reluctantly, to enter a drug rehabilitation program in California. He got on a plane to Los Angeles on March 30, but escaped the treatment center a couple of days later

continued overleaf

after telling staff he was going out for a cigarette break. Friends and family lost sight of him for the next few days, and attention from the search was briefly diverted when Love was arrested for suspected narcotics possession on April 6 in LA (charges were eventually dropped).

On the morning of April 8, however, an electrician doing work on the property found Cobain's body. The worker reported this to his dispatcher who, before dialing 911, called commercial rock station KXRX with the news, first declaring, "You're going to owe me some pretty good Pink Floyd tickets for this one." Cobain left behind a lengthy, rambling suicide note detailing his failure to enjoy success, his increasing lack of excitement regarding music, and his guilt over going through motions of being a superstar. "The worst crime I can think of would be to rip people off by faking it and pretending as if I'm having 100% fun," he wrote. The note, however, is most renowned for a chilling sentence inspired by a Neil Young lyric: "I don't have the passion anymore, and so remember, it's better to burn out than to fade away."

There's a small beach at Madrona, but if you want solitude – save for the occasional sea otter – head a few miles down the road to the grassy banks a few blocks past **Colman Park** (Map 2, B8), where swimmers have the water practically to themselves; sea otters are rare but not unknown visitors. Peninsular **Seward Park** (Map 2, G7) is a serene turnaround point for cyclists, pedestrians, and rollerbladers. Encircled by a two-and-a-half-mile loop path, there's an even more secluded forest preserve at the park's hilly center, full of Douglas firs, cedars, and maples.

BELLEVUE AND REDMOND

Large floating bridges dominate the strip of I-90 that whizzes from Seattle through small Mercer Island before reaching the Eastside, where **Bellevue** is the biggest of the region's suburbs – and actually the fourth-largest city in all of Washington, complete with downtown skyscrapers and thriving local business. Indeed, downtown Bellevue has become one of the hottest office real estate markets in the US, with less than five percent of its office space vacant. The city center is dominated by **Bellevue Square**, a several-square block shopping plaza that holds two hundred-plus shops and restaurants, where the small but worthy **Bellevue Art Museum**, on the third floor (Mon, Wed, Thurs & Sat 10am–6pm; Tues & Fri 10am–8pm; Sun 11am–5pm; $3, free Tues), cuts an incongruous figure atop the chain clothing stores and juice counters. Often spotlighting Pacific Northwest artists, it's devoted exclusively to rotating exhibits of contemporary work and has far more cutting-edge stuff than you'd expect from a museum in a supermall.

The unusual **Museum of Doll Art**, a few blocks away at 1116 108th Ave NE (Mon–Sat 10am–5pm, Sun 1–5pm; $6), is surprisingly worthwhile and tastefully executed, with appeal for both adults and children. The large, modern facility's two floors contain more than a thousand dolls of all sizes and nationalities from the last several centuries; among the most intriguing are Peruvian burial dolls, African fertility dolls, and Day of the Dead ceremonial figures. There are also some exquisitely crafted miniatures; look for the Japanese boy made from ground oyster shells. The dollhouse wing offers unexpected tableaux like a seventeenth-century Russian orthodox wedding and a 1930s simulation of an "Oriental Shop." More conventional doll culture is represented on the first floor, with vintage Barbies – including the first, from 1959, surprisingly fully clad – and celebrities from Elvis to Bart Simpson. A good antidote to the quaintness is the gruesome monkey violinist in the

BELLEVUE AND REDMOND

mechanical doll case on the second floor, and the "Jacqueline de la Colombiere and Her Beau" figure, made partially from animal skull, opposite the pop culture likenesses on the first floor.

A couple of miles south of Bellevue Square, **Mercer Slough Nature Park** is the largest remaining wetland on Lake Washington, containing some three hundred acres and more than five miles of trails and boardwalks through marshes and meadows. It's a favorite haunt for birdwatchers – more than one hundred species of birds inhabit the premises – though the loud hum of nearby I-405 makes it a less than idyllic retreat. Trail maps are available at the visitors center in **Winters House** at 2102 Bellevue Way SE (Mon–Sat 10am–4pm, Sun noon–4pm); park rangers lead free hour-long nature walks that meet outside the building on Sundays at 11am.

The rest of the Eastside is largely given over to bland modern housing developments and shopping malls. To the east, **Redmond** is dominated by the headquarters of computer giant Microsoft, though unless you have business on its campus, you're little more likely to get a first-hand look at its operations than you are to enter Bill Gates's lakefront mansion in Medina, another city suburb.

ALKI BEACH AND LINCOLN PARK

The anodyne neighborhoods of **West Seattle**, separated from downtown by the industrial piers and waterways of Harbor Island, hold little of interest other than **Alki Beach** (Map 2, B6), near the peninsula's western edge. It's Seattle's most popular beach, crowded on warm days with bathers, volleyball players, and other recreants, and the view across Elliott Bay is impressive, taking in the Space Needle, Magnolia, and Queen Anne Hill. A **pedestrian/bike path** leading eastward from the beach curves along the waterfront for a mile or two and also offers some of Seattle's best panoramas (bus #37 from downtown travels along this route). Apart from taking in the vista, however, the beach is only worth the trip if you're determined to take a swim in Puget Sound, and even then, the water is usually far too chilly for comfort.

In fact, the history of Alki is its most scintillating feature: the beach is where the first party of Seattle's white settlers landed in November 1851. Ten adults and twelve children were met by advance scout and fellow pioneer **David Denny**, who helped them ashore in the midst of heavy rain. The settlement – comprising a mere four cabins – was optimistically named New York in honor of settler Charles Terry's home state. This was quickly amended to the sardonic New York-Alki, roughly translated as "New York eventually" or "New York by and by," with the addition of the Chinook slang word "alki." It was soon determined that the deep-water harbor further north in Elliott Bay would be far more suitable for settlement, especially as ships could not dock at Alki, and the pioneers began staking claims around the area where downtown is situated today. Near 63rd and Alki a small column in Alki Beach Park, inscribed with the names of the settlers, commemorates the spot of the 1851 landing; its base includes a stone from another vaguely symbolic landing site – Plymouth Rock in Massachusetts.

As Alki Avenue curves south around Alki Point it turns into **Beach Drive**, a scenic coastal route with views of the Puget Sound and the Olympic Mountains. **Lincoln Park**, a few miles south down the road, holds a narrow beach with a paved promenade, picnic tables, and **Colman Pool** (Map 2, B6; late June–Aug daily noon–7pm), a heated outdoor saltwater swimming pool.

MUSEUM OF FLIGHT

Map 2, E8. Daily 10am–5pm, Thurs till 9pm; $8. Bus #174.

The largest air and space museum on the West Coast, the **Museum of Flight**, 9404 E Marginal Way S, is unfortunately sited in the midst of Seattle's unattractive industrial section, a thirty-minute drive or bus ride south from downtown. One of Seattle's best museums, it's certainly the most in-depth, with a few dozen military and civilian aircraft and several large complementary exhibits, although only those with an abiding fascination for aviation history may need the entire day to see it.

The museum's centerpiece is the hangar-like **Great Gallery**, which displays more than fifty full-size vintage aircraft, a number of which are suspended in air from the steel-and-glass roof. The first presidential jet (used by Eisenhower in 1959) is here, as well as some early commercial planes and bizarre manifestations of aviation design such as the Gyrodyne QH-50C Drone, a 1963 unmanned anti-submarine helicopter that looks not unlike an insect. When you tire of the bombers, take a look at the tiny early airmail carrier planes, accompanied by exhibits on that hazardous early twentieth-century trade. A more whimsical corner highlights homebuilt aircraft and transcontinental gliders, including the Gossamer Albatross II, whose propellers were connected through a series of gears to a constantly pedaling pilot.

The best of the exhibits on the floors overlooking the main gallery include a display on the US space program and a simulated air control tower, where you – or, more likely, your kids – guide mock takeoffs and landings with prompts from electronic screens and headsets. Aerospace films run throughout the day, but better are the free tours (check at admissions desk for details), sometimes given by ex-Boeing employees, which run through the highlights of the main galleries and add an in-the-know perspective.

In another wing of the museum the **Red Barn**, built in 1909 as the Boeing Company's original manufacturing plant and moved to its current location at the museum in 1975, offers a serious-minded, text-heavy spread of relics from the early days of flight. The achievements of the Wright Brothers get their due – there is a working replica of the wind tunnel they used – but the displays go back even further than 1900 to the ambitious designs of dreamers without the technology to enact their fantasies. There's also credit given to the substantial contributions of the French to the development of manned flight in the early 1900s (such as the crossing of the English Channel in Louis Bleriot's Model XI in 1909), when European advancements in the field were often outpacing those in the US. The impact of World War I and the early years of commercial flight are also traced, as is the birth of Boeing itself – still the most powerful company in the Northwest. The top floor, with its design workshop replica, gives you an idea of how the early Boeing brain trust worked.

For a free tour of Boeing's current operations at its Everett factory, north of Seattle, see p.115.

RAINIER BREWERY

Map 2, E6. Mon–Sat 1–6pm; free. Bus #130.

The omnipresent clouds of white steam from **Rainier Brewery**, 3100 Airport Way, are practically impossible to miss if you're on I-5 just south of downtown. Established in Seattle in 1878, the brewery was, by 1916, the sixth biggest in the world. Its dominance isn't what it used to be,

RAINIER BREWERY

and you'd be hard-pressed to find even locals who'd name Rainier as their beer of choice, but it still generates 5000 barrels of alcohol a day and offers free half-hour **tours** that give visitors a look at the operations, though nearly half of the time is devoted to a self-promoting video. Your payoff is the free beer you get to sample before and afterwards, so if you're not a big beer drinker, best skip the place altogether. A minimum of three people are needed for the tour, so you might be stuck here for a while if it's a slow day, although the hosts seem happy enough to let you soak up free booze while you wait. Also be warned that although the brewery looks close enough to touch if you take exit #163A heading south on I-5, the ensuing tangled streetplan actually makes it extremely difficult to get there via this route; stay on the highway and take exit #164 to Airport Way South.

JIMI HENDRIX GRAVESITE

At the southern edge of Lake Washington just south of the city limits, drab, flat **Renton** is notable only for **Greenwood Cemetery**, Monroe Ave NE and NE 4th St, where **Jimi Hendrix** – the most inventive guitarist in rock history – is buried. He was put to rest here on October 1, 1970, shortly after choking on his own vomit a continent away, in London. Although born and raised in Seattle, Hendrix had spent barely a day in his hometown over the last ten years of his life: he escaped Seattle by enlisting in the armed service at the age of seventeen, before he had graduated from Garfield High School in the Central District. Still, he had enough local time to attend rock'n'roll shows at the long-demolished Spanish Castle Ballroom halfway between Seattle and Tacoma, inspiring his "Spanish Castle Magic" track on the *Axis: Bold as Love* album.

The cemetery, just off I-405, is quite a schlep from downtown Seattle (reachable by bus on the #101 or #106 from downtown transferring to the #105 in Renton), and only worth the pilgrimage for devotees. Even so, it's surprisingly undervisited, with none of the nonstop partying found at Jim Morrison's grave at Père Lachaise Cemetery in Paris. Perhaps for that reason, the groundskeepers willingly give directions to the grave in the southeastern part of the grounds; look for benches grouped around a sundial. Engraved with a guitar, Hendrix's simple headstone is a few yards away, and usually embroidered with flowers and psychedelic stickers left behind by fans.

OUT OF THE CITY

Seattle has plenty to detain any visitor, but it's situated in one of the more fascinating regions of the US and so is an ideal base for **day-trips**. **Tacoma** and **Olympia**, within an hour or so of Seattle, are the only towns with anything faintly resembling the cultural attractions of the big city, though nothing is anything special. More spectacular is **Snoqualmie Falls**, the 270ft waterfall familiar from the *Twin Peaks* television series, 25 miles east of town. There's also the **Boeing factory** in Everett, thirty miles north of Seattle, maker of some of the world's biggest aircraft.

Otherwise, you're best off hopping a ferry (p.15) to any of the nearby fashionable islands in the Puget Sound. **Vashon**, **Bainbridge**, and **Whidbey islands** all offer a slower pace from the city – though not nearly as slow as that of the more distant **San Juan Islands**, which have some of the most tranquil countryside in western Washington.

For explanations of the accommodation and restaurant codes that appear throughout this chapter, see pp.142 & 170.

TACOMA

"The aroma of **Tacoma**" is not what the local tourist board likes to see on bumper stickers, but it's a popular slogan nonetheless, deriding the industrial town that most everyone in the Northwest loves to hate. It may no longer totally merit its bad reputation, considering its efforts to spruce up the city, but you can't help but be put off upon first sight of its downtown, a morass of smoky pulp and paper mills. It's particularly galling since downtown is perched above Puget Sound at **Commencement Bay**, a deep harbor whose appeal helped Tacoma be chosen as the western terminus for Northern Pacific Railroads transcontinental route in 1873.

Arrival and information

Tacoma is just a 25-mile drive down I-5 from Seattle. Greyhound **buses** from Seattle (℡253/383-4621) arrive downtown at 1319 Pacific Ave; Pierce Transit's Seattle Express lines (℡253/581-8000) are more pleasant alternatives, with frequent, and cheaper, bus service between downtown Tacoma and downtown Seattle. They also run buses for local transit. Tacoma's small **visitor information center**, at 440 E 25th St in Freighthouse Square (daily 10am–4pm), has maps and literature about sights in Tacoma–Pierce County.

Downtown Tacoma

Tacoma's central area in the 1980s was grim, with prostitutes and drug addicts lingering amidst the pawn shops and boarded-up businesses on the main drag, **Pacific Avenue**. But even cynics must admit that the strip looks better these days: the most down-and-out elements have largely vanished; the

TACOMA

University of Washington opened a local branch of its campus here in 1997; and further development is on the way, including plans for a contemporary glass art museum.

At 1717 Pacific Ave, **Union Station** (Mon–Fri 8am–5pm), which Amtrak vacated in 1983, has been reborn as a federal courthouse, its interior and exterior totally renovated for a cool $57 million. The copper-domed structure is the most elegant building in Tacoma, its marbled lobby featuring the largest exhibit of sculptured glass by native artist Dale Chihuly – be sure to see the 27 orange-and-henna-hued glass butterfly shapes in the Monarch Window at the rear. More of Chihuly's vibrant glasswork is on display at the nearby **Tacoma Art Museum**, at 12th Street and Pacific Avenue (Tues–Wed & Fri–Sat 10am–5pm, Thurs 10am–7pm, Sun noon–5pm; $4), though that's the best the museum has to offer, other than very minor works by Degas, Renoir, and Frederic Remington, in its small permanent holdings.

For more on Chihuly's glasswork, see p.268.

Next to Union Station, the excellent **Washington State History Museum**, 1911 Pacific Ave (June–Aug Tues–Wed & Fri–Sat 9am–5pm, Thurs 9am–8pm, Sun 11am–5pm; Sept–May Tues–Wed & Fri–Sat 10am–5pm, Thurs 10am–8pm, Sun 11am–5pm; $7), has a huge array of exhibits that stress interactivity without letting the technology dwarf the content. Large galleries recreate well the milieu of frontier towns and early logging industries, and it doesn't shy away from controversial topics, with exhibits on alcoholism among Native Americans and the 1919 general strike in Seattle (see p.282).

Past here the activity gets spotty: a few blocks north on Broadway is the pedestrianized stretch of **Broadway**

TACOMA

Plaza, with an **Antique Row** between S 7th and S 8th streets, but things fade out again to the west. Besides **Wright Park**, at 6th Avenue and South G Street, with its well-tended **conservatory** (daily 8am–4.20pm), nothing else in downtown is worth stopping for.

Point Defiance Park

About four miles north of downtown, at Pearl Street off Ruston Way, is picturesque **Point Defiance Park**, at 700 acres one of the largest urban parks in the USA. The **Five-Mile-Drive** loop has fine viewpoints of the Puget Sound at various pull-offs, from which you can also lose yourself on the park's numerous trails. Signs on the drive direct you to **Fort Nisqually** (April–May Wed–Sun 11am–5pm; June–Aug daily 11am–6pm; Sept–March Wed–Sun 11am–4pm; $1.50 summer, free rest of year), a reconstruction of a fur-trading outpost started in the 1830s with homes and storehouses that illustrate the stark lifestyles of residents of the original fort. The nearby **Camp Six** logging museum (mid-Jan–March & Oct Wed–Sun 10am–4pm; April–May Wed–Sun 10am–5pm; June–Sept Wed–Fri 10am–6pm, weekends till 7pm; free) is best on spring and summer weekends, when the logging train steam locomotive rides are running ($2). There's also a **zoo** and **aquarium** in the park (daily summer 10am–7pm, rest of year 10am–4pm; $7).

Eating and drinking

Antique Sandwich Company 5102 N Pearl St ©253/752-4069.
Mon–Sat 7am–7pm, Sun 8am–7pm. Budget.
The food's just okay here, but the ambience is laidback and inviting, and it's a good place to pick up free listings mags.

Engine No. 9 611 N Pine St ©253/272-3435. Kitchen open
Mon–Sat 11.30am–11pm, Sun 11.30am–10pm; bar usually
closes around 1 or 2am. Inexpensive.
Jovial tavern with fire station decor is a better place for drinking
or live music than eating; so-so pizza dominates the menu.

Shakabrah Java 2618 6th Ave ©253/572-4369.
Mon–Thurs 6am–10pm, Fri 6am–midnight, Sat 7am–midnight,
Sun 6am–9pm. Budget.
In Seattle this would be just another coffeehouse; here it
stands out for offering live music and Internet access.

Wendy's 430 E 25th in Freighthouse Square ©253/572-4678.
Mon–Sat 10am–7pm, Sun 10am–5pm. Budget
A quick and inexpensive Vietnamese restaurant, located in a
food court, started by a former Pike Place restaurant cook.

OLYMPIA

If Tacoma seems slow in comparison to Seattle, **Olympia**
is positively sleepy, having never grown into the metropolis
its founders – or those who named it state capital – hoped
for. About sixty miles south of Seattle and accessed by the
same I-5 route that gets you to Tacoma, it became capital
of the Washington territory in 1853, and though quickly
superseded as a commercial power when railroad routes
were placed elsewhere, it was officially named capital when
Washington gained statehood in 1889. Today it's dominated by the regal **state capitol** building and the legislators
and bureaucrats scampering around the surrounding
Capitol Campus.

The city has an eccentric streak, due in part to the presence just outside town of Evergreen State College, an
untraditional school that lets students design their own
courses of study. Cartoonists Matt Groening (creator of *The
Simpsons*) and Lynda Barry went to Evergreen, as did Sub

Pop Records co-founder Bruce Pavitt and numerous indie rockers; Kurt Cobain lived in Olympia for several years before his rise to fame in Nirvana.

Arrival and information

Greyhound is in the town center at 107 7th Ave SE (℃360/357-5541), just north of the Capitol Campus, and runs **buses** from Seattle to Olympia several times a day (2hrs). Intercity Transit serves the Olympia area (50¢ per bus ride, $1 for daily pass), plus free shuttles between downtown and the Capitol Campus from 7am to 6pm every business day; their customer service office is downtown at the Olympia Transit Center on State Street (Mon–Fri 7am–6pm, Sat 8am–5pm). The **visitors center** at the entrance to the Capitol Campus (Mon–Fri 8am–5pm) is stocked with maps and brochures.

Accommodations

Golden Gavel Motor Hotel 909 Capitol Way ℃360/352-8533. Standard-issue motor lodge near the center of things. ③.

Harbinger Inn 1136 E Bay Dr ℃360/754-0389. The best of Olympia's few B&B options is a five-room 1910 block mansion with balconies and Puget Sound views. ④.

Millersylvania State Park Tilley Rd ℃360/753-1519. Twelve miles south of Olympia, this campground has 120 tents, 47 RV hookups, and 4 primitive sites w/o vehicle, near a beach.

Downtown and the Capitol Campus

Downtown Olympia is made up of low-key blocks of restaurants, cafés, and the odd offbeat shop, with little in the way of sights bar the **Old State Capitol Building**, at

OLYMPIA

Washington and 7th Avenue, whose gothic turrets and arched windows overlook the green square of **Sylvester Park**. Just west of downtown is **Capitol Lake**, actually the southern part of Budd Inlet, on which you'll also find a waterfront **farmers' market** on weekends and some weekdays, April through December.

Just south of downtown, the **Capitol Campus**, a several-block string of government buildings starting at 14th Avenue and Capitol Way, is dominated by the capitol itself, the **Washington State Legislative Building**, an imposing Romanesque structure not far removed in grandeur from the US Capitol in Washington, DC. The original state capitol was constructed here in 1856 as a modest wooden building that didn't take long to decay, at which point operations were moved to the Old State Capitol; the present building, finished in 1928, is, at 287ft, only surpassed by St Paul's Cathedral in London, St Peter's in Rome, and St Isaac's in St Petersburg as the fourth tallest all-masonry domed building in the world. Free guided **tours** (daily 10am–3pm, on the hour) take you through an opulent interior highlighted by the Rotunda's five-ton Tiffany chandelier.

A few blocks further south, the **State Capital Museum**, at 211 W 21st Ave (Tues–Fri 10am–4pm, Sat–Sun noon–4pm; $2), houses two floors of marginally interesting exhibits in the Italian Renaissance revival-style Lord Mansion, best of which is an upstairs collection of Native American basketwork.

Tumwater and the Olympia Brewery

Heading south from downtown on Capitol Way for a mile or two leads into the first pioneer community in Washington – **Tumwater** – home to the large **Olympia Brewery**, until recently the biggest visitor draw in the area besides the state capitol. You used to be able to tour the brewery, but this hasn't been possible since early 1997, setting off anxieties that the operation, one of the biggest local employers, was about to close. Call ©360/754-5177 to see if the tours are on again.

Wolf Haven International

About eight miles south of Tumwater, following Capitol Way as it turns into Old Highway 99, a left turn on Offut Lake Road gets you to **Wolf Haven International** (May–Sept daily 10am–4pm, Oct–April Mon & Wed–Sun 10am–3pm; $5), a nonprofit organization offering sanctuary to more than forty wolves who would not be able to survive in the wild. You can walk within yards of the unexpectedly friendly animals, and the tour guides occasionally let loose with full-throated imitation wolf howls, setting off a blood-curdling frenzy of mournful baying among the resident population. The exchange is more surreal during a "**howl-in**" (May–Aug Fri & Sat at 6.30pm; ©1-800/448-9653 or 360/264-4695 for reservations; $6), a combination of storytelling and music that draws upon wolf-related myths and legends with call-and-response howls with the wolves when darkness falls.

Eating and drinking

Otto's 111 N Washington St ©360/352-8640. Mon–Sat 6am–7pm, Sun 7am–7pm. Budget.
Popular and reliable bagel bakery.

The Pleasant Peasant 113 4th Ave W ©360/705-3645.
Wed–Fri 4–10pm, Sat 9am–2pm & 4–10pm, Sun 10am–3pm.
Moderate.
Pricey by Olympia standards, with plain decor, but very good organic/vegetarian cuisine, especially strong on pasta.

OLYMPIA

Saigon Rendesvous 117 5th Ave W ℂ360/352-1989.
Mon–Fri 10.30am–10.30pm, Sat 10.30am–10pm, Sun
11.30am–9pm. Inexpensive.
Good Vietnamese food that's reasonably priced and well-
portioned, right in the city center.

The Spar 114 4th Ave E ℂ360/357-6444.
Sun–Thurs 6am–10pm, Fri–Sat 6am–11pm. Inexpensive.
Average American diner-styled cuisine, but in a funky old-time
setting, with long curving counter, old photos of Olympia on
the wall, and backroom lounge for smokers and drinkers.

SNOQUALMIE FALLS

Twenty-five miles east of Seattle down I-90, **Snoqualmie
Falls**, a dreamlike vision as pictured in the opening
sequence of David Lynch's cult TV show *Twin Peaks*,
exceed even Niagara Falls in height by a hundred feet.
They cascade 270ft in a rock gorge, and the mist is so dense
at points that you'd swear hidden technicians were billow-
ing fake clouds of fog from either side. The **observation
platform** is just across from the parking lot; for an equally
dramatic and less crowded viewpoint, take the half-mile
River Trail, which leads from the platform to the bottom
of the falls. Between the platform and the waterfall is the
Salish Lodge, the innocuous-looking structure that served
as the locale for many of the series' most dramatic scenes.

Non-fans of the series will be more interested in hiking
some of the nearby trails; the steep four-mile climb up **Mt.
Si**, which starts on Mt. Si Road in North Bend, is the most
popular, with summit views of the surrounding mountains
and Mt. Rainier. Forest shades the trail most of the way to
the stony area near the 4000ft peak, but the hair-raising
walk to the top of the nearby "Haystack" outcropping is
not advised for casual day-trippers.

SNOQUALMIE FALLS

THE BOEING TOUR CENTER

Boeing has more than 200,000 employees throughout the world, about 30,000 of whom work at their biggest plant in **Everett**, thirty miles north of Seattle. Noses of in-the-works planes can be seen when passing the factory on Hwy-526, but closer views are available at the **Boeing Tour Center** (Mon–Fri: Jan–May & Aug–Dec 8.30am–4pm; June–July 7.30am–4pm; ✆544-1264 or 1-800/464-1476), during ninety-minute tours that occur at least half a dozen times a day. It's a good idea to arrive early, as the first-come, first-served tickets (from the counter just inside the center) often run out fast, with waits of an hour or more not uncommon once you've gotten your time slot.

Don't expect to learn about the company's military contracts, the bumpy road to a merger with McDonnell Douglas, or lobbying in Washington to defeat a House measure that would have blocked Most Favored Nation status for China, thus imperiling one of the company's most important overseas markets; the tour's a smoothly executed PR exercise, focusing on Boeing's impressive technological features. You will get to see what's described as the largest manufacturing building in the world; and, looking around the 98-acre factory building, there's no reason to doubt that claim. Overhead platforms afford views of much of the floor space, cluttered by new planes in various phases of gestation. If it's break-time, you may see workers relieving stress by shooting hoops at the full-sized basketball poles dotting the grounds among the planes-in-progress underneath. The tour concludes with a bus ride on the "flight line" where finished 747, 767, and 777s are tested, giving you a glimpse of some of the newest models about to hit the skies.

THE BOEING TOUR CENTER

The rises and falls of Boeing

Boeing is the top public company in Seattle, with 1994 revenues that exceeded its closest local competitor by $5 billion. And, with its $16.3 billion acquisition of fellow aerospace giant McDonnell Douglas in 1997, it's looking more powerful than ever.

Seattle timberman William Boeing started the business as the Pacific Aero Products Company in 1916, changing the name to the Boeing Airplane Company in 1917. Boeing supplied the Navy with planes during World War I, but after the war the engineering staff was reduced to two, and Boeing resorted to making boats and furniture to survive. It bounced back in the early 1920s by modernizing war planes, and, with the vision of engineer Claire Egtvedt, designing original airplanes. In 1928, the company debuted the first American airliner, though it wouldn't truly reap the stakes for years to come. Boeing's fortunes fluctuated again with World War II, but hit a stride in the 1950s and 1960s, especially after diversifying into space technology. The boom slacked off in the 1970s, with the end of the Apollo space project, a 747 program plagued by problems, and a severe recession. Its workforce was cut by half between 1970 and 1971, a ripple that created bad times for all of Seattle; a billboard was even erected near the city limits reading, "Will the last person leaving Seattle turn out the lights?"

Yet Boeing has come back again: it cranks out more than forty commercial jets a month, and, with Lockheed Martin, it's developing the F-22, considered the most advanced tactical fighter in the world. Though its merger with McDonnell Douglas was opposed by the European Commission, who feared the alliance would threaten the Europe-based Airbus, a Boeing competitor, it managed to gain the EC's approval by dropping its plans to become the exclusive jetliner manufacturer for three US airlines. Not that the loss constitutes much of a dent – Boeing has a backlog of $80 billion in commercial orders alone.

VASHON ISLAND

Only 25 minutes from Seattle by ferry, **Vashon Island** lures visitors with its large patches of greenery, open fields, rocky beaches, and cyclable roads. The main highway is a ribbon threading most of the narrow island, while a sliver of sandbar and landfill connects it to adjoining **Maury Island**, less than half the size of its neighbor and not especially worth the trek.

Details on major Washington State Ferries routes are given in "Introducing the city," p.15.

A sleepy hamlet for most of Seattle's history, Vashon has become more popular recently as a residence for Seattle professionals, which longtime residents say you can measure by the increasing number of Mercedes and Jaguars loading onto the ferries. Indeed some affluent figures have vacation homes or residences here, including ex-*Cheers* mailman John Ratzenberger, and the presence of the **K-2** factory and the **SBC Coffee** headquarters offers more proof of the island's urban connections. You can check out the coffee company's old-fashioned building at 19529 Vashon Hwy SW (Mon–Fri 7am–6pm, Sat 9am–4pm; ☎463-3932), which sells the stuff and has a small museum-like section of old sorting and roasting machines; they also offer tours by appointment, for which you should call a week in advance. Otherwise, the gift stores, cafés, and suchlike lining the main road, **Vashon Highway**, are pleasant enough.

The best way to explore the island is to take a **bike** over from Seattle (note that only five bicycles are permitted on the passenger-only ferry that serves Vashon from downtown); *Vashon Island Bicycles*, at 17232 Vashon Hwy (☎463-6225), rents bikes for $9 an hour, $25 a day. If you plan on

VASHON ISLAND

sticking around overnight, your best options are *Lavender Duck*, 16503 Vashon Hwy SW (✆463-2592; ②–③), Vashon's most affordable bed-and-breakfast set in an 1896 farmhouse. There's also an excellent hostel, *Vashon Island Hostel*, 12119 SW Cove Rd (✆463-2592; ①), which offers log cabin dorm beds and teepees.

Eating and drinking

Dog Day Cafe 17530 Vashon Hwy SW ✆463-6404. Mon–Fri 7am–4pm, Sat 9am–4pm, Sun closed. Budget.
Good for both light healthy meals and coffeehouse-type refreshment, especially its fine juices.

Express Cuisine 17629 Vashon Hwy SW ✆463-6626. Wed–Sun 5pm until "when it dies down." Moderate.
Very informal, with large shared tables, but the dinners are delicious and filling, dominated by seafood dishes.

Sound Food Restaurant and Bakery 20312 Vashon Hwy SW ✆463-3565. Mon–Thurs 7am–8pm, Fri 7am–9pm, Sat 8am–9pm, Sun 8am–8pm. Inexpensive.
Basic but well-presented sandwiches, salads, and seafood/chicken–oriented entrees in an agreeable setting.

BAINBRIDGE ISLAND

Bainbridge Island's clumps of trees and scattered points of interest can't overcome the fact that nothing here beats the Seattle **ferry ride**, which sweeps by the Magnolia bluffs on the way over and gives a close-up of the Seattle skyline upon return. Despite the buildup of touristy shops and galleries near the ferry dock, it's not entirely welcoming to outsiders: public transit is sparse; there are no budget accommodations, other than the scrabbly state park campsite in the north; and the island's narrow roads aren't so great for biking. There are some artsy stores and comfortable diners in **Winslow**, a small harborside town, but this is more a place where you're happy to be a commuter rather than a visitor.

Accommodations

Cedar Meadow B&B 10411 NE Old Creosote Hill Rd ℂ842-5291. In a wooded space across the harbor from Winslow, with free bikes and pickup from the ferry if you call ahead. ③–④.

Fay Bainbridge State Park ℂ842-3931. Campground on the northeast tip of Bainbridge Island, with 36 sites and a beach. Closed mid-Oct–mid-April (but open for day use year round). ①.

Island Country Inn 920 Hildebrand Lane NE ℂ842-6861. Bainbridge's only hotel has 40 rooms, all with queen or king-size beds, and a pool and jacuzzi. ④.

Mary's Farmhouse 5129 McDonald Rd NE ℂ842-4952. The most affordable B&B on Bainbridge has two guest rooms in the $50–60 range. ③.

Winslow and the Bloedel Reserve

The ferry arrives in **Winslow**, Bainbridge's one town of note, loaded with specialty shops and restaurants that draw many people who never get past its main block, **Winslow Way**, which holds most of these spots. Behind Harold's Square mini-mall, a **farmers' market** sells produce and crafts on Saturday mornings from Easter to October; **Bainbridge Arts and Crafts**, 151 Winslow Way E, displays work by local artists.

A car is necessary to get to the island's only real attraction, the **Bloedel Reserve**, at 7571 NE Dolphin Dr, off

BAINBRIDGE ISLAND

the Agatewood Road exit of Hwy-305 (Wed–Sun 10am–4pm; reservations needed ©842-7631; $6). The natural conservatory contains nearly 150 acres of gardens, ponds, meadows, and wildlife habitats, including 84 acres of second-growth forest and abundant rhododendron, along with numerous varieties of trees, and more than 15,000 cyclamen plants. It's usually needle-drop quiet except for the birds (there's a refuge with swans, blue herons and more), and the perfectly geometric Japanese garden and large forest-enclosed reflecting pool add to the immaculate aura – almost overbearingly so.

Out from Bainbridge: Suquamish

If you've made it to the northern part of Bainbridge Island, you'll want to cross over to the **Kitsap Peninsula**, where the village of **Suquamish** is just a few miles down the road. **Chief Sealth**, aka Chief Seattle, the man after whom Seattle was named, is buried here near a white wooden church, his grave marked by two large dugout canoes. Half a mile away, **Old Man House State Park** was where the Suquamish's 500ft x 50ft longhouse stood, the longest one ever constructed on Puget Sound; it was burned in 1870 by the government.

Across Hwy-305, the **Suquamish Museum**, 15838 Sandy Hook Rd (daily: May–Sept 10am–5pm, Oct–April 11am–4pm; $2.50), movingly recounts the native population's forced Americanization after whites had established dominance in the Puget Sound. Among the various artifacts, look for the vintage – and very insensitive – advertisement hawking real estate in Chief Seattle Park that reads, "Just as this location was considered the finest on Puget Sound by the Indians, so is it today the finest property available in salt water."

Eating and drinking

Ruby's 4569 Lynwood Center ©780-9303.
Mon 5–9pm, Tues–Thurs & Sun 11am–2pm & 5–9pm, Fri–Sat 11am–2pm & 5–10pm. Moderate–expensive.
Good and somewhat unusual pastas and entrees, like wild mushroom fetuccini and hazelnut pork medallions.

Sawatdy Thai Cuisine 8780 Fletcher Bay Rd NE ©780-2429.
Tues–Sun 5–9pm. Inexpensive.
On the opposite side of the island from Winslow, this Thai place is the best restaurant if you're going beyond the harbor.

Streamliner Diner 397 Winslow Way E ©842-8595.
Mon–Fri 7am–3pm, Sat–Sun 8am–2.30pm. Inexpensive.
Neighborhood joint where most cooks and customers call each other by name, serving basic American breakfasts and hot meals; the peanut butter pie is a specialty.

Winslow Way Cafe 122 Winslow Way ©842-0517.
Mon–Tues 5–9.30pm, Wed–Sat 5–10pm, Sun 9am–2pm & 5–9.30pm; bar open until midnight. Moderate–expensive.
One of the more expensive Bainbridge restaurants, but also the best, good for classy pizza, pasta, and seafood.

WHIDBEY ISLAND

Whidbey Island is the first spot in the Sound to feel like a self-contained entity, and it's the longest island in the continental United States, nearly fifty miles from top to bottom. It's also not easily digested on a short ferry trip, needing at least a full day – preferably more – to appreciate its diverse qualities. **Langley** and **Coupeville** live up to stereotypes – in the good sense – of small-town getaways. However, **Fort Casey**, **Fort Ebey**, and **Deception Pass State Park** are more enticing, with their remote wooded trails and stark cliffside water views.

Arrival and information

Ferries to Whidbey Island leave from **Mukilteo**, about thirty miles north of Seattle off I-5. The twenty-minute ride terminates at **Clinton**, a tiny town near Whidbey's southern edge, from which Hwy-525 snakes through the middle of the island to Deception Pass at the top, turning into Hwy-20 halfway into the journey. Bringing a car is advisable, although Island Transit has free bus service serving the length of the island daily except Sundays (℃360/678-7771 or 360/321-6688). *All Island Bicycle Rentals*, 302 N Main St in Coupeville (℃360/929-8500), rents **bikes** for $19.95 a day, though cyclists should expect to contend with a fair amount of car traffic. The Coupeville **visitor information center**, 302 N Main St, is just a tiny self-service shack with free literature about B&Bs and island activities. A free visitors' guide, with a detailed map of the island, can be picked up on the ferry.

Accommodations

Captain Whidbey Inn 2072 W Captain Whidbey Inn Rd, Coupeville ℃360/678-4097 or 1-800/366-4097. Out of the way but worth it, with quiet rooms overlooking Penn Cove, as well as cottages and chalets in the forest, and a restaurant in the main lodge renowned for its seafood. ⑤-⑦.

Country Cottage of Langley 215 6th St, Langley ℃360-221-8709 or 1-800/460-7219. Five rooms in a restored 1920s farmhouse, on a bluff above Langley and the Puget Sound, approaching luxury-standard in the more expensive suites, with their jacuzzi tubs and fireplaces. ⑥-⑦.

Deception Pass State Park 5175 N Hwy 20 ℃360/657-2417. One of the most popular state parks in the US has 246 tent sites, as well as some primitive grounds. Still, it fills up quickly in the summer months, so call ahead. ①.

Drake's Landing 203 Wharf St, Langley ©360/221-3999. The least expensive of Langley's B&Bs, it's still very acceptable, with bathrooms in each room and views of the harbor. ③.

Fort Ebey State Park Coupeville ©360/678-4636. The best place to camp on Whidbey, with good hiking trails too. Fifty tent sites and three primitive ones (w/o vehicle). Reservations taken; closed Nov–Feb. ①.

The Inn at Langley 400 1st St, Langley ©360/221-3033. One of the poshest stopovers on the Puget Sound, this Frank Lloyd Wrightesque structure is built into a bluff overlooking the water; all 24 rooms have porches with waterfront views. ⑧.

Langley and Coupeville

Though the ferry lands at Clinton, a better first stop is **Langley**, a well-heeled seaside village just a few miles away off Hwy-525. There's not much doing here either, but it's a pleasant place, and **First Street** is lined with antique stores and galleries, such as the self-explanatory *Artists Cooperative of Whidbey Island*, at no. 314.

Sleepy **Coupeville**, in the island's center, is Whidbey's most historic district, with several dozen buildings from the late nineteenth and early twentieth centuries, and neighborhoods dotted with vintage Victorian homes – leftovers from its days as a flourishing seaport. It had been settled back in the 1850s by sea captains and merchants attracted by the protected harbor in **Penn Cove**, and by the plentiful oak and pine trees. Practically all of what's worth seeing today is found on the two blocks of waterfront on **Front Street** between Main Street and the pier, a stretch that also has most of Coupeville's shops and eateries. From the **Island County Historical Museum**, at Front and NW Alexander streets, ninety-minute guided

walking tours (May–Sept weekends 11am; $3) take you by the historic homes, churches, and what have you, though the most interesting of these, **Alexander's blockhouse**, just outside the museum, can be seen on its own for free. This small wooden structure was built by settlers to defend themselves from possible attack by the local Skagit Indians – which never occurred.

Fort Casey and Fort Ebey

Coupeville is actually part of **Ebey's Landing National Historical Reserve**, a series of farms, forests, and privately owned land named after one of the island's first white settlers, Colonel Isaac Ebey, who in an 1851 letter to his brother described his new home as "almost a paradise of nature . . . I think I could live and die here content." Ebey did indeed die here, but not with a smile on his face; in 1857 he was slain by Alaskan Tlingit in revenge for the killing of one of their chieftains.

On the western side of the island are two state parks in the reserve; the fort at one of these, **Fort Casey State Park**, was built at the turn of the century to guard the entrance to Puget Sound, though by the 1950s it was obsolete. Check out the grim cluster of dark **gun batteries**, whose World War II-era gun emplacements and spacious crannies can be freely explored.

If you have the legs, a seven-mile walk north along the beach leads from Fort Casey to the less militaristic – and more aesthetically pleasing – **Fort Ebey State Park** (reachable by car by turning left on Libby Road three or four miles northwest of Coupeville). Be warned, though: the walk is slow going, more stone than sand. An abandoned gun and bunker emplacement remain here, built in 1942 to defend against possible attack from the Pacific; the eerie atmosphere is enhanced by the remote location and heavy forest cover.

Deception Pass State Park

Pint-sized **Deception Pass State Park**, with its excellent hiking trails and campsites, occupies land on both Fidalgo and Whidbey islands, which are separated by Deception Pass itself, a narrow gorge spanned by an arching steel bridge. The turbulent waters in between were originally thought to be a small bay when charted by the Spanish. However, the British later discovered that the passage was actually a deep channel, and gave it its current descriptive name.

Grab a map from the Whidbey-side park office at 5175 N Hwy-20 and head to the **Lighthouse Point Trail** that begins right near the interpretive center, meandering along beach and forest for nearly a mile, leading to rocky bluffs with good views of the pass.

Eating and drinking

Christopher's 23 Front St, Coupeville ⓒ360/678-5480. Mon–Thurs 11.30am–9pm, Fri 11.30am–midnight, Sat 9am–midnight, Sun 9am–9pm. Inexpensive–moderate. Solid lunches and dinners that strike a good balance between basic café food and ritzier dining. Live music Thurs–Sat.

Knead & Feed 4 Front St, Coupeville ⓒ360/678-5431. Mon–Thurs 10.30am–4pm, Fri 10.30am–4pm & 5–9pm, Sat 9am–4pm & 5–9pm, Sun 9am–4pm. Inexpensive. Homemade breads, pies, and cinnamon rolls at its bakery, or sit-down lunches, and weekend breakfasts and dinners.

Langley Village Bakery 221 2nd St #1, Langley ⓒ360/221-3525. Mon–Sat 7.30am–5pm, Sun 8am–4pm. Budget. Great baked goods, pizza, and soup, either to go or to eat at the several small tables.

WHIDBEY ISLAND

Raven Cafe 197 2nd St, Langley ℗360/221-3211. Daily
7am–5pm. Budget.
Sandwiches and breakfasts in a coffeehouse-like setting, with
local musicians on weekend evenings.

Toby's 8 Front St, Langley ℗360/678-4222. Daily 11am–9pm.
Inexpensive.
Seafood, burgers, and microbrews at this wharfside joint.

THE SAN JUAN ISLANDS

The **San Juan Islands** are actually an archipelago of 743
islands, although only about 170 are visible during high
tide, and only 60 are populated. Regardless, the best of
them are exceptionally scenic getaways from the city.
Unless you've got your own boat or quite a bit of money,
your visits will be restricted to the four islands served by
Washington State Ferries – **San Juan Island**, **Orcas
Island**, **Lopez Island**, and **Shaw Island.** San Juan Island,
by far the largest, offers historic state parks and a busy port,
Friday Harbor; Orcas is the most scenic, especially in the
mountainous interior of **Moran State Park**; Lopez is the
calmest, its flat and largely empty roads a haven for bicyclists; there's barely anything – or anybody – to see on tiny
Shaw Island.

Explorer **Juan de Fuca**, believed to be a Greek sailing for
the Spanish, claimed to have found an inlet at 47 degrees
north latitude while searching for the mythical northwest
passage connecting the Pacific and Atlantic, but this went
unacknowledged until 1787, when Englishman Charles
Barkley found a strait at the approximate location and
named it in honor of de Fuca. It was the Spanish, though,
who first explored the Strait of Juan de Fuca in depth in
1790 under **Manuel Quimper**, accounting for the Spanish
names that grace several of the islands today.

Getting to the islands: Anacortes

Washington State Ferries run only to four of the San Juans, but you can see much of the archipelago on some of the routes. It pays to be early if you're bringing a vehicle, preferably two hours in advance, as the lines at the port can be long. You can just about manage a day-trip (Lopez is the closest), but it's better to plan on staying in the San Juans overnight – and **booking accommodations** well in advance – or at the very least spending the night before your departure in Anacortes before boarding the boats, the earliest of which leave at around 6am.

See "Introducing the City," p.15, for full San Juan
ferry timing and prices.

All the ferries – usually about a dozen daily – leave from the small port town of **Anacortes**, which is reachable from the convention center in downtown Seattle by Gray Line bus (daily 5.45am; $15.25 one-way; 1hr 45min; ✆626-5208 or 1-800/426-7532). As way-stations go, it's not bad, offering a few decent places to stock up on snacks and sandwiches before getting on the boat; try *Geppetto's*, 3320 Commercial Ave, with good Italian takeout food and baked goods, or *La Vie En Rose*, 418 Commercial Ave, serving tasty sandwiches and breads. If you need to stay overnight to catch a dawn ferry, the street is also lined with numerous budget hotels, the least generic of which is the *Islands Inn*, no. 3401 (✆360/293-4644), while the *Majestic*, at no. 419 (✆360/293-3355), is a nicely renovated, but more expensive, option.

Victoria Clipper (✆448-5000 or 1-800/888-2535) runs a passenger-only ferry from Pier 69 in Seattle to San Juan's Friday Harbor ($39 one-way, $54 return) and Orcas's Rosario ($43 one-way, $62 return). Boats leave once daily from mid-May through September, weekends and holidays

GETTING TO THE ISLANDS: ANACORTES

127

from mid-October to the end of the year, and just week-ends at other times.

Lopez Island

The first stop on the ferry trips is usually **Lopez Island**, the most pastoral and uncrowded of the strait's three prominent islands, with farms that formerly supplied much of western Washington. It's not the agricultural power that it used to be, but there are still plenty of orchards and cattle around, if not much else. There isn't much to do here except hike, camp, and bike, which is its appeal: Lopez is undeveloped, with a friendly population of less than two thousand. Residents did not entirely welcome, however, the recent construction of an opulent summer home for Microsoft billionaire Paul Allen on **Sperry Peninsula**, the remotest part of the island.

Arrival and information

The best way to see the small, mostly flat island is by **bike**. Rentals are available in **Lopez Village** – the island's tiny commercial district, down Fisherman Bay Road, about five miles from the ferry – from *The Bike Shop* on Lopez (ℂ360/468-3497), which will deliver bikes anywhere on Lopez, or further south on Fisherman Bay Road, at *Lopez Bicycle Works* (ℂ360/468-3700). At the latter location, *Lopez Kayaks* arranges **sea trips** ($37.25 a half-day) and rents **kayaks** ($15 per hr). Maps and information are available at many businesses in the village.

Accommodations

Inn at Swifts Bay Port Stanley Rd ℂ360/468-3636. The classiest lodgings on Lopez are nestled at the bottom of a little-traveled road near the ferry; turn left one mile south of the dock, and it's on the right, just past the fire station. ⑤.

Islander Lopez Fisherman Bay Rd ©360/468-2233, 1-800/736-3434. The only option if you don't want to camp or go for a pricey B&B, and quite a good one, with thirty spacious rooms (most with sunset views), swimming pool and hot tub, plus *Lopez Bicycle Works & Kayaks* on the same property. ④–⑤.

Odlin County Park ©360/468-2496. By the beach, just a mile from the ferry (follow signs from Ferry Rd). Charges $13 for campsites ($15 for premium sites on the beach), $10 for hikers/bikers. Closed Nov 1–March 15. ①.

Spencer Spit State Park Baker View Rd ©360/468-2251. Forty-one tent sites (along with three primitive ones w/o vehicle and one utility site) at an isolated park with good hiking and clamming available. Definitely the best place to camp on Lopez, but reserve ahead for peak season. Closed Nov–March. ①.

Around the island

Lopez's top destination is **Shark Reef Park**, at the island's southwest tip on Shark Reef Road, reached via Fisherman Bay and Airport roads. A ten-to-fifteen-minute walk through dense forest is rewarded by beautiful vistas at the water's edge, from where you can spot the occasional sea lion past the tidepools. Back on the northeast side of the island, **Spencer Spit State Park**, in addition to its camp-sites, offers good hiking among the trees or the spit, a slender strand of sand that juts out from the shore. Clam digging is an option here, although clam season was closed by the Department of Fisheries for nine months in mid-1997 to give the clams a chance to replenish themselves; indeed, the entire park was closed for three months in early 1997 due to high nitrate levels in the water.

LOPEZ ISLAND

Eating and drinking

The Bay Cafe Lopez Village ✆360/468-3700. Days and hours vary. Expensive.

The only spot in Lopez for class dining, but the eclectic entrees – in the $15–20 range, with at least one vegetarian choice daily – are worth the price. Best to reserve in advance.

Holly B's Bakery Lopez Village ✆360/468-2133. Mon 7am–5pm, Wed–Sat 7am–5pm, Sun 7am–4pm; fall closed Mon & Tues. Budget.

Small stop for buns, breads, lip-smacking pastries, and light snacks. Open "Aprilish–Decemberish."

South End Cafe Mud Bay Road, in the back of the store next to the gas station, ✆360/468-3198. Mon–Fri 11.30am–2pm, Fri–Sat 3–7pm; Sun closed. Budget.

A serviceable pitstop for burgers or pizza.

Orcas Island

Orcas Island is the most alluring destination in the San Juans for its striking scenery; as such, it's the best island to make your base. With rolling hills and leafy timber towering over the highways, beaches, and abundant wildlife, it's well-suited for either strenuous hiking or idle retreat. Its placid qualities have not escaped the notice of the outside world – there are only about 3500 full-time residents on the island, but three times as many property owners.

Accommodations

Beach Haven Resort Enchanted Forest Rd ✆360/376-2288.

An appealing refuge three miles west of Eastsound, with beachfront log cabins and wooded grounds. While remote, it's not undiscovered; reservations for summer stays (one week minimum) are needed a year in advance. ⑤.

Doe Bay Village & Resort Doe Bay Rd, turn right at the sign for *Doe Bay Natural Foods Cafe & General Store* ©360/376-2291. Six dormitory hostel beds for about $15/night, plus yurts and various types of cabins, some with basic amenities. Hot tubs and sauna are available for $5/night extra; $18 campsites cover a single tent (for two persons) and unlimited use of hot tubs and sauna. ①–⑤.

Orcas Hotel At the ferry landing in Orcas ©360/376-4300. A restored Victorian Inn whose plushest rooms have views of the harbor; the "modest Victorian" rooms on the sides and in the back don't, although they're considerably less expensive. ④–⑥.

Rosario Resort & Spa 1 Rosario Way ©1-800/562-8820. Former Seattle mayor and wealthy shipbuilder Robert Moran built this elegant, waterside mansion that now serves as a luxury resort expensive even by San Juan Island standards. ⑦.

Around the island

The ferry docks at the tiny town of **Orcas**, really just a street with a few shops; down the main road is **Eastsound**, a slightly larger town that divides the island roughly in half. Even here, there are no real sights, but it's the place on the island to eat and pick up necessities.

Past Eastsound, it's a few miles to the gates of **Moran State Park**, five thousand acres of forest and lakes, and thirty miles of trails. Overlooking the expanse is **Mt. Constitution**, at 2409ft the highest point on the island. A tough but exhilarating four-mile trail leads from Cascade Lake on the Horseshoe Highway to the top. The steep path twists around creeks, fields, and thick foliage, and there's a fair chance of spotting some of the nearly two hundred species of birds on Orcas. At the summit, a **stone tower** has the expected panoramic views.

ORCAS ISLAND

Otherwise, the best place to unwind is at **Doe Bay Village & Resort**, even if you're not staying there. Perched between forest and water at one of the calmest spots in the San Juans, its open-air, mineral spring-fed hot tubs are available for day use by non-guests ($5). A more adventurous dip into the water is provided by *Shearwater Adventures*, on kayak trips that leave from the resort ($39 half-day, $75 full; ℂ360/376-4699), yielding closer looks at the island's bald eagles, seals, and whales.

Eating and drinking

Bilbo's Festivo North Beach Rd and A St ℂ360/376-4728.
Daily 4.30–9.30pm; reservations advised. Moderate.
Reasonably good Mexican food, dished out in an affable, dining-roomish setting.

Cafe Olga Corner of Olga Rd and Doe Bay Rd ℂ360/376-5098.
March–Dec daily 10am–6pm. Moderate.
Enjoy good, if not big-portioned, meals and fruit pies either indoors or on an outdoor porch.

Doty's A-1 Cafe 7 North Beach Rd ℂ360/376-2593.
Daily 6.30am–6pm. Budget.
Just standard American diner food, but the place is amiable enough, and a good place to fill your belly before catching the ferry.

Garden Cafe 10 North Beach Rd ℂ360/378-5177.
Wed–Sat 11.30am–5pm. Inexpensive.
Appetizing pan-Asian fare that's a good deal, plus you get to walk through a yard and garden to enter.

San Juan Island

San Juan Island holds the San Juans' only incorporated town, **Friday Harbor**, whose wharfside blocks seem to conduct more commerce than the rest of the strait put together, though the balance of the island is rural and sparsely populated. There's plenty of good scenery, hiking, and, for a change, even some cultural sights – a **whale museum** and two national historic parks, **American Camp** and **English Camp**, which were military bases during a land dispute in the 1800s.

Arrival and information

Ferries arrive at **Friday Harbor**, which has a self-service **tourist info** booth on A Street, a good place to get a map of the island's irregular main roads. For personal assistance, the main office of the **San Juan Island National Historical Park**, 1st and Spring (Mon–Fri 8.30am–4pm; ☎360/378-2290), is not a visitors' center as such, but they'll be happy to answer questions about the island. A **car** is the best way to check out the scattered points of interest, though the sporadic San Juan Shuttle stops at most of the island's principal attractions ($4 one-way, $7 round-trip, $10 day pass; ☎360/378-8887 or 1-800/887-8387). **Bikes** can be rented at *Island Bicycles*, 380 Argyle St (☎360-378-4941); **mopeds** are available at *Susie's Mopeds*, corner of 1st and A streets (☎360-378-5244 or 1-800/532-0087), across from the ferry departure lanes. To get on the water, *San Juan Safaris* (☎360-378-2155 or 1-800/451-8910 ext 258) runs **kayak treks** and **whale watch cruises** from Roche Harbor.

Accommodations

Bed and breakfasts are most prevalent here, but there are some inexpensive **campsites**: *Lakeside Campground*, at 2627 Roche Harbor Rd (☎360/378-2350), and *San Juan County Park*, 380 West Side Rd (☎360/378-2992), both of which you should reserve ahead. For a cyclist-oriented camp, there's *Pedal Inn*, 1300 False Bay Rd (℗360/378-3049), five miles from the ferry dock.

Blair House 345 Blair Ave ℗360/378-5907 or 1-800/899-3030. Just up from the ferry right off of Spring Street, this is one of the less ostentatious B&Bs on the islands, nearly enclosed by trees, with a big front porch and hot tub. ④.

Friday's 35 1st St ℗360/378-5848 or 1-800/352-2632; *fridayharbor.com/~fridays*. Recently renovated 1891 hotel, convenient to the ferry, with agreeable ambience. ⑤.

Roche Harbor Resort Roche Harbor ℗360/378-2155 or ℗1-800/451-8910. At the opposite end of the island from Friday Harbor, in a town that consists of little besides the resort. But if you want old-style elegance during your stay, the *Hotel de Haro* (now part of the resort) is the place. ④.

Wharfside Slip K-13, Port of Friday Harbor, ℗360/378-5661; *www.rockisland.com/~pcshop/wharfside.html*. Two private staterooms on a 60ft motorsailor in the harbor make for an interesting change of pace from the usual B&B. ⑤.

Friday Harbor

With a population of nearly two thousand, **Friday Harbor** is by far the biggest town in the San Juans, though its prominence wasn't always a given – when it became the county seat in 1873 after the Pig War had ended (see p.136), it had a population of three. But its protected harbor and good anchorage allowed it to rebuild, and by the turn of the century the population had reached three or four hundred, continuing to grow through the first half of the 1900s, until a postwar decline refocused the town toward tourism and real estate.

With its numerous cafés and restaurants, the **waterfront** area is the place to eat before touring the island or heading back to the mainland. The commercial district near here is an unexceptional string of shops and cafés that makes for an okay stroll, hitting its peak at the **Whale Museum**, at 62 1st St N (daily: May–Sept 10am–5pm, rest of year 11am–5pm; $4), which has a small collection of whale skeletons and displays explaining the creatures' migration and growth patterns. The small room near the gift shop runs short video documentaries about research expeditions that include some good up-close footage of whale maneuvers. The volunteers at the museum can fill you in on the real thing, though: there are ninety-odd orcas that roam the 200-mile radius of San Juan Island, best seen at **Lime Kiln Point State Park** on the island's western side.

If you're interested in seeing the whales up close, *San Juan Safaris* (p.133) runs such tours.

American Camp and English Camp

At the island's southern tip is **American Camp**, a national park that played a role in the infamous Pig War. Morale among the US troops stationed here was quite low, and it's not hard to see why: the windswept, rabbit hole-strewn fields are bleak and largely shorn of vegetation. A self-guided, one-mile foot trail begins from the parking lot, passing the camp's few remaining buildings and what's left of a gun emplacement. Costumed volunteers re-enact life in both camps during the summer; call the park for details (©360/378-2902).

Up the island's western side is **English Camp**, the site of the only foreign flag officially flown by itself on American soil. Here forests overlook the pleasant green fields and big

SAN JUAN ISLAND

The Pig War

Both English Camp and American Camp were established on San Juan Island as the result of the **Pig War**, a dispute in which not a single shot was fired at a human being, the lone casualty being a pig that belonged to the British. Its death, however, sparked the resolution of a long-simmering border conflict between the US and the UK.

The Oregon Treaty of 1846 had given the United States possession of the Pacific Northwest south of the 49th parallel, extending the boundary "to the middle of the channel which separates the continent from Vancouver's Island." There were, however, two channels – Haro Strait and Rosario Strait – between Vancouver Island and the mainland, and San Juan Island lay between them. Citing different interpretations, both the British and Americans claimed the island and began settling it in the 1850s.

In 1859, American settler Lyman Cutlar shot a British-owned pig that was rooting in his garden. When the British threatened to arrest him, 66 American troops were sent in; the governor of British Columbia responded by sending three warships. Eventually, US President James Buchanan sent Winfield Scott, commanding general of the US Army, to cool things down. An agreement was reached allowing for joint occupation of the island until the dispute could be settled.

This co-ownership lasted for twelve years, during which a number of deaths resulted from the tough conditions faced by the forces on both sides, though none via warfare. Finally, the dispute was referred to Kaiser Wilhelm I of Germany in 1871, who ruled in favor of the US the following year.

leaf maple trees near the shore, where four buildings and a small formal garden have been restored. A slide show in the barracks (summer daily 8.30am–5pm, rest of year

Mon–Fri 8.30am–4pm) explains the Pig War – a tale that will begin to seem as familiar as a White House scandal over the course of your San Juan visit. From here you can hike an easy loop to **Bell Point**, or retreat to the parking lot to mount the short (one mile round-trip) but steep, wooded trail to **Young Hill**, passing the small English Camp **cemetery** on the way. The 650ft summit has views over much of the island.

Roche Harbor

At the island's northwest tip is **Roche Harbor**, established in the 1880s around the limestone quarrying business, but the gracious white **Hotel de Haro**, built over the harbor in 1886 to lodge visiting lime-buyers, set a more affluent tone. The hotel's now part of the **Roche Harbor Resort**, and unless you're staying here, it's only worth a quick peek at the building and a stroll around the minuscule wharf. When you head back up to Roche Harbor Road, however, veer off to the left just before the arch welcoming visitors to Roche Harbor and park at the small lot by the cemetery a bit down the road. Signs from here put you on the path to the haunting mausoleum of **John Stafford McMillin**, founder of the hotel. Set far back from the street in the woods, with seven crumbling pillars surrounding a chipped roundtable and chairs honoring various members of the McMillin clan, you expect the werewolves to start howling at any moment.

Eating and drinking

Cannery House 174 N 1st St ℂ360/378-2500.
Mon–Wed 11am–7pm, Thurs–Sun 11am–9pm. Moderate.
Interesting menu and good views of the harbor.

Electric Company 175 1st St ℂ360/378-4118.

Daily 11am–9.30pm. Inexpensive.

A meat-and-potatoes-type tavern that has live music on weekends.

Garden Path Cafe in Churchill Square at 232 A St ℂ360/378-6255. Mon–Sat 10.30am–4.30pm; Sun closed. Inexpensive. Reasonable lunches and dinners, but the big bonus is the view of the harbor, with both indoor and patio seating.

San Juan Donut Shop 209 Spring St ℂ360/378-2271.

Mon–Sat 5am–3.30pm, Sun 6am–1pm. Budget.

The most popular breakfast place in town (not just donuts), opening its doors at 5am to serve riders before the first ferry.

LISTINGS

ACCOMMODATION

Seattle has plenty of **accommodation** to handle its increasing number of visitors; indeed, the problem is not so much getting a room as finding good mid-range deals. In downtown in particular, there's not much middle ground between the **luxury hotels** and bottom-end **budget lodgings**, most of which are a bit grim. If you want something attractive and centrally located, with modern conveniences, you're looking at $80 a night at the least. Good alternatives are **B&Bs**, most of them around the Capitol Hill area, offering much more character and better value for the money, often around $70 a night. **Hostels** offer the best deals for the budget traveler, with dorm beds going for $15 a night or less, along with inexpensive private rooms for which you should always call ahead. **Campsites** are few and far between in the city and are not much of an option.

Lodgings in Olympia, Whidbey Island, Bainbridge Island, Vashon Island, and the San Juan Islands are included in "Out of the City," p.106.

As in any large city, it's advisable to arrange a place to stay **in advance**, at least for the first night of your visit. During

Price codes

━━━━━━

All accommodation prices have been coded according to the least expensive double rooms in each establishment, and only including local taxes where indicated.

① up to US$30
② US$30–45
③ US$45–60
④ US$60–80
⑤ US$80–100
⑥ US$100–130
⑦ US$130–165
⑧ US$165–200
⑨ US $200+

summertime, popular festivals and big sports events can make rooms scarce, and you might be forced to settle for an out-of-the-way motor lodge. Rates sometimes dip **off-season** (notably winter), and there are often discounts for multi-day visits. Bear in mind that a steep **hotel room tax** of 15.6 percent is imposed in Seattle, a figure that lessens outside the city, notably on the islands, where it's below 10 percent.

HOSTELS

All Seattle **hostels** are close to the downtown action. IYHF/AYH memberships are useful in a few of them for procuring space or reduced rates, but not necessary to qualify for a bed in most cases. The Ys and the AYH Pike Place Market hostel have more regulations (though not onerous ones) than the private ones; at all hostels there's usually a limit to the number of consecutive days you can stay, though at the private hostels these rules are sometimes relaxed off-season. Most of the hostels offer **private rooms** for couples and singles, although you'll be paying about two or three times the dorm rate. Regardless, you shouldn't take space for granted; though you may be able to get a space just by showing up, there's no harm in calling ahead.

American Backpackers Hostel

Map 5, C6. 126 Broadway Ave E ©720-2965.
Reached via an alley near the busiest corner in Capitol Hill, this hostel has 45 beds, including four-to-a-room dorms ($13.50) and a few private rooms ($30 single, $35 double). No curfew and lots of extras: free breakfast, downtown pickup, club passes, and parking (in off-season). It also runs bus tours, from camping trips to visiting the graves of Jimi Hendrix and Bruce Lee, with a pit stop at Kurt Cobain's former house. ①–②.

Green Tortoise

Map 3, C4. 1525 2nd Ave ©340-1222.
Relocated from their former site near Seattle Center to downtown, a block away from Pike Place Market, these old-style digs now function as four-to-a-room dorms ($15), plus some more expensive singles and doubles. They "will come and fetch you anywhere in the Seattle area within reason" (ie anywhere in or near downtown); they also do walking tours of the city. ①–②.

Hosteling International Seattle (AYH)

Map 3, B4. 84 Union St ©622-5443; *www.hihostels.com.*
Locationwise this is hard to beat: just a block from Pike Place Market, with Pioneer Square minutes away. Modern, comfortable dorms, with about 200 beds ($15–17, add $3 for non-members), but reservations are still advisable June–Sept, and full AYH membership is required during those months. ①.

HOSTELS

Vashon Island Hostel (AYH)

12119 SW Cove Rd, Vashon Island ℂ463-2592.

As Vashon is only a short ferry ride away from downtown Seattle, you may want to consider this spot; see p.118 for more.

Vincent's Backpackers Guest House

Map 5, D5. 527 Malden Ave E ℂ323-7849.

This comfortable house on a quiet, tree-lined street in Capitol Hill has 38 beds, most in six-bunk dorm rooms ($12), as well as a few doubles for $45. There is a bathroom with shower in all rooms, abundant kitchen facilities, and a backyard with picnic tables. Free pickup from *Greyhound*, *Amtrak*, ferry terminals, and anywhere in downtown if you call in advance. ①–②.

YMCA

Map 3, D5. 909 4th Ave ℂ382-5000.

More sterile than the average hostel, but it's safe, clean, and in the middle of downtown, with singles, doubles, and a dozen dorm beds. Open to both men and women; dorm beds ($17) reserved for AYH members. ①–②.

YWCA

Map 3, D4. 1118 5th Ave ℂ461-4888.

Open to women only, and a bit more upscale than YMCA, with some rooms including private bath. ②.

HOTELS

Seattle's **hotels** are mostly geared toward the business traveler, with many four-star accommodations downtown that run $150 or more a night. There are few good mid-level options, and if you want budget hotels for under $50 a night, the levels of service and cleanliness tend to drop dramatically, as does the desirability of the location. There are actually very few hotels at all outside the downtown and Seattle Center areas, and those that do exist are usually fairly bland, though otherwise amenable. Further out, there are the usual chain options on Aurora Avenue (Highway 99) and near the Sea-Tac airport, both fairly inconvenient bases for exploring the city.

The King County Convention and Visitors Bureau's **Seattle Hotel Hotline** makes reservations at local hotels (April–Oct Mon–Fri 8.30am–5pm; ℂ461-5882 or 1-800/535-7071). The rest of the year, the service (retitled **Seattle Supersaver**) specializes in off-season discount deals. Still, it's often easier to get information about special deals and amenities by dialing the businesses directly.

DOWNTOWN

Alexis

Map 3, C5. 1007 1st Ave ℂ624-4844 or 1-800/426-7033.
Plush decor in this renovated early twentieth-century building, as well as a spa, steam room, complimentary continental breakfast, and the refined *Bookstore Bar & Cafe* in the lobby. Nearly half the rooms are suites that, at their largest, add touches like fireplaces and dining rooms. ⑧.

The Edgewater Inn

Map 4, C6. Pier 67, 2411 Alaskan Way ℂ728-7000 or 1-800/624-0670.
Seattle's only waterfront hotel has nice rooms, the best of which have windows right on the bay – though for those you'll need to both pay some more and reserve well in advance. ⑦.

DOWNTOWN

Four Seasons Olympic

Map 3, D4. 411 University St ✆621-1700 or 1-800/223-8772.
The standard for top-of-the-line luxury accommodations in
Seattle. About half of the residential-styled rooms are suites,
frequented by visiting celebrities and politicians (this is where
Bill Gates held his summit of CEOs from around the world in
1997). The prices are geared toward the CEO crowd as well:
the Presidential Cascade Suite costs $1250 per night. ⑨.

Hotel Monaco

Map 3, D5. 1101 4th Ave ✆621-1770 or 1-800/945-2240.
This one-time Pacific Northwest Bell switching office was
recently converted into a boutique hotel. The exterior still
looks like something out of the Eastern bloc, but inside are
luxurious guest rooms, with two-line phones and fax
machines. ⑧.

Hotel Seattle

Map 3, D5. 315 Seneca St ✆623-5110.
A good deal for those looking for a central location and
modern, but not antiseptic, ambience in the upper-middle
price range. ⑤.

Pacific Plaza

Map 3, D5. 400 Spring St ✆623-3900 or 1-800/426-1165.
Pleasant if unremarkable rooms in a renovated 1928 building
near the middle of the business district. ④.

The Paramount

Map 3, D3. 724 Pine St ✆292-9500 or 1-800/426-0670.
One of the more impressive of the new luxury hotels sprouting
up downtown, with an attractive European-styled exterior and

DOWNTOWN

decent rates. There's a popular pan-Asian restaurant, *Blowfish* (see p.138), on the ground floor. **⑧**.

Pioneer Square Hotel

Map 3, D6. 77 Yesler Way ⓒ340-1234.
This recently restored turn-of-the-century brick hotel, originally built by Seattle founding father Henry Yesler, is the best (if not the only) choice in Pioneer Square for mid-price accommodations with a good level of comfort. There's also a juice bar on the lobby floor, as well as a saloon with fifteen microbrews on tap. **⑤**.

Renaissance Madison

Map 3, E5. 515 Madison St ⓒ583-0300 or 1-800/468-3571.
Formerly known as the *Stouffer Madison*, this gigantic (more than 500-room) luxury hotel towers over I-5 at the southeast edge of downtown. Tasteful marble and wood room decorations, but not as special as the other places with similarly high rates. **⑧**.

Sorrento

Map 3, F4. 900 Madison St ⓒ622-4400 or 1-800/426-1265.
Just on the east side of I-5 from downtown, but still within easy walking distance, this 76-room 1908 hotel, recently modernized with in-room faxes and two-line phones, has top-drawer accommodations in fairly intimate surroundings. The regal exterior surrounds a circular courtyard with palm trees; some rooms have Puget Sound views. **⑨**.

WestCoast Camlin

Map 3, D2. 1619 9th Ave ⓒ628-0100 or 1-800/426-0670.
This 1926 building with a brick-and-terracotta-tower is one of the cheaper downtown hotels and has a nicely faded charm.

However, the rooftop *Cloud Room* lounge – one of the city's favorite romantic landmarks – is due to be converted into luxury suites, and the rest of the hotel is slated for a four-star upgrade, so you should call to see if the prices have changed. ⑥.

WestCoast Vance

Map 3, C2. 620 Stewart St ✆441-4200 or 1-800/663-1144. Administered by the same chain as the *Camlin*, this is also a newly renovated 1920s building, though with not so much character. Try to get a room with a Space Needle view. ⑥.

BELLTOWN AND THE SEATTLE CENTER

Best Western Loyal Inn

Map 4, F4. 2301 8th Ave ✆682-0200.
The cheapest of this chain's downtown Seattle locations is within walking distance of the Space Needle; free parking, too. ④–⑤.

Commodore

Map 4, F6. 2013 2nd Ave ✆448-8868.
Functional rooms – but not much else – on the border between Belltown and downtown. Also has eight hostel beds, although that alternative should only be employed if the far superior nearby downtown hostels are full. ①–②.

The Inn at Queen Anne

Map 4, A2. 505 1st Ave N ✆282-7357 or 1-800/952-5043; *www.pacificws.com*.
Small but comfortable studio apartment-style lodgings on the

edge of Seattle Center, with queen-sized beds. There are kitchenettes with microwaves as well. ⑤.

Moore

Map 4, F6. 1926 2nd Ave ☎448-4851 or 1-800/421-5508. Ancient, large building that offers little in the way of charm, but is well placed to take advantage of both downtown sightseeing and Belltown nightlife. ②.

Seattle Inn

Map 4, E3. 225 Aurora Ave N ☎728-7666. A few blocks east of Seattle Center, and compensating for its lack of personality and nearby Hwy-99 traffic with free parking and free rates for children under 16 staying in their parents' room. ③.

CAPITOL HILL

Eastlake Inn

Map 5, B2. 2215 Eastlake Ave E ☎322-7726. Average motor lodge, but more conveniently situated (a few blocks away from Lake Union's houseboat community) than most, and cheaper than the ones around Seattle Center; some units are mini-suites with kitchens. ②.

UNIVERSITY DISTRICT

University Inn

Map 6, A5. 4140 Roosevelt Way NE ☎632-5055 or 1-800/733-3855. Average modern hotel just off University Way. Some rooms have kitchens; there's also a pool and whirlpool spa. ⑥.

CAPITOL HILL AND THE UNIVERSITY DISTRICT

LAKE WASHINGTON AND OUTLYING DISTRICTS

Mercer Island Travelodge

7645 Sunset Hwy, Mercer Island ℭ232-8000.

Basic, satisfactory motel doubles on Mercer Island, an attractively green suburb in Lake Washington between Seattle and Bellevue, only five miles from downtown and right off I-90. ④.

The Salish Lodge

Snoqualmie Falls, Snoqualmie ℭ1-800/826-6124 or 888-2556.

If you're looking for accommodations with dramatic views, you can't beat this place, which served as *The Great Northern Hotel* in the *Twin Peaks* TV series, and overlooks the Snoqualmie Falls about thirty miles east of Seattle. They pour on the luxuries, too, like woodburning fireplaces and a rooftop spa. ⑥-⑦.

Woodmark

1200 Carillon Point, Kirkland ℭ425/822-3700 or 1-800/822-3700.

In the Eastside suburb of Kirkland (just north of Bellevue), this high-priced luxury hotel on the edge of Lake Washington has some of the best waterside views around, though you'll pay plenty, and not every room overlooks the lake – those that do cost about $50 extra. Also houses a popular (and expensive) lakeside seafood restaurant, *Waters*. ⑧.

BED AND BREAKFASTS

Seattle's **bed and breakfasts** offer the best balance of comfort and value in accommodations. Rooms are almost always bigger and nicer than hotel units going for the same rates, and many are in converted turn-of-the-century mansions – mostly grand old Capitol Hill homes. There are usually fewer than ten rooms in each, making reservations a good idea, and there's often a two-night minimum stay. Proprietors tend to be a friendly lot who know when not to overdo the hospitality, and are often a good source of information about the area and its history.

B&Bs are especially popular in the Puget Sound and the San Juan Islands, and not just for out-of-state travelers. Seattleites will often spend weekends or even vacations there, and with good reason, as many offer splendid rural isolation within easy drive of the big city. See "Out of the City," p.106, for listings of the best of these.

If you're looking for assistance, call *Seattle & Surrounding Region: A Pacific Reservation Service* (✆784-0539), which makes reservations throughout Washington State and British Columbia and has a list of guest homes available for $5; or *A Travelers' Reservation Service* (✆232-2345), which also has B&Bs throughout the Northwest (a $5 booking fee may apply to some accommodations).

DOWNTOWN

Pensione Nichols

Map 3, B3. 1923 1st Ave ✆441-7125 or 1-800/440-7125.
Downtown B&B that could hardly be more centrally located, on a rundown, noisy street. The ten or so rooms are comfortable, if small. ⑤.

QUEEN ANNE

Green Gables Guesthouse

1503 W 2nd Ave ✆282-6863.
These rather preciously appointed dwellings at the top of Queen Anne Hill, a mile from Seattle Center, are actually two

houses with seven rooms, three with private baths; antique beds, stained glass, and hardwood floors throughout. The Rose Room suite has a private entrance and holds up to four people. ④.

Bed & Breakfast on Broadway

Map 5, C5. 722 Broadway Ave E ✆329-8933 or 1-888/329-8933. Next to a huge unsightly vacant lot on the rotary where the commercial part of Broadway ends. Otherwise this turn-of-the-century house, with hardwood floors, oriental rugs, and four rooms is attractive enough and near the main action on Capitol Hill. ⑤.

Gaslight Inn

Map 5, D7. 1727 15th Ave ✆325-3654.
Nine rooms in this popular guest house, as well as large common areas and more expensive suites for longer-term stays. Friendly proprietors, homemade scones, swimming pool, hot tub, and a prime Capitol Hill location make this one of the best in town. ④–⑤.

Hill House

Map 5, C6. 1113 E John St ✆720-7161.
Handsome turn-of-the-century brick house with garden and covered patio, with lower-priced rooms than most Capitol Hill B&B options; children welcome. ③–④.

Prince of Wales

Map 5, D6. 133 13th Ave E ✆325-9692 or 1-800/327-9692.
A bit noisy due to the traffic, but the rooms are up to snuff, with views of the Space Needle and Puget Sound, and the

front porch swing is a good bonus. The attic suite has a private rooftop deck; there's also a two-room suite that can hold three or four guests. ⑤.

Roberta's Bed & Breakfast

Map 5, D4. 1147 16th Ave E ©329-3326.
Five rooms with queen-size beds, all but one with private baths. In an elegant home near Volunteer Park, and on one of the quieter streets in Capitol Hill. ⑤.

Salisbury House

Map 5, E5. 750 16th Ave E ©328-8682;
www.salisburyhouse.com.
Four doubles in this 1904 Capitol Hill mansion with maple floors, high ceilings, and a quiet but convenient location. Ask for the "Blue Room" if you want morning sun, or the "Lavender Room" if you want the biggest space. ⑤.

Shafer-Baillie Mansion

Map 5, D4. 907 14th Ave E ©322-4654 or 1-800/922-4654.
A sprawling, historic home in Capitol Hill, on Millionaires' Row, that also hosts weddings and the like. Eleven handsomely furnished rooms, most with private baths, all with refrigerators; large lawns and gardens too. ⑥.

UNIVERSITY DISTRICT

Chambered Nautilus

Map 6, D3. 5005 22nd Ave NE ©522-2536 or 1-800/545-8459.
Early twentieth-century Georgian home with six rooms, four of which have porches; apple quiches are the breakfast specialty. Reservations a month or two ahead of time are advisable in the summer months. ⑤.

UNIVERSITY DISTRICT

The College Inn

Map 6, B6. 4000 University Ave NE ℂ633-4441;
www.speakeasy.org/collegeinn.
The most budget-friendly Seattle B&B has comfortable singles
and doubles on the edge of UW's campus. Twenty-seven
rooms in all; full breakfast buffet included. Reservations
advisable, especially around graduation/orientation times at the
university, when things book up far in advance. ③.

MAGNOLIA, BALLARD, AND FREMONT

Chelsea Station on the Park

Map 7, D4. 4915 Linden Ave N ℂ547-6077.
Suites and double rooms, all with private bath, on a quiet block
across from the Woodland Park Zoo. One of the more restful
and neighborly Seattle B&B options; smoke-free environment.
⑤.

Dibble House

Map 7, A1. 7301 Dibble Ave NW ℂ783-0320.
Fairly cheap rates in a 1920s-style house that's a short drive
from the zoo and the Locks. Three bedrooms with queen beds,
two with twins, though all but one have shared bath. ③.

Lake Union B&B

Map 7, G7. 2217 N 36th St ℂ547-9965.
These two rooms near the edge of Lake Union are splendidly
sited, although they're often booked; reserve well in advance.
⑤.

CAFÉS

I n Seattle, **cafés** are more than just places to drink coffee (though that's certainly part of it); they are the centers of social life, attracting all kinds of people and often exhibiting art or staging cutting-edge live music. Indeed, one of the great pleasures of Seattle cafés is their multipurpose nature, which also shows up in the decor – at its most extreme, it may mean you're not quite sure whether the voodoo doll lamp on your table is a featured artwork or a garage sale relic.

There's still plenty of coffeehouse culture, and a variety of brews (including tea) are in abundance almost everywhere. Ordering one cup of coffee pretty much gives you carte blanche to park yourself in a seat all day if you so wish. The *Starbucks* and *Seattle's Best Coffee* chains are ubiquitous but don't give the real Seattle experience; regardless of what you think of the coffee, they have little more charm or personality than a fast-food joint. If you want bohemian, hit **Belltown**; for boisterous socializing, **Capitol Hill** is best. Whatever your preference – near-solitude, wacky art damage, convivial social interaction, or a wired caffeine buzz – there's a café to suit your needs, or several to hit as your mood changes.

As a crucible of computer technology, it's an obvious place to find plenty of **cybercafés**, which rent terminals for browsing the Internet or playing state-of-the-art digital games, usually at $5–10 per hour. Many cafés that don't specialize in digital culture will nonetheless have a terminal or two available to play around on (again for a fee).

Most cafés serve at least some light food, but for **snacks**, there are spots that specialize in **baked goods**, **bagels**, and **desserts**; bagel houses especially are taking off in Seattle. There are also tons of **espresso carts**, one of the most interesting being *On the Ave*, on the sidewalk in front of *The Dawghouse* at 4511 University Way NE, which has what may be the smallest seating area of any eating or drinking establishment in town: a small, circular table barely large enough to hold two coffee mugs. Another cart, *TNT*, in the parking lot of *Baskin and Robbins* at Broadway and Harrison in Capitol Hill, does a big business in drive-through orders.

Cafés that serve meals on par with the best restaurants are listed in "Restaurants," p.168. Many serve alcohol, too, and those that are more bar than café are listed starting on p.191.

COFFEEHOUSES AND CAFÉS

Allegro Espresso Bar

Map 6, B5. 4214 University Way NE, in alley between University and 15th Ave NE ⊘633-3030.

Mon–Fri 6.30am–11pm, Sat 7.30am–11pm, Sun 8am–1pm.

One of the favored haunts of those who take their coffee seriously, this is also something of a hangout for the university's more intellectual and international element. Computer terminals with free Internet access are available if you're also having something at the café.

B&O Espresso

Map 5, B6. 204 Belmont Ave E ☏322-5028.
Mon–Thurs 7.30am–midnight, Fri 7.30am–1am, Sat 9am–1am, Sun 9am–midnight.

For those who want some classiness without sacrificing a casual atmosphere, this is the place, with its cool dark interior, outdoor seating, and a fine assortment of drinks and desserts (the brownies are excellent). With locations at 401 Broadway E (in Broadway Market) and 103 Cherry St (Pioneer Square).

Bauhaus Books & Coffee

Map 5, B7. 301 E Pine St ☏625-1600.
Mon–Fri 6am–1am, Sat–Sun 8am–1am.

A Capitol Hill hangout for the dressed-in-black crowd, dispensing coffee and some teas in a somber interior, with high chairs at the windowside counter. The small, artsy used-book section is largely devoted to architecture volumes.

The Burke Museum Cafe

Map 6, B4. 17th Ave NE and NE 45th St (in the basement of the Burke Museum) ☏543-9854.
Mon–Wed 7am–5pm, Thurs 7am–8pm, Fri 7am–5pm, Sat–Sun 9am–5pm.

Also known as *The Boiserie*, this café has high ceilings, wood-paneled walls, wooden armchairs, and classical music, yielding an ambience that approximates a nineteenth-century drawing room. Not a place for chatty socializing, but the best quiet spot in town.

Cafe Paradiso

Map 5, C7. 1005 E Pike St ☏322-6960.
Mon–Thurs 6am–1am, Fri 6am–2am, Sat 8am–2am, Sun 8am–1am.

The snacks are unexciting; most folks come here for the

serious java and to hang out in the dark atmosphere. Smokers can lounge upstairs; downstairs is a somewhat sunnier and less secluded space.

Creative Cafe

8516 Greenwood Ave N ⓒ**706-7074.**
Sun–Thurs 8am–8pm, Fri–Sat 8am–9pm.
A café with the usual espresso, juices, and light food, but distinguished from the norm by its "paint it yourself pottery studio," which is available at no hourly charge.

Espresso Roma

Map 6, B5. 4201 University Way NE ⓒ**632-6001.**
Mon–Fri 7am–10pm, Sat–Sun 8am–10pm.
Numerous large tables and benches don't compensate for the sullen service and bland atmosphere at this establishment, which serves coffee, tea, and baked goods on one of the busiest corners of the U District. The one reason to consider a quick one here is the outdoor porch, a good viewpoint for the passing foot traffic on University Way.

Grand Illusion Espresso and Pastry

Map 6, B3. 1405 NE 50th St ⓒ**525-9573.**
Daily 11am–11pm.
The homiest of the popular U District cafés, with a living-room feel and good snacks, as well as basic light meals and some outdoor seating, this is a great place to thumb a newspaper or book for a couple of hours. Adjoins the *Grand Illusion* rep house cinema (p.219), and has live music sometimes.

Habitat Espresso

Map 5, C6. 202 Broadway Ave E ℂ329-3087.
Mon–Thurs 7am–midnight, Fri 7am–2am, Sat 9am–2am, Sun
9am–midnight.
Organic coffees and teas, served in a low-key avant-garde
atmosphere; half the profits are donated to nonprofit
organizations. There's also a small stage for music and spoken
poetry events.

Last Exit on Brooklyn

Map 6, B3. 5211 University Way NE (no phone).
Sun–Thurs 9am–midnight, Fri–Sat 9am–2am.
Longtime countercultural hangout in the U District where the
gentle hippie/slacker crowd philosophizes in a sparsely
decorated space.

Pegasus Coffee

Map 3, D6. 711 3rd Ave ℂ682-3113.
Mon–Fri 6.30am–4.30pm.
In the lobby of the Dexter Horton Building, and a more
relaxing place to imbibe java than the usual coffee bar, with
brews of *Pegasus* beans – whose roasting facilities are on
Bainbridge Island (on which there's a branch at 125 Parfitt Way
SW ℂ842-3113).

Sit & Spin

Map 4, E5. 2219 4th Ave ℂ441-9484.
Sun–Thurs 9am–midnight, Fri–Sat 9am–2am.
Justly renowned café/laundromat/performance-space with
diner booths, kitschy found art, and lamps that double as
sculpture. The drinks and food are not bad either, especially
the fresh juices. Plus there's the "Poetic and Literary Fuck-All"

COFFEEHOUSES AND CAFÉS

spoken word free-for-all on the first Wednesday evening of the month.

Speakeasy Cafe

Map 4, E5. 2304 2nd Ave ℭ728-9770.
Mon–Thurs 9am–midnight, Fri 9am–2am, Sat 10am–2am, Sun 10am–midnight.
This multipurpose space screens films, holds poetry readings, runs Internet workshops, stages community meetings, and often has ambient, jazz, and improvised music (events calendar online at *www.speakeasy.org*). Judged simply as a café, it's plenty worthwhile as well, serving tea, coffee, beers, pastries, salads, and soup in a convivial, culturally energized atmosphere.

Teahouse Kuan Yin

Map 7, G5. 1911 N 45th St ℭ632-2055.
Sun–Thurs 10am–11pm, Fri–Sat 10am–midnight.
In the same building as the *Wide World Books* travel bookstore (see p.255), this is a necessary antidote in coffee-happy Seattle, serving several dozen varieties of black, oolong, green, and herbal teas as well as light snacks in a comfortable if subdued setting.

Torrefazione Italia

Map 3, D7. 320 Occidental Ave S ℭ624-5847.
Mon–Fri 6.30am–6pm, Sat 8am–6pm, Sun 9am–5pm.
Pioneer Square espresso bar which may have the best Seattle coffee experience, with top-notch roast coffees in an old-world setting, heightened by the outdoor seating area on the pedestrianized part of Occidental Avenue. Also at 622 Olive Way (ℭ624-1429) and Rainier Square, 1310 4th Ave (ℭ583-8970).

Coffee: bean there, drink that

There's no ready explanation for the astonishing proliferation of **coffee bars** and **espresso carts** in Seattle in the 1980s and 1990s. Regardless, more than two hundred licensed espresso carts operate from sidewalks and store entrances. The Capitol Hill café *Coffee Messiah*, crammed with Christian religious icons and crucifixes, sports a sign declaring "Caffeine Saves." There's even an "Espresso Dental" office that serves lattes to waiting patients.

Much of Seattle's coffee culture was generated by **Starbucks**, which has gone from a single store in Pike Place Market, begun in the early 1970s, to the leading retailer and roaster of brand coffee beans in the US, running about a thousand stores in North America, and recently expanding into Japan and China as well, with yearly revenues of $1 billion. Their closest competitor in the Seattle area, *Seattle's Best Coffee*, is no slouch either, with a half-dozen outlets in downtown alone; and even some of those who schlep around their own coffee carts gross as much as $100,000 a year.

There is no surer way of identifying an out-of-towner than overhearing someone ordering an unembellished "espresso" or "latte." Locals are obsessive about coffee preparation, specifying type of milk, number of shots of espresso, even requesting leaf-shaped designs for their foam. You'll catch on quickly once you're there, but if you're determined to start off by passing for a local, just ask for a "double tall skinny," a tall latte made with 1 percent or nonfat milk, with a double shot of espresso.

Vivace Espresso

Map 5, C6. 901 E Denny Way ℡860-5869.
Daily 6.30am–11pm.
Large-sized haunt for Capitol Hill's most serious coffee drinkers by

self-proclaimed "espresso roasting and preparation specialists." More chic is their sidewalk café at 321 Broadway E (next to the Washington Mutual Bank parking lot), the prime people-watching perch on Broadway, with a few outdoor tables, perennial takeout lines, and no interior – open daily from 6.30am "till late."

Zeitgeist

Map 3, D7. 161 S Jackson St ✆583-0497.
Daily 6am–midnight.

Mostly coffee, a few sweet snacks, and a bit of art at this small haunt at the heart of Pioneer Square's gallery scene. Just the right levels of moody darkness make this a good escape from the more genteel and pretentious environs of the surrounding galleries.

Zoka

Map 7, G4. 2200 N 56th St ✆545-4277.
Mon–Sat 6am–midnight, Sun 6am–10pm.

Classic-style coffee house with basic, comfortable decor; not as weird or edgy as the ones in the hipper districts, but just fine for brews and relaxation.

CYBERCAFÉS

Book & Bean Espresso Co.

Map 5, B6. 1635 1/2 E Olive Way ✆325-1139.
Daily 24 hours.

A definitive only-in-Seattle café that feels more like someone's living room than a commercial enterprise, with a few agreeably comfy chairs in the tiny main area, a back room of tattered used books, and computer terminals (Internet access $5 per hr).

CapitolHill.Net

Map 5, C6. 219 Broadway E ©860-6858.
Mon–Sat noon–10pm, Sun noon–8pm.

The best of Seattle's growing roster of virtual cafés dispenses muffins and espresso, but the chief attraction is the Web browsing, graphic design, computer games, and other hi-tech activities, available for ten cents a minute in a pleasant, low-key, two-tiered lofty space.

Virtual Commons

Map 4, B1. 200 Roy St #101 ©281-7339 *vcommons.com.*
Mon–Thurs 9am–1am, Fri–Sat 9am–2am, Sun 9am–midnight.

An upscale, serious atmosphere, but still nice, in a loungy and spacious setting, with coffee, snacks, and beer available. Internet and software activities for $3.50 per half-hour; "premium software" games for $4.50 per half-hour.

SNACKS: BAGELS, BAKERIES, AND DESSERTS

Bagel Oasis

Map 7, D7. 462 N 36th St ©633-2676.
Mon–Fri 6.30am–5.30pm, Sat–Sun 7am–4pm.

More imaginative bagel sandwiches than the usual (try the "Rainy Day" combo of portobello mushroom and red peppers), as well as a good variety of bagels, an assortment of bagel spreads, and baked goods. Also downtown at 1125 4th Ave (©624-9063).

Bruegger's Bagels

Map 3, D6. 107 1st Ave S ©621-8933.
Mon–Fri 6am–7pm, Sat–Sun 7am–7pm.

Consistent winners of local bagelry polls, dishing out an

impressive range of bagels and spreads at several locations throughout the city. Also branches at Columbia Seafirst Center on 701 5th Ave (②682-6722), 1301 Madison St (②382-0881), 23 Mercer St (②284-9684), 4517 University Way NE (②545-0828), and 1815 N 45th St (②633-7768).

Cafe Dilettante

Map 5, C5. 416 Broadway E ②329-6463.
Daily 10am–midnight.
Though they do serve coffee, people come here more for the chocolate treats, the best in town.

Cinnamon Works

Map 3, B4. 1530 Pike Place ②583-0085.
Daily 7.30am–6pm.
Delicious oat-fruit bars, sticky buns, and aptly named "Monster" cookies at this bakery counter in the heart of Pike Place Market.

The Erotic Bakery

Map 7, G5. 2323 N 45th St ②545-6969.
Mon–Sat 10am–7pm, Sun noon–5pm.
Custom-designed erotic cakes, cupcakes, and chocolates in a store that also has an extensive selection of risqué greeting cards and naughty novelties.

Honey Bear Bakery

Map 7, G4. 2106 N 55th St ②545-7296.
Daily 6am–11pm.
Though it draws some smirks for its appeal to the Birkenstock crowd, this Wallingford/Green Lake institution gets customers from all over town for its delicious breads, desserts, and all-veggie

snacks, available for takeout or on-site consumption in a spacious café with large wooden tables. Try their famous white chocolate brownie, or a loaf of wholewheat bread to take with you.

Juice Plant

Map 5, B7. 801 E Pike St ℃324-7722.
Mon–Fri 7.30am–8pm, Sat–Sun 9am–7.30pm.
Juice bar that mixes dozens of healthy smoothies and fruit juices, including exotic combos like "Guava Lava" and "Rocket Chocolate." The "wild berry squeeze" is a refreshing blast on hot days. Also branches at Wallingford Center, N 45th St and Wallingford Ave N, and downtown, at 2nd & Madison behind the First Interstate building.

Le Panier

Map 3, B4. 1902 Pike Place ℃441-3669.
Mon–Sat 7am–6pm, Sun 8am–5pm.
French bakery cooks up a wide variety of breads and pastries, and also serves as one of the more popular hangouts in Pike Place Market.

Marble Top Creamery

Map 6, B4. 4507 University Way NE ℃547-3436.
Mon–Thurs noon–11pm, Fri–Sat noon–1am, Sun noon–10pm.
The best place in the U District for ice cream and frozen yogurt, offering a bewildering variety of flavors and toppings, with patient staff to guide you. The cheesecake-brownie combo is a particularly rich and worthy treat.

Noah's New York Bagels

Map 5, C6. 220 Broadway E ℃720-2925.
Mon–Sat 7am–7pm, Sun 8am–7pm.

SNACKS: BAGELS, BAKERIES, AND DESSERTS

This Bay Area-based chain has made big inroads into Seattle's bagel market, and rightly so. The sweet varieties (cranberry-orange, blueberry, and cinnamon raisin) are especially good, as are the accompanying cream cheese "shmears," such as sun-dried tomato and basil. Also at 2746 NE 45th Ave (ⓒ522-1998) and 2135 Queen Anne Ave N (ⓒ282-6744).

Pacific Dessert Company

Map 5, C5. 516 Broadway E ⓒ328-1950.
Mon–Thurs 4–11pm, Fri 4pm–midnight, Sat 11.30am–midnight, Sun 1–11pm.
A high-quality dessert spot with a variety of sweets and cakes, most notably the "Chocolate Decadence" specialty cakes. Also near Seattle Center at 127 Mercer St (ⓒ284-8100).

Piroshky-Piroshky

Map 3, B4. 1908 Pike Place ⓒ441-6068.
Daily 8am–7pm.
Yummy Russian bakery has pastries and piroshki that satisfy urges for something between a snack and a full meal. Get something with potato inside and you can't go wrong; good apple cinnamon and cheese rolls, too.

Simply Desserts

Map 7, D7. 3421 Fremont Ave N ⓒ633-2671.
Tues–Thurs noon–11pm, Fri–Sat noon–11.30pm, Sun noon–6pm.
Fine Fremont dessert specialist that's low in square feet but high in quality, where the white chocolate cakes are a specialty.

Touchstone Bakery

Map 7, D7. 501-A N 36th St ⓒ547-4000.
Sun–Tues 7.30am–6pm, Thurs–Fri 7.30am–6pm, Sat 7.30am–5pm.

Wholegrain organic collective with a small but enticing street counter of pastries that are just as good as those in less health-conscious outlets, but better for you; try the vanilla rolls.

RESTAURANTS

Seattle has **restaurants** to suit all tastes and budgets. The breadth of styles available, in fact, is considerably wider than one might expect given the city's fairly white demographics. Asian, Italian, Ethiopian, seafood, vegetarian, and conventional American cooking are all well represented, and the number of more exotic establishments is on the rise.

The term "Northwest cuisine" is bandied about quite a bit in Seattle, but it doesn't add up to much more than tastefully prepared dishes centered around locally caught **seafood**, which is of a high standard, especially the salmon. The International District has tons of inexpensive **Asian** spots, while **Pan-Asian** food, which fuses different kinds of Asian cuisine into the same menu, or mixes Asian and North American styles, has become trendy here in recent years. On the other hand, **Mexican** food in Seattle is a consciously Americanized derivation that seems to have been specifically designed to smooth out its tangiest and most exciting properties. **Vegetarians** will not have a problem in Seattle, which is approaching coastal California standards in providing a wealth of meatless alternatives.

Dining in Seattle is a fairly casual affair, with dress codes rare even in some of the pricier places. Reservations aren't a bad idea at the most popular establishments, especially on weekends, but it's fine just to turn up; indeed quite a few places don't take reservations at all. **Non-smoking** laws aren't quite as stringent as they are in California, but most restaurants don't allow it, even at selected tables, and legislation is being considered to ban it altogether.

Places that open early usually offer **breakfast** not only in the morning, but for lunch hours as well, which in Seattle usually run from about 11am to 3pm. **Lunches** can be anything from $5 sandwiches to high-powered downtown affairs. Also, if you want to enjoy some of the fancier restaurants without the high cost, lunch prices are often drastically lower for dishes of similar quantity and quality to those served after 5pm. If you're on a really tight budget, head for the numerous all-you-can-eat **lunch buffets** for $5 or so, often at Indian restaurants. Weekend **brunches** are also popular, though the lines can be out the door at the best spots.

The boundary between a **café** and a restaurant can be thin in many instances in Seattle. Quite a few of the city's cafés are great places to have full dinners, not just to sip beverages and munch pastries. Wholefood and vegetarian enthusiasts in particular are in for inexpensive treats at many cafés; others will have savory soups, massive sandwiches, fragrant breads, or the odd delicious entree special. By law, **bars** are required to serve meals, but their menus are largely uninspired.

There are better options for **fast food** in Seattle than most anywhere else, especially in **Pike Place Market**.

For Seattle bars, see p.191; for cafés, see p.155. A few cafés that offer a good range of full meals are included in the listings below.

RESTAURANTS

With numerous tasty ethnic foods available in the $5 range, it's by far the top place for a quick bite downtown.

In the listings below, prices are coded according to an average three-course meal, drinks not included: **budget** (under $8); **inexpensive** ($8–15); **moderate** ($15–25); **expensive** ($25–35); **very expensive** (over $35).

Athenian Inn

Map 3, B4. Pike Place Market, main floor of Main Arcade Ⓒ624-7166.
Mon–Sat 7am–7pm. Budget–inexpensive.

Serviceable food (breakfast is best), but a good place to check out views of Puget Sound and the local character of the clientele. Try the seafood platter if you're coming for a proper meal.

Blowfish

Map 3, D3. 722 Pine St. Ⓒ467-7777.
Mon–Fri 6.30–10.30am, 11.30am–1am, Sat–Sun 8am–1am.
Moderate.

Good pan-Asian restaurant that recently opened on the ground floor of the *Paramount* hotel, with the accent on tapas-style dishes, such as grilled chicken yakisoba, marinated in a spicy Korean red bean paste, and sugar snap peas stir-fried with shiitake mushrooms in black beans, garlic, and ginger.

Common Meals

Map 4, F6. 1902 2nd Ave Ⓒ448-6422.
Mon–Fri 11am–2pm. Budget.

This roomy restaurant, dedicated to providing job training to the homeless, serves up excellent $5.95 lunch buffets. The constantly varying spreads are topped off by extremely good desserts.

Copacabana

Map 3, B4. Triangle Building, Pike Place Market ℡622-6359.
Daily summer 11.30am–9pm, shorter hours other seasons.
Moderate.
This Bolivian restaurant is one of Pike Place's most offbeat eateries, with a concentration on dishes with pie-type fillings (the *huminta*, or corn pie, and fish soups are especially recommended). The outdoor balcony seating has a good view of the hubbub on Pike Place below.

Crepe de France

Map 3, B4. 93 Pike St, Economy Row of Pike Place Market ℡624-2196.
Mon–Wed 10am–5pm, Thurs–Sun 10am–6pm. Budget.
Over a dozen varieties of meat, veggie, and sweet crepes are whipped up before your eyes at this Pike Place stall with five counter seats, a great place for taking in the Market ambience.

Dahlia Lounge

Map 3, C3. 1904 4th Ave ℡682-4142.
Mon–Fri 11.30am–2.30pm, Mon–Thurs 5.30–10pm, Fri–Sat 5.30–11pm, Sun 5–9pm. Expensive.
One of downtown's most established upscale restaurants, and most famed for its seafood, of which the crab cakes are a specialty. It also offers other imaginative main courses like squash tamales and apricot chicken.

El Puerco Lloron

Map 3, B4. 1501 Western Ave ℡624-0541.
Mon–Thurs 11.30am–8pm, Fri–Sat 11.30am–9pm, Sun noon–6.30pm. Budget.
A rare restaurant in Seattle, with convincingly authentic

DOWNTOWN

Mexican fare (and decor), serving tamales, tostadas, and excellent chile rellenos in a cafeteria-style set-up.

Elliott Bay Cafe

Map 3, D7. 1st Ave S and S Main St ⓒ682-6664.
Mon–Fri 9am–10.30pm, Sat 10am–10.30pm, Sun 11am–5.30pm.
Budget–inexpensive.

In the basement of *Elliott Bay Book Company*, and one of the most popular rendezvous points in the city, with a good assortment of moderately priced, wholefood-oriented soups, salads, quiches, and the like. Newspapers and weatherbeaten old hardcover books are available for perusal while you eat.

Etta's Seafood

Map 3, A3. 2020 Western Ave ⓒ443-6000.
Mon–Thurs 11.30am–10pm, Fri–11.30am–11pm, Sat 9am–11pm, Sun 9am–10pm. Expensive.

Fine regional fish dominates the menu of this restaurant a block from Pike Place Market, owned by Tom Douglas, who established himself with the *Dahlia Lounge*. Indeed this is similar to the *Dahlia*, but a bit more casual. The most distinctive dish – king salmon pit-roasted and rubbed in spices, and served with cornbread pudding – is also the most expensive, but worth it.

Gravity Bar

Map 3, B3. 113 Virginia St ⓒ448-8826
Sun–Thurs 11am–9pm, Fri–Sat 11am–10pm.

Map 5, C5. 415 Broadway E ⓒ325-7186.
Sun–Thurs 10am–10pm, Fri–Sat 10am–11pm.
Inexpensive–moderate.

The last word in postmodern vegetarian cuisine, serving delicious rice-and-veggie dishes, pizza, and more complex dishes in

Bauhaus-ish surroundings: lamps on steel poles run from floor to ceiling, while sheet steel rattles when your legs touch the table. The "Mayan Calendar" pizza, topped with black bean spread and avocado, makes a great light meal; there's also a juice bar.

Ivar's

Map 3, C6. Pier 54 on the waterfront ℗624-6852.
Daily: summer 11am–11pm, winter 11am–10pm, outdoor fish bar open 11am–2am every day.

401 NE Northlake Way ℗632-0767.
Mon–Thurs 11.30am–2.30pm & 4.30–10pm, Fri 11.30am–2.30pm & 4.30–11pm, Sat noon–3.30pm & 4–11pm, Sun 10am–2pm & 3.30–10pm. Budget–moderate.

A local institution, *Ivar's* has several fish bars around town, but for sit-down dining stick to either the *Acres of Clams* branch at Pier 54 or the *Salmon House* at Northlake on the north shore of Lake Union. Smoked salmon is the thing to eat at the Northlake location, which has a 45-item Sunday brunch.

The Kaleenka

Map 3, B3. 1933 1st Ave ℗728-1278.
Mon–Thurs 11am–9pm, Fri–Sat 11am–10pm. Moderate.

This well-established Russian restaurant at the edge of Pike Place Market dishes out fine – and extremely filling – ragu (casserole), borscht, piroshki, as well as Uzbek specialties.

Lowell's Restaurant

Map 3, B4. Main floor of Main Arcade, Pike Place Market ℗622-2036.
Daily 7am–5pm. Inexpensive.

Along with the *Athenian Inn*, the most popular of the Pike Place restaurants with waterfront views, renowned for its

DOWNTOWN

seafood and breakfasts. There may be a wait to get a seat on the upper floor.

Metropolitan Grill

Map 3, D6. 820 2nd Ave ✆624-3287.
Mon–Fri 11am–3.30pm & 5–11pm; Sat 4–11pm; Sun 4.30–10pm.
Very expensive.

The steak-lover's best bet in town, with a good choice of top cuts, in a place that's heavy on power suits and has one of the longest bars in Seattle. The filet mignon is a standout.

Pabla Indian Cuisine

Map 3, C4. 1516 2nd Ave ✆623-2868.
Daily 11am–3pm & 5–10pm. Budget–inexpensive.

The $5.99, sixteen-item buffet lunches (daily 11am–3pm) make this one of the best downtown budget choices, although they also serve more expensive dinners.

Red Sea Restaurant

Map 3, D7. 206 1st Ave S ✆233-9157.
Mon–Sat 11am–3pm & 5–10pm, Sun 5–10pm. Inexpensive.

Decent Ethiopian food in spacious, simply decorated surroundings, and with frequent reggae, soukous, and African music on stage. Opt for a combo plate, with assorted lentils, lamb, and spicy potatoes to sop up with spongy *injera* bread.

Sabra

Map 3, B4. 1916 Pike Place ✆441-4544.
Mon–Sat 10.30am–5pm. Budget.

Cafeteria-style Middle Eastern augments the usual falafel with more unusual dishes like squash patties, available for takeout or on-the-spot consumption in a small, pleasant outdoor courtyard.

Saigon Restaurant

Map 3, B4. 1916 Pike Place, on ground floor of Soames-Dunn Bldg in Pike Place Market ⓒ448-1089.
Mon–Sat 11.30am–6pm. Budget–inexpensive.
One of the best inexpensive places to eat in Pike Place, with a menu of Vietnamese seafood and vegetarian dishes that features some sweat-breaking curries.

Sound View Cafe

Map 3, B4. Flower Row of Main Arcade in Pike Place Market ⓒ623-5700.
Mon–Fri 7am–5pm, Sat 7am–5.30pm, Sun 9am–3pm. Budget.
Nothing earthshaking about the food here, though it's healthy, filling serve-yourself fare (small salad bowl $2.50, large salad bowl $5), but the views of Puget Sound come at a price considerably lower than elsewhere in Pike Place Market.

Three Girls Bakery

Map 3, B4. Lower floor of Sanitary Market, Pike Place Market ⓒ622-1045.
Daily 7am–6pm. Budget–inexpensive.
Endure the long lines at this well-loved haunt for the large, tasty sandwiches (the hummus is good), available either at a takeout counter or for sit-down eating at the small adjoining café. Get the jalapeno bread, or one of their crumbly fruit pastries, if you want some good snacks for the road.

Wild Ginger

Map 3, B4. 1400 Western Ave ⓒ623-4450.
Sun–Thurs 11.30am–3pm & 5–11pm, Fri–Sat 11.30am–3pm & 5pm–midnight. Moderate–expensive.

DOWNTOWN

This trendy pan-Asian restaurant is one of Seattle's biggest restaurant success stories of the 1990s, and has extensive daily specials to supplement their already lengthy and ambitious menu – though it's best to go with dishes that don't try to do too much at once, like the tuna manada (yellowfin tuna fried in spicy Indonesian sauce). Good, if a tad overrated and overpriced.

INTERNATIONAL DISTRICT

Bangkok House

Map 3, F8. 606 S Weller St ✆382-9888.
Daily 11am–10pm. Inexpensive.
Solid Thai restaurant with lightning-fast service. Anything with peanut sauce here is succulent, and the pad thai (noodles with chunks of meat and/or vegetables) is also recommended.

Chau's Seafood Restaurant

Map 3, E7. 310 4th Ave S ✆621-0006.
Mon–Thurs 11am–midnight, Friday 11am–1am, Sat 4pm–1am, Sun 4–11pm. Budget–inexpensive.
Well-regarded Chinese place on the downtown–International District border does mostly seafood dishes – though it's also a good place for duck – and has weekday lunch specials for around $5.

Hon's

Map 3, F7. 416 5th Ave S ✆623-4470.
Daily 11am–10pm. Budget–inexpensive.
Cheap and filling Chinese Szechuan and Vietnamese cuisine, right across from the International District Metro Tunnel.

House of Hong

Map 3, G7. 409 8th Ave S ☎622-7997.
Mon–Thurs 11am–10pm, Fri 11am–midnight, Sat
10.30am–midnight, Sun 10.30am–10pm. Inexpensive.

Dependable Chinese food in a large establishment that's open
relatively late on weekends, making it a good option for dining
after events in the Pioneer Square/Kingdome area. It also has
good dim sum, with carts moving through every few minutes
offering you samples from the extensive menu.

Mikado

Map 3, F7. 514 S Jackson St ☎622-5206.
Mon–Fri 11.30am–2pm & 5.30–10pm, Sat 5.30–10pm. Expensive.

The most popular Japanese restaurant in town, and with good
reason: its classy surroundings hold a fresh and extensive sushi
bar, much pricier at dinner than at lunch.

Tai Tung

Map 3, F7. 659 S King St ☎622-7372.
Sun–Thurs 10am–11.30pm, Fri–Sat 10am–1.30am. Inexpensive.

One of the district's oldest Cantonese restaurants, which has
an incredibly extensive menu; to get a dose of a few things
at once, opt for one of the combo meals, which run around
$7.

Viet My

Map 3, E7. 129 Prefontaine Place S near 4th & Washington
☎382-9923.
Mon–Fri 11am–9pm, closed weekends. Budget–inexpensive.

Superb inexpensive Vietnamese lunches and dinners on the
edge of one of the area's shabbiest blocks, with many dishes
under $5.

INTERNATIONAL DISTRICT

BELLTOWN AND THE SEATTLE CENTER

Bahn Thai

Map 4, D1. 409 Roy St ℘283-0444.
Mon–Thurs 11.30am–3pm & 4.30–10pm, Fri 11.30am–3pm & 4.30–11pm, Sat 4–11pm, Sun 4–10pm. Inexpensive–moderate.
This Thai spot has a relaxed, decorous atmosphere, with a long menu of well-spiced dishes – the seafood selection is especially varied and good, with imaginative salmon and squid options.

Bamboo Garden

Map 4, D1. 364 Roy St ℘282-6616.
Daily 11am–10pm. Inexpensive–moderate.
Though a quick glance at the menu might lead you to believe this Chinese place has standard dishes, everything in fact is made from vegetable protein products and 100-percent vegetable oil. Though fake meat may not be your thing, it's all pretty good, best topped with a peanut pudding (actually peanut soup) dessert.

Chinese Wok

Map 4, E5. 2311 5th Ave ℘441-8488.
Mon–Sat 11am–8pm. Inexpensive.
Underneath the monorail, this Belltown neighborhood favorite offers friendly service and bountiful portions. The orange-flavored beef, spinach with fillet chicken, and fried eggplant with garlic sauce are all winners.

Crocodile Cafe

Map 4, E6. 2200 2nd Ave ℘448-2114.
Tues–Thurs 8am–11pm, Fri–Sat 8am–midnight, Sun 9am–3pm. Budget.
Best known as one of Belltown's prime nightlife haunts for alternative music, the *Crocodile Cafe* is a diner by day, serving the

biggest breakfasts in the city. Enjoy the enormous ratatouille omelets under the gaze of odd stuffed animals, hanging papier-mâché sculptures, cheesy thrift-store album sleeves, and the like.

Noodle Ranch

Map 4, E5. 2228 2nd Ave ℗728-0463.
Mon–Thurs 11.30am–10pm, Fri–Sat 11.30am–11pm.
Inexpensive–moderate.
Delicious pan-Asian cuisine in the $10 range, offering imaginatively spiced noodle-based dishes and other creations in a casual Belltown atmosphere. The green curry here packs quite a punch, better than at most Thai restaurants.

QUEEN ANNE

Chutneys

Map 4, B2. 519 1st Ave N ℗284-6799.
Sun–Thurs 11.30am–2.30pm & 5–10pm, Fri–Sat 11.30am–2.30pm & 5–10.30pm. Inexpensive.
The best place in town for a sit-down Indian meal, equally adept at meat tandooris and vegetarian curries, and also dishing out all-you-can-eat $7 lunch buffets for the budget conscious. It also has locations in Capitol Hill, 605 15th Ave E (℗726-1000), and Wallingford, 1815 N 45th St (℗634-1000).

The 5 Spot

1502 Queen Anne Ave N ℗285-SPOT.
Sun–Thurs 8.30am–10pm, Fri–Sat 8.30am–11pm.
Budget–inexpensive.
The most colorful of Queen Anne's inexpensive eateries, this southern-style diner has specialties like the Tennessee Mountain Pone platter of corn-vegetable patties, the Truck Stop Pork Chop sandwich, and Coca-Cola cake.

QUEEN ANNE

611 Supreme

Map 5, B7. 611 E Pine St ©328-0292.

Tues–Thurs 8am–10pm, Fri 8am–11pm, Sat 4–11pm, Sun 4–10pm.
Budget–inexpensive.

This French creperie has many dinner and dessert crepes, best
of which are the *saumon-chèvre*, with smoken salmon and herb
butter, and the *èpinard*, with spinach, roasted peppers,
cambozola, and walnuts.

Byzantion

Map 4, E5. 601 Broadway E ©325-7580.

Mon–Thurs 11am–11pm, Fri 11am–midnight, Sat 10am–midnight,
Sun 10am–11pm. Inexpensive–moderate.

The best Greek restaurant in town, reasonably priced, and
served with enough pita bread to make the prospect of dessert
unthinkable; good spinach pie and souvlaki.

Cafe Septieme

Map 5, C6. 214 Broadway E ©860-8858.

Sun–Thurs 9am–11pm, Fri–Sat 9am–midnight. Inexpensive.

Large spot with booths and some sidewalk seating in the heart
of Capitol Hill's main drag serves tasty, somewhat unusual
breakfasts and lunches like vegetable fritattas and eggplant steaks.

Coastal Kitchen

Map 5, D5. 429 15th Ave E ©322-1145.

Sun–Thurs 8.30am–10pm, Fri–Sat 8.30am–11pm. Inexpensive.

One of the most popular breakfast and brunch spots in Capitol
Hill, although they're open for other meals too, when the
menu approximates Gulf Coast-styled cuisine, with grilled
prawns, rock shrimp cakes, and beans and rice.

Caffe Minnie's

Map 5, C5. 611 Broadway E ℂ860-1360.
Daily 24 hours. Inexpensive.

The American-style food here is just adequate, but it is open all
night, and has sidewalk seating on Broadway. Named by *Seattle
Weekly* readers as the "best restaurant for getting attitude from
waitstaff" – not necessarily a compliment. Also has another 24-
hr location near the Space Needle at 101 Denny Way (ℂ448-
6263).

Globe Cafe

Map 5, D7. 1531 14th Ave ℂ324-8815.
Tues–Sun 7am–7.30pm. Inexpensive.

For food or ambience, this is hard to beat for a Seattle café
experience, with a tasty all-vegan menu of full meals,
drinks, and desserts, and an unpretentiously goofy decor of
globes, oddly shaped painted salt shakers, blackboards for
patrons to draw on, comfy booths, and offbeat music on
the sound system. Also hosts poetry performances twice a
week or so.

Kingfish Cafe

Map 5, E5. 602 19th Ave E ℂ320-8757.
Mon, Wed–Fri 11.30am–2pm & 6–9pm, Sat 6–9pm, Sun 11am–2pm.
Inexpensive–moderate.

Southern-styled food like griddle cakes and beans and rice
in casual setting, with terrific vintage soul and R&B music
playing as you munch beneath large sepia-toned photos.
The sisters who run this place grill catfish and shrimp with
as much flavor as you'll find in New Orleans; and it's a
good change of pace from the usual Capitol Hill
restaurants.

CAPITOL HILL

Kokeb

Map 5, D8. 926 12th Ave ☎322-0485.

Daily 5–11pm. Inexpensive.

The city's most popular Ethiopian restaurant, with several dozen inexpensive and filling seafood, poultry, beef, and vegetable combinations, served on a bed of *injera* bread.

Machiavelli

Map 5, B7. 1215 Pine St ☎621-7941.

Mon–Thurs 5–10pm, Fri–Sat 5–11pm. Moderate.

Good Italian food, featuring tangy and creative pasta sauces (though the portions aren't huge), at the foot of Capitol Hill in a cozy ambience falling somewhere between a pizzeria and a bistro. Try the penne with roasted red pepper pesto, sundried tomatoes, walnuts, and cream.

Museum Cafe

Map 5, B7. 1530 Bellevue Ave E ☎329-5388.

Mon–Fri 11am–4pm. Budget.

A comfortable enough place to stop in for a burger or a sandwich, as well as "endless pour" (ie free refill) coffee or iced tea. The requisite bohemian touch is provided by a decor of vintage gas station pumps, signs, and oil cans.

Piecora's

Map 5, D7. 1401 E Madison St ☎322-9411.

Daily 11.30am–11pm. Inexpensive.

The best pizza parlor in a city not known for its pizza joints, with satisfyingly gooey pies and a friendly neighborhood atmosphere.

CAPITOL HILL

Siam on Broadway

Map 5, C5. 616 Broadway E ✆324-0892.
Mon–Thurs 11.30am–10pm, Fri 11.30am–11pm, Sat 5–11pm, Sun 5–10pm. Inexpensive.

Perennially crowded and reasonably priced, this open-kitchen Thai restaurant has both counter and table seating for digging into dishes that rank among the spiciest in the city.

EASTLAKE

14 Carrot Cafe

Map 5, B1. 2305 Eastlake Ave E ✆324-1442.
Mon–Thurs 7am–3pm, Sat–Sun 7am–4pm. Budget–inexpensive.

In the Eastlake area near the shores of Lake Union, this place is most patronized for its breakfasts, with weekend crowds often spilling onto the sidewalks for several dozen yards. For something a bit off the wall, try the Tahitian French toast, prepared with tahini.

Louisa's Bakery & Cafe

Map 5, B1. 2379 Eastlake Ave E ✆325-0081.
Mon–Sat 7am–7pm, Sun 8am–2pm. Budget–inexpensive.

A good place to either order a sit-down breakfast at the register or get some snacks to take on the road from their extensive selection of baked goods. More casual than most Seattle cafés serving full meals, but no less appealing for that.

UNIVERSITY DISTRICT

Araya's

Map 6, B4. 4732 University Way NE ✆523-3220.
Mon–Thurs noon–10pm, Fri–Sat noon–11pm, Sun noon–6pm. Budget–inexpensive.

Decent Thai restaurant, but the real reason to come here is for

EASTLAKE AND UNIVERSITY DISTRICT

the $6 all-you-can-eat vegetarian buffet lunch, a refreshing change from the standard Indian buffet special.

Black Cat Cafe

Map 6, B5. 4110 Roosevelt Way NE ✆547-3887.
Tues–Sat 10.30am–8.30pm, Sun 10.30am–3pm. Budget.
Unpromising-looking shack in the back of a parking lot has tons of bohemian allure, with its rickety tables, motley assortment of garage sale furniture, and leftist literature lining the walls. The food at this vegetarian collective kitchen is basic but good.

Flowers

Map 6, B4. 4247 University Way NE ✆633-1903.
Daily 11am–2am. Inexpensive.
A bar and restaurant most notable for its lunchtime vegan buffet (daily 11am–3pm); choose from about twenty items for $5.50. The best all-you-can-eat option in town, especially strong on pasta dishes.

Himalaya

Map 6, A1. 6411 Roosevelt Way NE ✆526-9670.
Mon–Thurs 11am–2.30pm & 4.30–10pm, Fri 11am–2.30pm & 4.30–10.30pm, Sat 11.30am–3pm & 4.30–10.30pm, Sun 11.30am–3pm & 4.30–10pm. Budget–inexpensive.
One of the better Indian restaurants, which outside of its daily lunch buffet serves up more seafood specialties than the usual Indian joint; the prawn coconut, for example, is a good choice.

Marco's Filipino Cuisine

Map 6, B5. 4106 Brooklyn Ave NE ✆633-5696.
Daily 11am–8pm. Inexpensive.

In the midst of a blockful of Asian restaurants on the edge of the U District, this offers filling portions of food in the $5 range; its mild curries are similar in character to Vietnamese food.

Saigon Deli

Map 6, B5. 4142 Brooklyn Ave NE #103 ©634-2866.
Mon–Fri 11am–10pm, Sat–Sun 11.30am–9pm. Budget–inexpensive.
Hole-in-the-wall diner that whips out fine Vietnamese dishes, most under $5. You won't go away hungry.

Silence Heart Nest Vegetarian Restaurant

Map 6, B3. 5247 University Way NE ©524-4008.
Mon–Tues 11am–9pm, Thurs–Sat 11am–9pm. Inexpensive.
Indian-oriented vegetarian menu, with daily specials and rotating desserts, served in a placid, New-Agey atmosphere. They have things like a vegetarian meatloaf, but it's better to stick with the Indian dishes, especially the masala dosai – crepes of spicy potatoes.

MAGNOLIA, BALLARD, AND FREMONT

Chinook's

Map 8, F7. Fishermen's Terminal ©283-HOOK.
Mon–Thurs 11am–10pm, Fri 11am–11pm, Sat 7.30am–11pm, Sun 7.30am–10pm. Moderate.
Popular both for its fresh seafood and its floor-to-ceiling view of the boats in Fishermen's Terminal; *Little Chinook's* next door is a much less expensive fish bar. The menu is vast and offers a lot of other stuff besides fish, but you may as well try the salmon dishes such as "Baked Salmon Chinook," cooked with sundried tomato-basil butter.

El Camino

Map 7, D7. 607 N 35th St ☎632-7303.
Mon–Thurs 5–10pm, Fri 5–11pm, Sat 10am–3pm & 5–11pm, Sun
10am–3pm & 5–10pm. Moderate–expensive.

Regional Mexican cuisine that's stronger on the nouvelle
cuisine than the regional aspect, but nonetheless offers a tasty
assortment of elaborately prepared dishes and homemade sodas
in the moderate-to-expensive range. The rock shrimp
quesadilla, with a frosty margarita, is a nice start. Weekday
happy hours 3–5pm on their outdoor patio.

Fremont Noodle House

Map 7, D7. 3411 Fremont Ave N ☎547-1550.
Tues–Thurs 11am–9.30pm, Fri 11am–10.30pm, Sat noon–10.30pm,
Sun noon–9.30pm. Inexpensive.

A Thai restaurant with the avowed goal of serving dishes
similar to Bangkok street food, though the results are a bit
chicer and cleaner than what you'd find at the average Bangkok
roadstand. However, it does offer a good menu of moderately
priced noodle soups, rice dishes, and appetizers.

Kinnaree

3311 W McGraw St ☎285-4460.
Sun–Thurs 11.30am–9pm, Fri–Sat 11.30am–10pm. Inexpensive.

Fine Thai restaurant in Magnolia with a menu in which each
item can be ordered in vegetarian, meat, or seafood formats
according to individual preferences. Any of the above, in green
coconut milk curry, is recommended.

Longshoreman's Daughter

Map 7, D7. 3510 Fremont Pl N ☎633-5169.
Mon–Thurs 7.30am–10pm, Fri–Sat 7.30am–10.30pm, Sun
7.30am–2.30pm. Inexpensive.

Valued not so much for the diner-style food, which is okay, as its funky vibe, with counter seating and heart-shaped chairs, which make it one of the best places to hang out in central Fremont.

Pontevecchio

Map 7, D8. 710 N 34th St Ⓣ633-3989.
Mon–Fri noon–3pm & 6–10pm; Sat noon–4pm & 6–10pm.
Inexpensive.
Dark, cozy eight-tabled Italian bistro near the Fremont Bridge serving light but authentic meals of panini sandwiches and pasta, served with disarming exuberance. The chef/owner will get out his guitar and serenade when time allows.

Szmania's

3321 W McGraw St Ⓣ284-7305.
Tues–Sun 5–9pm. Moderate–expensive.
One of the few reasons to journey into Magnolia Village, this is one of the finest neighborhood restaurants in Seattle, mixing German, Continental, and Northwest cuisine on a menu that changes according to the season, with inventive and tasty entrees – like stuffed boneless quail with grape demi-glace and gorgonzola polenta; the chocolate bread pudding dessert is killer.

WALLINGFORD

Jitterbug

Map 7, G5. 2114 N 45th St Ⓣ547-6313.
Daily 8am–3.30pm & 5–11pm. Inexpensive.
A hot spot for breakfast on Wallingford's main drag, with chummy waitstaff and adventurous "cactus cooker" and wild mushroom omelettes; get here early for weekend "blunch," when the small diner quickly reaches capacity.

WALLINGFORD

Kabul

Map 7, G5. 2301 N 45th St ©545-9000.
Mon–Thurs 5–9.30pm, Fri–Sat 5–10.30pm. Inexpensive.
One of the more offbeat ethnic restaurant choices in town, this
Afghan establishment in the heart of Wallingford has a menu of
moderately priced kebabs and both veggie and meat entrees, as
well as live sitar music on Tuesdays and Thursdays. Try the
Qoorma-I Tarkari, an Indian-like stew of cauliflower, carrots,
potatoes, and rice.

GREEN LAKE

Carmelita

Map 7, C1. 7314 Greenwood Ave N ©706-7703.
Sun, Tues–Thurs 5–10pm, Fri–Sat 5–10.45pm, Sat–Sun brunch
9am–1.30pm. Moderate.
Opened in late 1996, and already ensconced as Seattle's second
favorite vegetarian restaurant (after *Cafe Flora*). Mostly organic
ingredients, with well-executed dishes like wild mushroom and
polenta, and chickpea pizza.

Red Mill Burgers

Map 7, C2. 312 N 67th St ©783-6362.
Tues–Sat 11am–9pm, Sun noon–8pm. Inexpensive.
Seattle's favorite burger joint, with a wide variety of classic and
adventurous combinations to choose from; they make their
own tangy mayonnaise, too. There are veggie burgers as well,
though it's questionable as to whether a vegetarian would feel
comfortable here.

Twin Teepees

Map 7, E1. 7201 Aurora Ave N ©783-9740.
Sun–Thurs 8am–9pm, Fri–Sat 8am–10pm; lounge open for two
hours after kitchen closes. Inexpensive.

GREEN LAKE

An obligatory stop for devotees of kitsch architecture, the two connected teepee-shaped buildings of this place are easily visible from Aurora Ave/Highway 99. They serve up fairly standard American diner-style steak, seafood, omelettes, and pasta.

LAKE WASHINGTON AND OUTLYING DISTRICTS

Cafe Flora

Map 5, G5. 2901 E Madison St ℂ325-9100.
Tues–Fri 11am–10pm, Sat 9am–2pm & 5–10pm, Sun 9am–2pm & 5–9pm. Expensive.

The best vegetarian restaurant in Seattle, attracting even devout carnivores for its creatively crafted soups, salads, and entrees, like the wild mushroom curry and grilled seitan; the white chocolate raspberry cheesecake is amazing. A pleasant setting, too, especially the stone patio wing, which surrounds diners with trees and a fountain under a pyramid skylight.

Fasica's

808 S Edmunds St ℂ723-7971.
Daily 11am–10pm. Budget.

One of the best values in Seattle, with huge family-style Ethiopian platters that can easily feed two for $8. The vegetable combos, with the usual elements of lentils, carrots, potatoes, and greens, are better options than the ones with ground beef. Out of the way near Seward Park, but worth the trek.

Hi-Spot

1410 34th Ave ℂ325-7905.
Sun–Mon 8am–2pm, Tues–Sat 8am–2pm & 5.30–9.30pm. Inexpensive.

In a converted Madrona house with wooden floors, this serves lunch and dinner on most days, but remains most famous for its sumptuous breakfasts, especially fatty creations like the Mexi-fries, a heap of potatoes, cheese, sour cream, and tasty garnishes. Also has an espresso café downstairs that opens at 7am.

BARS

lthough cafés have edged ahead of **bars** in popularity, you still don't need to look far to find a watering-hole in any Seattle neighborhood. There are plenty of typically raucous joints and sedate neighborhood hangouts, but above all Seattle's bar scene is distinguished by its diversity, particularly in the neighborhoods a few miles from the city center. Bars here are often more like British pubs, or cafés that happen to serve alcohol, complete with singer-songwriters, art displays, and nonsmoking environments. Others cater to discriminating palates by specializing in wines, whiskeys, or house microbrews.

Gay-oriented bars in Seattle are listed on pp.224–226.

Microbreweries are big in the Northwest, and some of them run their own bars on the premises, many of which are listed in this chapter. Downtown and Fremont in particular have a few good ones, and some also offer tours with tastings. The most popular of these, the *Redhook Brewery* in Fremont, is actually not a microbrewery (defined as an operation that produces less than 15,000 barrels a year) but a craft brewery, as its increased success has led to a greater, if still relatively small, output. If you want to get truly soused,

Brew Hops Tours (✆283-8460; $35) take in three small breweries either around lunch or dinner.

In Washington State, you must be **21 or older** to drink legally. All establishments with liquor licenses are required to have a minimum of five dishes available for five hours a day, and must have some type of food available, besides nuts and pretzels, during all the hours in which they serve alcohol. This accounts for the wealth of pub-styled grub in bars and taverns, though it's usually mediocre. Bars generally close around 2am, when they must, by law, stop serving alcohol.

DOWNTOWN

Central Saloon

Map 3, D7. 207 1st Ave S ✆622-0209.
Daily 11.30am–2am.
Bills itself as "Seattle's oldest saloon" (established 1892), and consistently crowded owing to its location at the epicenter of the tourist district. The live music is standard energetic bar-band fare.

Doc Maynard's Public House

Map 3, D6. 610 1st Ave ✆682-4649.
Fri–Sat 8pm–1.30am.
The meeting point for Bill Spiedel's Underground Tours (p.31) is also a good turn-of-the-century style (gargantuan) bar, but is only open to the larger public on weekend nights (it does serve those waiting to take the tour at other times). Not the place to go, however, if you want to avoid hordes of tourists.

Larry's

Map 3, D7. 209 1st Ave S ✆624-7665.
Daily 8am–1.45am.
Part of Pioneer Square's joint cover scheme (see p.202), and the

most blues-oriented bar involved, though no one's going to confuse the performers with Muddy Waters.

Owl 'n' Thistle

Map 3, D7. 808 Post ℂ621-7777.

Daily 11am–2am.

Guinness is the drink of choice at this Irish pub, packed out on weekends for live music, Irish and otherwise.

The Pike Pub & Brewery

Map 3, B4. 1415 1st Ave ℂ622-6044.

Daily 11am–midnight.

This small craft brewery serves its own beers, which are respectable, as well as numerous bottled brands, along with a large wine list and an extensive fish- and pizza-oriented menu. The sprawling multileveled, nonsmoking premises are slick but still fairly unpretentious, and it's one of the only worthwhile places open at night in Pike Place Market.

Pyramid Alehouse

Map 3, D9. 1201 1st Ave S ℂ682-3377.

Mon–Sat 11am–11pm, Sun 11am–10pm.

Near the Kingdome, an excellent small brewery with a warehouse-like space that serves a dozen of their brands, including some fruit-flavored beers. Some of their specialties are only available here, too, like their extra-special bitter (ESB). Tours, Mon–Fri 2pm & 4pm, Sat–Sun 1pm, 2pm, & 4pm.

Virginia Inn

Map 3, B3. 1937 1st Ave ℂ728-1937.

Mon–Thurs 11am–midnight, Fri–Sat 11am–2am, Sun noon–midnight.

A good blend of young professionals and bohemian types drink microbrews and some unusual bottled beers at this bar on the fringe of Pike Place Market. The small outside patio is a great spot for Puget Sound views, although space at these tables can be hard to come by at peak times.

BELLTOWN AND THE SEATTLE CENTER

Belltown Billiards

Map 4, E6. 90 Blanchard ✆448-6779.
Mon–Fri 11.30am–2am, Sat–Sun 4.30pm–2am.
The best hangout for those who like to play pool and drink at the same time – Seattle Mariners stars Alex Rodriguez and Jay Buhner have been spotted inside. A dozen pool tables are available for $6–12 an hour depending upon the time of day; on Ladies Pool Night (Wed 7–9pm) all-women tables can play for free. Live blues and jazz on Sunday nights for no cover.

Lava Lounge

Map 4, E5. 2226 2nd Ave ✆441-5660.
Daily 3pm–2am.
Belltown's concession to 1990s exotica revival is this 'tiki lounge, with South Pacific-inspired decor of lava lamps and sea creatures that (consciously) reeks of inauthenticity, giving it a kitsch value that attracts a large number of youngsters. There's live music on Wednesday nights, and a shuffleboard to help pass the time.

Two Bells Tavern

Map 4, E5. 2313 4th Ave ✆441-3050.
Mon–Sat 11am–2pm, Sun 11am–10pm.
Not as hip as it once was, but the *Two Bells* is still a Belltown institution, drawing arty types as well as overflow from the

downtown business crowd. It has microbrews on tap, and the burgers, served on French rolls, make for a good low-cost meal during the day.

The Comet Tavern

Map 5, C7. 922 E Pike St ✆323-9853.
Daily noon–2am.
The oldest bar in Capitol Hill is a smoky dive and a bit of a rocker's hangout, with a couple of pool tables. The front entrance is papered over with band posters, which will give you a good idea of the more subterranean happenings around town.

The Deluxe Bar and Grill

Map 5, C5. 625 Broadway E ✆324-9697.
Mon–Fri 11am–1am, Sat–Sun 10am–2am.
At the north end of Broadway, this is one of Capitol Hill's more mainstream spots, but it's relatively uncrowded and has outdoor seating for drinking beer and eating burgers.

Eastlake Zoo

Map 5, B1. 2301 Eastlake Ave E ✆329-3277.
Daily 11.30am–2am.
A worker-owned co-op for more than twenty years, this spot in Eastlake, near the shores of Lake Union, numbers some old hippies among its drinkers. However, it's really just a good neighborhood bar, favored by Seattleites of all ages who like to shoot pool – free until 5pm – while they drink.

Elysian Brewing Co.

Map 5, D7. 1221 E Pike St ✆860-1920.
Daily 11.30am–midnight (Sat & Sun sometimes till 2am).

Brewpub of one of the better local microbreweries, with an industrial-type decor that fits in well with the Capitol Hill boho vibe, and a menu featuring a mix of international cuisines. Their house ales, including a wild rice ale, are the best selections from the tap.

Hop Scotch

Map 5, D6. 332 15th Ave E ✆322-4191.
Mon–Fri 11am–midnight, Sat–Sun 8am–midnight.
More than fifty varieties of scotch, as well as a sizable wine list, are what make this recent Capitol Hill addition stand out from the typical bar. Upscale in both decor and clientele.

Hopvine Pub

Map 5, D5. 507 15th Ave E ✆328-3120.
Daily 11am–midnight (sometimes until 2am).
Live acoustic-oriented folk, blues, jazz, singer-songwriter, and open-mike performers to drink microbrews to, for little ($1) or no cover. A good outing for the mellow crowd.

Linda's Tavern

Map 5, B7. 707 E Pike St ✆325-1220.
Daily 4pm–2am.
One of Capitol Hill's most happening bars, and attracting an underground rock crowd mainly for its excellent jukebox, stocked with both old classics and current indie rock acts rarely available on bar sound systems. DJs spin every Tuesday and Sunday night; the nights when rare blues and soul are the theme (check ahead to see when they're scheduled) are recommended.

Big Time Brewery and Alehouse

Map 6, B5. 4133 University Way NE ⊘545-4509.
Sun–Thurs 11.30am–12.30am, Fri–Sat 11.30am–1.30am.

A relatively long-established microbrewery (circa late 1980s) that is a big student hangout. Ales are their stock in trade – try their Bhagwan Bitter – but there are other drinks as well, such as the potent Old Wooley barley wine, in a large space with hardwood decor and a shuffleboard in the back room.

Blue Moon Tavern

Map 6, A4. 712 NE 45th St.
Daily noon–2am.

A well-loved dive with a literary reputation: Dylan Thomas, Allen Ginsberg, and Lawrence Ferlinghetti are some of the celebrities said to have passed through its doors. It sometime hosts readings and stages a Grateful Dead night every Sunday.

College Inn Pub

Map 6, B5. 4006 University Way NE ⊘634-2307.
Mon–Fri 11.30am–2am, Sat–Sun 2pm–2am.

The basement pub affiliate of an adjoining B&B and restaurant, drawing a young university crowd that's more clean-cut than the norm. A good place to play pool and darts.

MAGNOLIA, BALLARD, AND FREMONT

74th Street Ale House

Map 7, C1. 7401 Greenwood Ave N ⊘784-2955.
Daily 11.30am–midnight.

Out in Green Lake, this British pub-styled joint has a slightly (but not annoyingly) gentrified air and a wide selection of draft beers served in "true English imperial 20-ounce pints." There are several local microbrews to choose from, and a more extensive and higher-quality menu than most Seattle bars offer.

Bitters

Map 7, D7. 513 N 36th St *©*632-0886.
Tues–Sat 11am–11pm, Sun 11am–5pm; wine bar open Tues–Sat 5–11pm.

The decor is typically eccentric Fremont, down to the model toy cars in the window with crushed beer-can frames. After working hours, though, the emphasis is the wine bar, which serves a good assortment of reds and whites in addition to beer and coffee.

BYOB

Map 7, C7. 102 NW 36th St *©*634-BREW, *www.634brew.com*.
Tues–Fri 11am–10.30pm, Sat 10am–10.30pm, Sun 10am–4pm, Mon by appointment only.

You can brew your own beer and wine here, with step-by-step guidance from the employees, though you may not want to cart around your experiment for months afterward while it ferments. You can also drink at the bar – try the apricot ale, or the *very* bitter Rainy Day Bitter – or take in the sun on the deck.

Hale's Ales

Map 7, A5. 4301 Leary Way NW *©*782-0737.
Sun–Thurs 11am–11pm, Fri–Sat 11am–midnight.

Handcrafted English-styled ales from the third oldest microbrewery in the Northwest (and largest draft-only brewery in Washington), as well as a decent menu of pub-styled food. The gracefully designed, spacious interior is highlighted by a bar with porcelain tap fixtures; there's live music on Friday and Saturday nights in the back room.

Latona

6423 Latona Ave NE ℗525-2238.

Daily 11.30am–2am.

Run by the owners of *Hopvine* (see p.196), this nonsmoking Greenlake pub often showcases live jazz, folk, and blues, and has a rotating selection of exclusively Northwest beers on tap.

Murphy's

Map 7, G5. 1928 N 45th St ℗634-2110.

Daily 11.30am–2am.

Actually out in Wallingford, adjacent to Fremont, and often featuring live Irish music on Friday and Saturday nights for a $2 cover. They pour a nice Guinness, the Irish coffee is good, and there's also a wide selection of Northwest beers.

Traveler's Pub & Cafe

Map 8, F5. 5327 Ballard Ave NW ℗789-5265.

Mon–Fri 11.30am–3pm & 5–10pm or closing, Sat 4pm–closing; Sun closed.

An aptly named Ballard joint that presents travel slide shows and lectures some nights for no cover charge. On other nights, there are often singer-songwriters, sometimes for a small cover charge.

Triangle Tavern

Map 7, D7. 507 Fremont Pl N ℗632-0880.

Daily 11.30am–2am.

So-named because of the small triangular outdoor seating area, Fremont's best tavern is a relaxed affair that attracts a youthful, occasionally artsy local clientele, and serves grilled fish and salads along with microbrews and pear cider. The outdoor tables are great for people-watching on sunny days.

Trollyman Pub

Map 7, C7. 3400 Phinney Ave N ⓒ548-8000.
Mon–Thurs 8.30am–11pm, Fri 8.30am–midnight, Sat 11am–midnight, Sun noon–7pm.

Inside the *Redhook Brewery*, this is the best brewpub in Seattle, pumping out all varieties of the Northwest's favorite craft brewery (the ESB, or extra-special bitter, is especially recommended) in a casual, living room-like setting with a convivial Fremont crowd. This is also where you meet to take tours of the *Redhook Brewery* (see p.88).

NIGHTLIFE

S eattle's **nightlife** can seem provincial when you consider the city's hip reputation. But there's plenty going on here most nights, and the scene is only sleepy in comparison to those of the biggest American metropolises. Music and dancing are staged in friendly and comfortable settings; cover charges are low; and dress codes are rarely enforced.

Seattle's **live music** scene has gotten a lot of notice in the 1990s, but you'll rarely find a local gig by the likes of Pearl Jam, the Foo Fighters, or other big grunge acts. The scene peaked at the beginning of the decade, but it helped spawn an enormous number of local alternative rock bands that play mostly their own material. It has also obscured the fact that Seattle has other good popular music available if you want something beyond alternative rock, such as blues, R&B, Cajun, reggae, or acoustic folk.

Seattle **clubs** are largely not raging all-night affairs, but they are a refreshing change for those who want to dance and drink in fairly laidback surroundings. The usual disco and funk still blare away at some places, but it's also easy to find more cutting-edge electronic/DJ fare as well.

LIVE MUSIC

It wasn't until the 1990s that Seattle assumed a prominent place in popular music, largely due to the explosion of **grunge** bands such as Nirvana, Pearl Jam, and Soundgarden. The scene is pretty much ancient history now, but the punk/heavy metal crossover that characterized grunge can still be heard in many of the city's underground acts, although these days the city hosts a wider array of **alternative rock** bands, with literally hundreds of bands playing a large and diverse local circuit. The network of venues isn't as extensive as you might imagine, but they're usually small and informal, with the best spots concentrated downtown and in Belltown and Capitol Hill. Lots of bands also play at cafés and bars where the cover charge will be minimal or nonexistent. If you're under 21, you won't legally be able to enter a music show where liquor is being served – though there are a couple of "all-ages" places (*Velvet Elvis* and *RKCNDY*).

Other types of music are pretty easy to find as well. Pioneer Square is the place to head for if you want **blues** or, to a lesser extent, **jazz**. The Pioneer Square **joint cover night** scheme allows you into ten bars and clubs – *Bohemian Cafe, Central Saloon, Colourbox, Doc Maynard's, Fenix, Fenix Underground, Larry's, New Orleans Creole Restaurant, Old Timer's Cafe,* and *Zasu* – most of which usually feature run-of-the-mill live music, for one blanket fee ($5 weekdays, $8 weekends). **Folk** and **singer-songwriter** attractions are easy to find throughout the city in cafés and the more genteel bars. **Reggae** and **international world music** bands play with less frequency, but are scattered around in reasonable quantity.

National touring acts of varying degrees of commercial stature almost always stop in Seattle if their itinerary is comprehensive, so there's sure to be a renowned international act or two during a visit of any duration. You can see a lot of cool stars and locals if you're in town for one of Seattle's music or arts **festivals**. Bumbershoot (on Labor Day Weekend) and the Northwest Folklife Festival, both of which take place at Seattle Center, are the biggest of these; the Earshot Jazz Festival, spread out over a few weeks in the fall, also draws a lot of major players.

The Rocket and *Seattle Weekly* are the best places to check for up-to-date listings; for ticket information to the big venues, see "City directory," p.273.

Anomalous Records

Map 5, D7. 1402 E Pike ⓒ328-9339.
A tiny record store (see p.261) that also occasionally hosts some of Seattle's most uncompromising experimental/ improvisational music performances in its loft-like space.

Ballard Firehouse

Map 8, F5. 5429 Russell Ave NW ⓒ784-3516.
Nightly live music, mostly standard good-time rock and blues, at a venue with a large dance floor. There are occasional Brazilian nights, and the odd big-name mainstream act, though most of these are way past their prime.

Bohemian Cafe

Map 3, D6. 111 Yesler Ave ⓒ447-1514.
Far from the most bohemian place in town, though they do feature reggae, blues, funk, and jazz several nights a week.

Colourbox

Map 3, D6. 113 First Ave S ☏340-4101.

Average rock club that at least provides some variety from the neighboring blues/R&B bars in Pioneer Square, with whom they participate in joint cover nights. Lots of local alternative bands who have yet to record or make a national reputation.

Crocodile Café

Map 4, E6. 2200 2nd Ave ☏441-5611;
www.seattlesquare.com/croccafe.

By day a diner (p.178), by night a hip and intimate rock club, this relatively small Belltown fixture is one of the best Seattle spots to see most any kind of music. The action centers on the booth-filled backroom bar, which presents a wide range of acts, from well-known indie fixtures to unknown up-and-comers.

Dimitriou's Jazz Alley

Map 4, G5. 2033 6th Ave ☏441-9729.

The best jazz venue in Seattle, if a bit mainstream, presenting a steady march of notable out-of-towners; heavy on established veterans, who often headline for a week or so.

Fenix

Map 3, E7. 315 2nd Ave S ☏467-1111.

Hip by Pioneer Square standards, and passé by those of the Seattle underground, it's hard to predict what you'll see here, though the acts are often well-known. There's also a dance club (*The Fenix Underground*, p.208) on the same premises.

Moore Theater

Map 4, F6. 1932 2nd Ave ☏443-1744; *www.themoore.com*.

Past-its-prime former vaudeville auditorium seats nearly 1500 and sometimes hosts famous touring acts who can't fill arenas.

LIVE MUSIC

New Orleans Creole Restaurant

Map 3, D6. 114 First Ave S ℂ622-2563.
Lots of roots rock, blues, jazz, and Cajun, best when zydeco is featured. The Cajun cuisine isn't bad either.

The OK Hotel

Map 3, C7. 212 Alaskan Way ℂ621-7903.
All sorts of live music and entertainment here, often in different rooms and all at once, so loud guitars bleed into poetry contests. Local avant-garde hero Wayne Horvitz plays here with some frequency; perhaps apocryphally, this is also where Nirvana first performed "Smells Like Teen Spirit" (in April 1991).

Old Timer's Cafe

Map 3, D8. 620 1st Ave S ℂ623-9800.
A crowded tavern where blues is featured almost nightly.

Paramount

Map 3, E2. 911 Pine St ℂ682-1414.
On the eastern edge of downtown, this large movie palace-like hall hosts shows by star or near-stellar touring acts.

Red Sea Restaurant

Map 3, D7. 206 1st Ave S ℂ233-9157.
This decent Ethiopian restaurant often features reggae bands on the weekends.

RKCNDY

Map 3, E1. 1812 Yale Ave ℂ667-0219.
An unimpressive facility that's tolerated because it stages regular all-ages shows. And *RKCNDY* has plenty of them, with both local and international acts.

LIVE MUSIC

Serafina

Map 5, B2. 2043 Eastlake Ave E ☎323-0807.

An Italian-oriented restaurant out in Eastlake that often has live Latin and jazz music in the evening.

The Showbox

Map 3, C4. 1426 1st Ave ☎628-3151.

With a capacity of nearly 1000, this renovated space near Pike Place Market is the best place to catch touring acts yet to graduate to the bigger arenas. There's also DJ/dance music for Saturday's "Electrolush" events, and some rap and jazz.

Sit & Spin

Map 4, E5. 2219 4th Ave ☎441-9484.

The live music at this combination cafe/laundromat/ performance space tends toward the way underground, with occasional CD release parties by bands on Seattle's numerous tiny labels.

Speakeasy Cafe

Map 4, E5. 2304 2nd Ave ☎728-9770.

Multipurpose space with film screenings, poetry readings, and Internet workshops also often has ambient, jazz, and improvised music of an interesting, uncommercial nature (events calendar on-line at *www.speakeasy.org*).

Tractor Tavern

Map 8, F6. 5213 Ballard Ave NW ☎789-3599.

Roots music of all kinds is the specialty – zydeco, Irish, blues, bluegrass – with the occasional high-profile act. A much better alternative than similar spots in Pioneer Square.

Velvet Elvis

Map 3, D7. 107 Occidental S ✆624-8477.

Seattle's leading all-ages venue, specializing in cool alt-rock acts. It's also used for theatrical performances, meaning that most of the floor is occupied by permanent sloped seating, making dancing quite difficult.

CLUBS

Seattle's **clubs** aren't many in number, and though several are the standard kind – loud, crowded, and pretentious – that you find in most large cities, the majority are very relaxed, with nonexistent dress codes, and all musical tastes and sexual orientations welcomed. Almost all of the noteworthy clubs are situated in downtown or nearby Capitol Hill. The clubs usually specialize in different music and/or DJs on a night-by-night basis, and it's not at all unusual for the same venue to feature gothic-industrial, 1980s new wave, and electronica in the same week. With these changes, not to mention the way some clubs will mix in live music nights or poetry readings, consulting the entertainment listings in the *Seattle Weekly* or *The Stranger* is essential.

For listings of gay clubs in Seattle, which are some of the most happening in town, see pp.224–226.

Alibi Room

Map 3, B4. 85 Pike St ✆623-3180.

Experimental club fare that makes a refreshing change from the norm, in a space in the bowels of Pike Place Market where you can either groove to some of the town's more adventurous DJs or hang out in quieter, more café-like sections.

CLUBS

Art Bar

Map 3, C4. 1516 2nd Ave ℘622-4344.

Not as arty as the name implies, with a youthful crowd at a space that opens every Saturday at 6am (yes, 6am) for the "Mega Watt Palace" morning of drinks and DJs.

Beso Del Sol

Map 7, E5. 4468 Stone Way N ℘547-8087.

Beso is usually a Mexican restaurant, but they have salsa DJ music featured on Saturday nights.

The Fenix Underground

Map 3, E7. 315 2nd Ave S ℘467-1111.

Unexceptional but reliable dance DJs devoted to music from the 1970s to today, with some retro theme nights like "1980s Underground" or "Club Hi-Dee 'Ho" (swing dance & lounge).

Machine Werks

Map 4, D3. 112 5th Ave N ℘441-0715.

For those who like their beats-per-minute loud and furious, with detours into poetry and lounge jazz, particularly on the beatnik throwback "Club Dig" nights on Thursdays.

Romper Room

Map 4, B3. 106 1st Ave N ℘284-5003.

Dance music with a decade-by-decade specialization, most popular on "Eighties Nights."

Rupert's

Map 3, D7. 309 1st Ave S ℘628-7703.

Two floors and two bars at a nightspot that's more eclectic than most – you might have a choice between lounge DJs on the bottom floor and world groove up top, with Seventies and Eighties "oldschool disco" on Fridays.

Vogue

Map 4, E6. 2018 1st Ave ⊘443-0673.
One of the older Seattle club scene institutions, and still packing in youthful, edgy crowds to sounds that vary from new wave, reggae, and gothic to the more industrial-oriented, ever-popular Sunday Fetish Night.

THE PERFORMING ARTS AND FILM

Seattle is fairly strong in the **performing arts**, especially considering the city's modest size. The **theater** has long been a major force in the city's arts community; indeed Seattle probably has the most vibrant theater scene of any similar-sized metropolis in the US, both for big-budget and fringe productions. It's also one of six US cities to have its own major **opera**, **symphony**, and **ballet** companies, and lesser-known quality **dance** and **classical** organizations stage performances in the area as well.

There aren't a wealth of screens in town showing offbeat **films** on a regular basis, but there's a respectable clutch of art houses, and the springtime Seattle International Film Festival brings hundreds of foreign and independent movies to the area. The local **comedy** scene is quite small, but Seattle supports live **readings**, **poetry**, and **spoken word** performances with gusto, mostly taking place in bookstores, lecture halls, and cafés.

THEATER

Seattle has more equity **theaters**, and more annual theater performances, than any city in the US save New York. Its Actors Equity Guild has nearly five hundred members, and plenty of non-union actors and actresses make the city their home too, filling out the ranks of the numerous offbeat productions. As such, there's never a shortage of options, from reinterpretation of the classics to big-budget musicals to tiny experimental works.

Ticket prices can clear the $30 mark for prestigious performances in the Seattle Center, but entry to many smaller shows costs $10 or less, and certain theaters offer tickets for half-price right before showtime. Ticketmaster sells tickets for some of the bigger productions, and Ticket/Ticket sells day-of-show theater and concert tickets at half price; see p.273 for more details.

The **Fringe Theater Festival** (℡320-9588, *www.SeattleSquare.com/FringeFest*) stages dozens of productions in more than half a dozen Capitol Hill locations over about two weeks of early spring; tickets are usually in the $10 range. Otherwise, check the listings in the alternative weeklies for the most offbeat productions, since some are held where you'd least expect them.

A Contemporary Theater (ACT)

Map 3, D3. Kreielsheimer Place, 700 Union St ℡292-7676.
A bit mainstream for a contemporary drama specialist, but there are world premieres and adventurous adaptations mixed

THEATER

211

in with new productions of Tennessee Williams, Chekhov, and the like. The season runs April to November, in a 1925 downtown auditorium.

Annex Theatre

Map 3, C3. 1916 4th Ave ℗728-0933.
One of Seattle's most established theaters for alternative/fringe works. It's very unpredictable what you'll see.

Belltown Theatre

Map 4, E6. 115 Blanchard St ℗728-7609.
One of the more freewheeling spaces in town, and one of the least expensive, offering everything from stand-up comedians and adult puppet theater to new plays from Northwest playwrights.

Cornish College of the Arts

Map 5, C5. 1501 10th Ave E ℗726-5066.
Quality modern fare that's decently risktaking. Housed in the Ned Skinner Theater on the Cornish College campus.

Empty Space

Map 7, D7. 3509 Fremont Ave N ℗547-7500;
www.seattlesquare.com/emptyspace.
This Fremont institution is one of the city's bolder playhouses, presenting both contemporary material and the classics.

Fifth Avenue Theatre

Map 3, D4. 1308 Fifth Ave ℗625-1900;
www.5thavenuetheatre.org.
Seattle theater is at its glitziest in this gigantic 1926 ex-vaudeville house that replicates the throne room of China's

Forbidden City and presents mainstream musicals with big-name stars.

The Group Theatre

Map 4, C2. Center House, Seattle Center ✆441-1299.
Long-lived Seattle theater dedicated to spreading the gospel of progressive multicultural politics.

Intiman Theatre

Map 4, C1. Seattle Center ✆269-1900.
Classics and premieres of innovative new works, along with the occasional surprise like a Spalding Gray monologue.

Mystery Cafe

Map 6, A4. University Plaza Hotel, 400 NE 45th St ✆324-8895.
"Interactive" mystery dinner theater where audience mingles with the actors over a two-and-a-half-hour performance. Prices include a three-course meal. Ticket office is at 4105 E Madison St, Suite 310; performances Fridays and Saturdays at 8pm ($40).

New City

Map 5, C7. 1634 11th Ave ✆323-6800.
Capitol Hill playhouse that commissions a lot of new works for performance, and often shows works-in-progress.

Northwest Actors Studio

Map 5, C7. 1100 E Pike St ✆324-6328.
A theater arts center that, in addition to offering acting courses, puts on a performance calendar with a wide scope: comedy, Shakespeare, and the ultra-avant-garde are all fair game. Tickets are usually $10 and under.

THEATER

Northwest Asian American Theatre

Map 3, G7. 409 7th Ave S ✆340-1445.

Works written, performed, and directed by Asians and Asian-Americans.

On the Boards

153 14th Ave ✆325-7901.

In addition to its contemporary dance program, this also puts on challenging contemporary theater, often mixing dance and theater in the same production. It's moving to the former home of *ACT* (Queen Anne Hall; ✆285-7977 for info) in fall 1998.

Open Circle

429 Boren Ave N (in back off the alley) ✆382-4250.

A fifty-seater theater that's one of the city's more intimate playhouses; its own company gives several shows and workshop performances each year, with content from Jean Genet to rock musicals.

Paramount Theatre

Map 3, D2. 911 Pine St ✆682-1414.

Along with the *Fifth Avenue Theatre*, this fellow ex-vaudeville house is the main place in town to see extravagant musicals and big-budget mainstream Broadway-type affairs.

Seattle Repertory Theater

Map 4, B2. Seattle Center ✆443-2222.

Seattle's oldest and most established theater company mixes revivals of classics with sometimes daring newer works in the Bagley Wright Theater in Seattle Center. A second stage in the same facility, the *Leo K. Theatre*, was recently opened for new and smaller-scaled works.

University of Washington School of Drama

Map 4, B5. 4001 University Way NE ℗543-4880.
A dozen shows from late October to early June, presented at
the Meany Studio Theatre, Playhouse Theatre, and Penthouse
Theatre (all on the UW campus). Mixes classics, contemporary
works, and premieres, and the price ($7–8) is right.

Velvet Elvis

Map 3, D7. 107 Occidental Ave S ℗624-8477.
Small Pioneer Square theater that doubles as an all-ages rock
club. Of late it's become the seemingly permanent home of
Vince Balestri's solo show, *Kerouac*, based on Jack Kerouac's
writings, and sometimes performed with jazz accompaniment.

CLASSICAL MUSIC, OPERA, AND DANCE

Much of the city's **classical music**, **opera**, and **dance**
revolves around the Seattle Center's Opera House, which
hosts major performances by the Seattle Opera, Seattle
Symphony, and Pacific Northwest Ballet, although a new
building for the Seattle Symphony, Benaroya Hall, is scheduled to open downtown at 2nd and University in the fall of
1998. There's nothing too remarkable about the building
itself, which seats more than 3000 and was originally the
Civic Auditorium before being made over for the World's
Fair in the early Sixties; ticket prices range from $10 to $55.
In any case, they often sell out in advance, although there
are occasionally half-price day tickets for students and
seniors on the day of performance, about fifteen minutes
before showtime.

These professional companies get the lion's share of
press, but more affordable – and sometimes more inter-

esting – classical music and dance is offered at the *Meany Theater* on the University of Washington campus. The multidisciplinary arts organization *On the Boards* puts on respected modern dance productions, and the Northwest Chamber Orchestra has a varied classical program at far less expensive prices than the symphony commands.

Meany Theater

Map 4, B5. 4001 University Way ©543-4880 or 1-800/859-5342; *www.meany.org*.

As the home of the UW World Series, the *Meany Theater* stages most classical music, world dance, opera, and world music events on the campus, often featuring performers of international repute. The 1200-seat hall is known for its wide proscenium stage; all seats cost the same, though the best ones have usually been taken by subscribers. The *Meany* is also often used for UW's Musicfest seasons, which present classical performances and occasional operas by UW faculty and students, as well as some guest artists. Tickets for those are much more affordable than either the Opera House events or UW World Series, some running as low as $5.

Northwest Chamber Orchestra

Map 3, D4. 1305 4th Ave, Suite 522 ©343-0445.

Having celebrated its twenty-fifth anniversary season in 1997, the NCO presents concerts at the University of Washington's Kane Hall, as well as the Seattle Art Museum and Volunteer Park. Fairly affordable, with a wide repertoire ranging from baroque, Mozart, and Shostakovich to brand-new pieces.

Seattle Symphony

Map 4, C2. 4th Floor, Seattle Center House ℂ215-4747;
www.seattlesymphony.org.

Now under conductor Gerard Schwarz, esteemed as the music
director of New York's Mostly Mozart Festival. In addition to a
varied program of the classics, the symphony has also hosted
special concerts by such noted performers as pianist Van
Cliburn and violinist Isaac Stern; special performances range
from Handel's *Messiah* to the Kronos Quartet. The acoustics
are expected to be superior at Benaroya Hall, at 2nd and
University, when the symphony moves downtown in mid-
1998. The season runs from September to June.

OPERA

Seattle Opera

Map 4, B3. Box office 1020 John St ℂ389-7699,
www.seattleopera.org.

Five to ten performances each of five or so productions, from
October through May. The Seattle Opera has the biggest
budget of any arts organization in the city, and it shows in the
elaborate staging. The selection includes classics such as *La
Bohème*, but there have been newer works such as *Florencia in the
Amazon*, inspired by the writings of Gabriel García Màrquez.

DANCE

On the Boards

153 14th Ave ℂ325-7901; *www.ontheboards.org.*

In addition to its theater program (see p.214), *On the Boards*
stages cutting-edge dance events, often of a multidisciplinary
nature. It's awaiting the renovation of its new home in Queen
Anne Hall, but it also gives occasional performances in bigger
venues such as the *Moore Theater*, *Paramount*, and *Seattle Opera
House*.

OPERA AND DANCE

Pacific Northwest Ballet

Map 4, C1. 301 Mercer St ℗441-2424, *www. pnb.org*.

When not touring internationally, the *PNB* puts on six programs a year at the Opera House from September to June. Founded in 1972, and under the artistic direction of Kent Sowell and Francia Russell since 1977, its company has an active repertory of seventy works, the most popular production being a December staging of Tchaikovsky's *Nutcracker*, with set and costume design by Maurice Sendak (*Where the Wild Things Are*).

Spectrum Dance Theater

800 Lake Washington Blvd ℗325-4161.

One of the more prominent jazz dance companies in the US, and giving performances on Fridays and Saturdays in the $15–25 range; $16 ($8 children and seniors) for Sunday matinees.

FILM

There's a shortage of good **film** houses in Seattle, where most of the cinemas show general-release Hollywood productions. More interesting – and more atmospheric – are the rep theaters in Capitol Hill and the U District, most housed in old buildings that are either comfortably dilapidated or spruced up with recent renovations. Ticket prices are in line with those in most major US cities: around $7 for most first-run shows and a few dollars less for matinees.

....

There are several film festivals in Seattle, headed by the Seattle International Film Festival in the spring. See "Festivals," p.228, for details.

....

911 Media Arts

Map 5, A6. 117 Yale Ave N ✆682-6552.

A nonprofit media center that holds regular screenings of experimental films and videos. Erratic but challenging, and the first place to go for work that's too avant-garde for even the rep houses.

Egyptian

Map 5, C7. 801 E Pine St ✆323-4978.

Old Masonic temple with a 1920s feel that is the most charming cinema in town. The program matches the high standards of the architecture, focusing on offbeat current releases and independents, and hosting much of the Seattle Film Festival.

Grand Illusion

Map 6, B3. 1403 NE 50th St ✆523-3935; *www.wigglyworld.org*.

Seattle's best rep house isn't much in the way of decor – a hundred or so seats in a comfortably worn theater – but the programming is first-rate: director retrospectives, little-seen foreign films, and independents. Next door to the *Grand Illusion Café* (see p.158).

Harvard Exit

Map 5, C5. 807 E Roy St ✆323-8986.

Well-worn building at the northern edge of Broadway in Capitol Hill shows a consistent program of left-of-center current releases.

The Sanctuary

Map 6, A3. 5030 Roosevelt Way NE ✆524-8554.

The best video store in town, *Scarecrow Video*, also screens classics and cult flicks in its small (19-seat) upstairs space. More

FILM

of a projection room than a theater, really, but you'll see some things here that you'll have a hard time coming across elsewhere.

Seven Gables

Map 6, A3. 911 NE 50th St ℰ632-5545.
Attractive converted home at the edge of the U District showing quality current films.

Varsity

Map 6, B4. 4329 University Way NE ℰ632-3131.
This place runs one or two art house movies every day, including old classics, documentaries, foreign films, and newly released independents. And, of course, regular screenings of *The Rocky Horror Picture Show* on Saturdays at midnight.

POETRY AND SPOKEN WORD

Poetry and spoken word performance has taken off in Seattle, with several clubs and cafés offering a regular schedule of poetry "slams" and open-mike nights; the big-name

Comedy

Seattle doesn't have too many **comedy** clubs, though standup does occasionally take place at several theaters (such as the *Market Theatre* in Pike Place Market and the *Belltown Theatre*), which offer nights of improv and the like. The two top places are *Pioneer Square's Comedy Underground*, 222 S Main St (Map 3, E7; $6–10), and *Giggles*, 5220 Roosevelt Way NE (Map 6; A3; Fri–Sat 4.30pm–1am), out in the U District.

published poets tend to do their readings at bookstores or lecture halls. There are also numerous author readings/ appearances at local bookshops, especially *Elliott Bay Book Company* and the *University Book Store*. For performance listings, check out the free monthly publication *Wordscape* (available in many cafés); the alternative weeklies also usually have listings.

Globe Cafe

Map 5, D7. 1531 14th Ave ℘633-5647.
One of Seattle's best cafés, with free "open mikes" every Sunday and Tuesday nights, as well as featured readings to ensure some dependable quality.

The O.K. Hotel

Map 3, C7. 212 Alaskan Way ℘621-7903.
Weekly "slam" poetry competitions on Wednesdays for $3, plus open-mike and scheduled readings on the same bill.

Queen Anne Coffee House

1625 Queen Anne Ave N ℘907-5081.
"Noise" is an all-ages open mike every Thursday night, open to rap, improvisation, and prose as well as poetry. Slam competitions are held for cash prizes on the last Thursdays of the month.

Sit & Spin

Map 4, E5. 2219 4th Ave ℘441-9484.
This laundromat/café holds a "Poetic and Literary Fuck-All" on the first Wednesday evening of the month that is one of Seattle's most freewheeling performance art nights.

POETRY AND SPOKEN WORD

Seattle Slams

The **poetry "slams"** held regularly in Seattle are not mosh pits of young punks bumping bodies to the cadences of local wordsmiths. They do, however, share some of indie rock's in-your-face energy and lack of respect for artistic convention. Slams are verbal poetry contests in which competitors read in bang-bang sequence, the winners determined by the audience. It's not poetry NEA-style, for sure.

Slam poetry started at the *Get Me High Saloon* in Chicago, when poet Marc Smith decided hecklers could be used to his advantage by asking them to rate his performance on a one-to-ten scale. The genre has spread through cities across the US, but Seattle is still pretty much at the forefront. The city's top venue is the *OK Hotel*, which holds weekly slams and stages regional semifinals.

There are four basic rules: no props, do your own (original) poem, don't go over three minutes, and "check your ego at the door." Judges are chosen from the audience, and could be anyone, from slackers to Microsoft drones (an occupation bound to draw whoops of disapproval from the rest of the crowd); their judgments and scores are subject to the same catcalls that the performers endure. As the night advances, the contestants with the higher scores advance to succeeding rounds until only one is left, usually winning a modest cash prize.

While purists may complain that the genre dumbs-down poetry to the level of a sports contest, there's no doubt that slams have brought poetry to an audience of clubgoers that would otherwise be loathe to seek it out. And the quality of the readings is actually fairly high; after all, if you're willing to be graded on your art – and, if you do well, forced to extemporize on the spot – there's a fair chance you'll have a little native talent in the first place. Failing that, a whole lot of guts.

POETRY AND SPOKEN WORD

Speakeasy Cafe

Map 4, E5. 2304 2nd Ave ©728-9770.

This eclectic venue stages a monthly "Real to Reel" series that combines cinema with poetry, spoken word, and performance art, and also schedules other regular poetry/spoken word events.

GAY SEATTLE

G**ay and lesbian** culture in Seattle centers around Capitol Hill – unsurprising given the neighborhood's history of progressive politics. In fact, many gays have moved to Seattle from other parts of the Northwest (and indeed the US) due to the entire city's longstanding liberalism and increasingly cosmopolitan character.

The top **publication** for the gay community is the weekly *Seattle Gay News* (25¢), available at newsstands and larger bookshops throughout the city. It includes an events calendar and coverage of both political and arts activity; it also has a Web site, *www.sgn.org/sgn*, with additional material. *Beyond the Closet*, 518 E Pike St (Map 5, B7; ✆322-4609), is the best-stocked gay/lesbian **bookstore** in the Pacific Northwest and is also a good source of information for local events and news.

Gay City (✆860-6969; *www.speakeasy.org/GayCity*) organizes social events and services for the gay community, ranging from support groups and educational outreach for HIV-positive males to participant sport contests for gay males at Volunteer Park in Capitol Hill. Seattle's **Gay Pride parade** (p.232) takes over a dozen blocks on Capitol Hill's main strip, Broadway, on the last Sunday in June; it's now one of the city's most exuberant events.

Lesbian and gay resources

Arcadia Women's Health Center 1300 Spring St ✆323-9388. Feminist clinic open to all women, but clients can request a lesbian health care provider if they wish.

Connections Line ✆323-0220. Counseling and crisis intervention.

Gay/Lesbian Youth Info Line ✆322-7900.

Lesbian Resource Center 1808 Bellevue Ave ✆e322-3953. General information on lesbian groups and events.

Parents and Friends of Lesbians and Gays ✆325-7724.

Seattle AIDS Support Group ✆322-2437.

Seattle Bisexual Women's Network ✆783-7987.

Seattle Counseling Service for Sexual Minorities ✆282-9307.

Seattle Gay Clinic 500 19th Ave E ✆461-4540. Health services and information for gay males.

GAY BARS

The Easy

Map 5, C7. 916 E Pike St ✆323-8343.

Daily 11am–2am.

Two-level, Capitol Hill lesbian-oriented establishment that draws a youthful crowd. By night it becomes as much a dance club as a place to drink, with a good-sized dance floor; there's also live music sometimes, including jazz on Sundays.

R Place

Map 5, B7. 619 E Pine St ✆322-8828.

Daily 2pm–2am.

Three-floor bar on the lower part of Capitol Hill that's a prime cruising spot for young professional gay men – a little yuppie-

GAY BARS

ish for most hip-minded folks, but a decent alternative for those who want avoid the dance club environment; with pool and darts.

Wild Rose

Map 5, C7. 1021 E Pike ℗324-9210.
Sun–Thurs 11am–midnight, Fri–Sat 11am–2am.

Seattle's most popular lesbian bar is a comfortable mixing point for eating (the menu has a pretty wide selection), playing pool or darts, or just hanging out. If you want something livelier, Thursday through Saturday evenings are dance nights.

GAY CLUBS

Neighbours

Map 5, C7. 1509 Broadway ℗324-5358.

Broadway's most popular gay hangout, and the place to go if you want to dance yourself into delirium to loud, beat-heavy sounds. Not as musically adventurous as many other dance clubs, though variety is ensured by drag, disco, and 1980s nights. It's one of the best club deals in the city on weeknights, when the cover is only $1 (Weds are free); it's $5 on Fridays and Saturdays.

Re-Bar

Map 5, A7. 1114 Howell St ℗233-9873.

Seattle's hottest dance spot, with a wall dividing the bar from the dance floor, and drawing big gay and straight crowds with an ever-shifting nightly focus that encompasses acid jazz, hip-hop, funk, soul, and Latin. And for those who never tire of Sylvester records, there's the long-running Queer Disco Night every Thursday at 9pm. There are also some live music acts, as well as occasional theatrical productions in the early evening.

GAY CLUBS

Timberline Tavern

Map 3, D3. 2015 Boren Ave ⓒ622-6220.
A country and western line-dancing club for the gay crowd,
drawing both men and women (including a decent number of
straights) to its large wooden floor. If you're not schooled in
the dance styles yet, come for line-dancing and two-stepping
lessons at 7.30pm on Tuesdays (for beginners) and Wednesdays
(for intermediates), although the clientele's pretty friendly
about helping novices out once the proper dancing starts at
9pm. On Sunday afternoon more conventional music takes
over for the 4pm Disco Tea Dance, where 75¢ beers are served.

FESTIVALS

Festivals in Seattle vary greatly in scale from the enormous Bumbershoot arts and music festival held around Labor Day to Vincent Price filmfests. The city's strong sense of neighborhood and ethnic pride results in dozens of small festivals throughout the year targeted toward very special interests. Also good are several free music concert series, mostly spanning parts of the summer – during which time even a brief stay is likely to coincide with an event that piques your curiosity. Not surprisingly, festivals are less frequent in the colder months.

JANUARY

Chinese New Year

The International District is at its most colorful around late January, when parades are staged and dragon costumes come out in full force. ℂ382-1197.

Women in Cinema Film Festival

For a week in late January, this screens several works a day by women filmmakers from all over the world at the *Harvard Exit*. Check the Seattle International Film Festival Web site (*www.seattlefilm.com*) for information. ℂ324-9996.

FEBRUARY

Festival Sundiata

Held at Seattle Center during Black History Month, and named after a Mali king who rescued a kidnapped griot (storyteller), this is the largest African-American festival in the Northwest, with music, workshops, food, crafts, and children's activities. Most events at the three-day festival are free. ℰ684-7200.

MARCH

Fringe Theater Festival

Dozens of productions in more than half a dozen Capitol Hill locations for a couple of weeks in March. Tickets are usually in the $10 range. ℰ320-9588 (*www.SeattleSquare.com/FringeFest*).

St Patrick's Day Parade

St Patty's is not that big a deal here, but there's still a downtown parade, March 17, starting from City Hall. ℰ425/865-9134.

APRIL

Cherry Blossom and Japanese Cultural Festival

This free event takes place at Seattle Center in late April and features historical and cultural exhibits, food, martial arts, music, calligraphy, tea ceremonies, and children's games. ℰ684-7200.

MAY

Worldfest

This multicultural music and crafts fair, representing more than one hundred ethnic groups, takes place in early May in the *Crossroads* shopping center in Bellevue. ℰ644-1111.

Seattle International Film Festival

More than two hundred films from all over the world are shown at this prestigious May festival and are often accompanied by director appearances. Shows take place at the *Egyptian*, *Harvard Exit*, *Guild 45th*, and *Broadway Performance Hall*; tickets are $7 ($5 matinees), and sell out fast for the prime-time slots. ℗325-6150 (*www.seattlefilm.com*).

University District Street Fair

Held around mid-May, this is the biggest event of its kind in Seattle, taking over the main section of University Way with hundreds of booths, food vendors, and lots of live entertainment. ℗523-4272.

Northwest Folklife Festival

This free Memorial Day weekend bash attracts 200,000 visitors and around 6000 participants, for all types of rootsy music, including bluegrass, Celtic, and world music, along with crafts, ethnic foods, dance, and storytelling. Whatever your musical interests, check out the Music Emporium, an exhibit of unusual folk instruments. ℗684-7300 (*www.nwfolklife.org/folklife*).

JUNE

International Music Festival

Not, as the name might indicate, world music, but classical music performances, held over the last half of June, most of which take place in Seattle's *Meany Theater*, the Seattle Art Museum auditorium, and the Meydenbauer Center in Bellevue. ℗233-0991.

FESTIVALS

Summer music festivals

Out to Lunch Summer Concert Series Free weekday music concerts of all sorts, noon to 1.30pm, at various downtown plazas and parks all summer long. ✆623-0340.

Pain in the Grass This series presents rock bands, mostly local, for free at Seattle Center's Mural Amphitheater, 6–8.30pm every Friday night, mid-June through late August. Previous bills have included Seattle alternative vets like Mudhoney and the Young Fresh Fellows. ✆684-7200.

Seattle Peace Concerts Staged throughout the summer at various local parks, mostly Volunteer Park and Gas Works Park, these feature rock, blues, zydeco, jazz, and other kinds of rock and roots-oriented artists. Shows are free, but the audience is asked to bring food bank donations for the Northwest Harvest organization. ✆789-5651.

Seward Park Concert Series Summer jazz, Shakespeare plays, and ethnic events, most notably Hispanic Seafair (late July) and the Pista Sa Nayon Filipino-American festival (early August). ✆723-SEED.

Summer Fun at the Locks Near the parade of ships entering the Lake Washington Ship Canal at the Ballard Locks. It's a mixed bag, from the Boeing Employees Concert Band to gospel choirs. ✆783-7059.

Summer Nights at the Pier About a dozen evening waterfront concerts at Piers 62/63 from late June through mid-August, usually of pretty big rock, blues, and pop names. It's often as expensive as big-name shows in standard arenas, though. ✆628-0888 (*www.summernights.org*).

artsEdge

Inaugurated in 1997, this is one of Seattle's most daring arts festivals, showcasing several hundred experimental Northwest artists and performers for a free weekend of events at Seattle Center in late June, taking in both the conventional (Shakespeare puppet drama) and the outrageous (Seattle Chainsaw Ensemble). ☎684-7197.

Fremont Fair & Solstice Parade

The most enjoyable Seattle neighborhood celebration. The highlight is the parade itself, full of outrageous human-powered floats and costumes. ☎633-4409.

Pride Parade and Freedom Rally

Also known as Gay Pride Parade, this is a popular event with Seattle residents of all sexual orientations, held on Broadway in Capitol Hill on the last Sunday of June. ☎324-4297 or 292-1035.

JULY

Independence Day

Fourth of July fireworks on the Lake Union waterfront. Gas Work Park is the most popular viewing location, but get there early if you want a good seat. ☎292-8028.

Seafair

A three-week celebration of Northwest maritime culture, kicking off in late July and held at various locations. It includes maneuvers by the Navy's Blue Angels, hydroplane races on Lake Washington, and milk-carton races on Green Lake. ☎728-0123.

Bite of Seattle

Seattle's most popular food festival, with restaurants setting up outdoor booths in Seattle Center at the end of July. ☎232-2982.

FESTIVALS

Central Area Community Festival

Held in Seattle's Central District in late July, and oriented toward the neighborhood's large African-American community, featuring youth poetry readings, African-American history exhibits, and booths from local sports teams. ℭ253/288-1441.

Pacific Northwest Arts and Crafts Fair

The most prominent Eastside festival, in Bellevue Square on the last weekend of July, and something of a local legend for never having been rained out in its fifty-year-plus history. ℭ454-4900.

San Juan Island Dixieland Jazz Festival

An event that takes place on San Juan Island for three days near the end of July, the antidote to those who think popular music here begins and ends with grunge. If you're interested, make plans and reservations way in advance. A pass for admission to all three days costs $50 ($42 if you order it before June 30), and $15–28 for one day. ℭ360/378-5509 (*www.rockisland. com/~jazz*).

AUGUST

Chief Seattle Days

In Suquamish, just over the bridge from Bainbridge Island, the Suquamish Tribe celebrate this August weekend festival of Native American culture and canoe races. ℭ360/598-3311.

Hempfest

This hippie-type street fair unsurprisingly attracts folks sympathetic to the legalization of marijuana, a hemp product, and it's a pretty mellow affair, with crafts, information booths,

FESTIVALS

and the same sort of rock bands you'd find at most any live festival. Location varies. ℂ781-5734 (*www.hempfest.com*).

SEPTEMBER

Bumbershoot

A mammoth several-hundred event extravaganza that takes over the Seattle Center complex on Labor Day weekend. Acts range from the famous (the Sex Pistols played their reunion tour here) to the obscure; there's also a lot of film, comedy and theater. Around $10 for an all-day ticket (discounts if you buy multiday passes). ℂ281-8111 (*www.onereel.org/bumbershoot.html*).

Salmon Homecoming Celebration

Held around the second weekend of September, this free festival on Piers 62/63 at the waterfront focuses on Northwest Indian groups, with storytelling, food and craft booths, and other Native American cultural exhibits. ℂ386-4320.

OCTOBER

The Earshot Jazz Festival

Held over several weeks, the focus here is on progressive contemporary jazz notables. ℂ547-9787 (*www.earshot.com/earshot*).

Asian-American Film Festival

For about five days in October, works by Asian-American directors; it's especially strong on short subjects. ℂ525-0892.

Lesbian and Gay Film Festival

Runs for a week in late October at the *Harvard Exit* in Capitol Hill, from feature dramas to avant-garde shorts, and including selections from several continents. ℂ323-4274.

DECEMBER

Jewish Film Festival

Jewish-related movies and work by Jewish filmmakers, including Israeli titles. Some events also feature live music, and there have also been "bagel and film fiestas." ©622-6315.

SPORTS AND OUTDOOR ACTIVITIES

With temperatures that seldom dip below freezing and a close proximity to some of the most scenic mountains and waterways of North America, Seattle is well-suited for year-round **outdoor activities**. Rain barely dampens the pace of hiking, climbing, and biking during the colder months, and it takes something close to a hurricane or blizzard to dissuade many weekend campers and sailors. Major **sports franchises** didn't arrive here until the 1960s and 1970s, and were slow to catch on, but the city has now embraced its professional athletic teams with fervent enthusiasm, particularly the Mariners (baseball) and the SuperSonics (basketball).

Indeed, the excitement generated by those teams means tickets are often hard to come by, and Sonics games are always sellouts. The prices aren't always such bargains either, at least if you want to be close to the action. Baseball remains a reasonable alternative for weekday and weeknight games, when decent seats are usually available until game time; for weekend and big series, though, you'll probably be consigned to the outer reaches of the outfield, or may not be able to get in at all.

Advance tickets for major Seattle sporting events can be purchased over the phone from *TicketMaster* (✆628-0888), which also sells them in person at a few places throughout the city, including *Tower Records* outlets and the Westlake Center mall downtown (see "Tickets", p.273, for more details). It charges a fee on top of the ticket price, which can be avoided by contacting the teams' box offices, most of which are conveniently located in either the Kingdome, the Seattle Center, or the University of Washington campus.

BASEBALL

When the Seattle Pilots brought major league **baseball** into town in 1969, the franchise was a miserable failure, lasting only a year before moving to Milwaukee – just long enough for the Pilots' relief pitcher Jim Bouton to pen his bestselling diary, *Ball Four*, in which he observed, "A city that seems to care more for its art museums than its ballpark can't be all bad." Times have changed. In 1997, the **Seattle Mariners** were among the most successful operations in all of sports, drawing more than three million fans to the Kingdome, while featuring two of the most exciting players in the game: outfielder Ken Griffey Jr and shortstop Alex Rodriguez. There's also a lot of care being put into the construction of new open-air baseball and football stadiums to replace the Kingdome, at an expense that may exceed $1 billion.

BASEBALL

For more on the Kingdome, see p.43.

The Mariners (ticket information ☎622-HITS) will continue to play indoors in the Kingdome until a new natural grass, open-air stadium with a retractable roof is completed nearby – scheduled for 1999. The cheapest seats (in the outfield) cost $6, box seats (the most expensive) $25; premium seats are getting scarce, however, as the team is now selling more than 15,000 season tickets.

Minor league baseball is available within thirty miles or so of town in both Tacoma, where the triple-A-level **Rainiers** (☎253/752-7700 or 1-800/281-3834) play at Cheney Stadium, and in Everett, where the single-A-level **Aquasox** (☎258-3673) play from mid-June to early September. Both teams are Mariner affiliates, and good seats are pretty easy to get; plus, it's outdoors and cheap (under $10, sometimes under $5).

BASKETBALL

The **SuperSonics** (usually abbreviated to the "Sonics") are the only Seattle team to win a major league championship, back in the late 1970s. They've come close again in recent years, and have remained a consistent contender, led by star point guard Gary Payton. They play at Key Arena in Seattle Center (ticket info ☎283-DUNK), a 17,000-seater venue where tickets are hard to come by. Prices run $7–100, and you can forget about getting space near the floor level at the center of the court, unless you have connections. Across Seattle Center, the **Reign** ushered Seattle into the women's professional hoops circuit, the American Basketball League, in 1996, playing at the Mercer Arena, which seats about 4500. Tickets cost $11–35 (info ☎285-5225), and are also usually snapped up quickly; indeed some games in the Reign's inaugural season ended up as sell-outs.

FOOTBALL

Until the mid-Nineties, the **Seahawks** (ticket information ℂ827-9766) were also among the hottest tickets in town, but the football squad's lackluster record in recent years – not to mention the concurrent surge of interest in Seattle's other pro teams – has diverted attention elsewhere. There was speculation that the franchise would be leaving town, until Paul Allen stepped in as a buyer, on the condition that a new open-air stadium be built in the Kingdome's place. Tickets are easier to get these days, but they're still not cheap, ranging from $10 to $50. The new stadium will be constructed in almost the same location as the old one, and during the demolition, the team will play in Husky Stadium at UW.

UW's football players, the **Huskies**, have enjoyed a lot more success than the Seahawks, usually ranking among the nation's top twenty college outfits. They play in the Pacific-10 conference at the 72,000-seat Husky Stadium on the edge of the campus, near Lake Washington; tickets (ℂ543-2200) cost $26–28 for reserved seats, $13–14 for general admission to the bleachers. The same ticket office, incidentally, sells seats for several other UW sporting events, the most popular of which are the men and women's basketball contests; tickets for those are $6–10.

SOCCER, HOCKEY, AND HORSE RACING

Soccer enthusiasts can watch the **Sounders**, 1995 and 1996 champions of the A-League, the highest US pro soccer level other than major league soccer; they play at

Memorial Stadium in Seattle Center (©622-3415 or 1/800-796-KICK for ticket information). **The Seattle SeaDogs** (©282-3647) play indoor soccer at the Key Arena, an outing which young kids might find more memorable, as children are allowed on the field before and after games to meet players and kick balls around. There's no major league **hockey** team in Seattle, but the **Thunderbirds** (©448-PUCK) of the minor Junior A Western Hockey League play in Key Arena too. In the Tacoma suburb of Auburn, **horse racing** is held at **Emerald Downs** (©288-7000), which opened in the spring of 1996. The racing season runs late March through September, Wednesdays through Sundays (Thurs–Sun until mid-May).

BIKING

Despite the rainy climes, hilly topography, and jammed motorways, Seattle has one of the highest percentages of **bicycle** commuters in the country: there are about thirty miles of bike/pedestrian trails and nearly one hundred miles of signed bike routes. Though you'll have a hard time finding level routes unless you stick close to the lakes, the semi-mountainous terrain guarantees a good workout, and the scenery is often magnificent.

The most popular route is the twelve-mile **Burke-Gilman Trail**, which starts near 8th Avenue NW and NW 43rd Street and follows the banks of the Lake Washington Ship Canal and northern Lake Washington. The path is also open to joggers and walkers; at its northern end, it connects to the ten-mile Sammamish River Trail, which brings riders over to Redmond in the Eastside.

Another good route is the stretch of **Lake Washington Boulevard** that starts at the Arboretum and goes by the lake's edge for a few miles before terminating at Seward Park; the southern end of the route is closed to traffic from 10am to 6pm on the second Saturday and third Sunday of the month between May and September. Far more challenging, but very beautiful, is **Magnolia Boulevard**, which climbs a steep hill from the Magnolia Bridge to Discovery Park, passing gorgeous cliffside views of the Puget Sound en route.

For a more rural experience there's great biking in Vashon Island (p.117) and Lopez Island (p.128).

Bikes can be **rented** at *Gregg's*, at 7007 Woodlawn Ave NE (✆523-1822), *Bicycle Center*, at 4529 Sandpoint Way NE (✆523-8300), or *Al Young*, 3615 NE 45th St (Map 6, G4; ✆524-2642); rates tend to be $3–5 per hour, $15–25 per day. If you're planning on doing a lot of cycling while you're in the area, call the bicycle division of the city's **transportation department** (✆684-5374); leave your name and address, and they'll send you the free and very handy *Seattle Bicycling Map*, which outlines bicycle routes and lists cycling regulations. Bicycle activists can join Seattle's **Critical Mass**, which meets at Westlake Center at 5.30pm on the last Friday of the month for rides through downtown to promote nonmotorized transportation. Whatever your political stance, helmets should be worn in Seattle at all times; there are more than two hundred car-bicycle accidents every year.

RUNNING

Jogging is big in Seattle in all weather, and every lunch-break finds the waterfront populated with office workers who have changed into running gear to take in a few miles along the Puget Sound. Seattle's numerous parks and water-side lanes offer a lot of choices for the fitness enthusiast, and some of the better routes are multipurpose bike/running/walking paths, such as the Burke-Gilman Trail (see p.240) and routes along Green Lake, Lake Washington, and Myrtle Edwards Park. Discovery Park has a challenging 2.8-mile loop trail that goes through dense forest and along bluffs with great views of the Puget Sound. Competitive races are held in town throughout the year, highlighted by November's **Seattle Marathon/Half-Marathon** (&729-3660 or 729-3661; *www.seattlemarathon.org*). *Northwest Runner*, available at sporting goods outlets, prints a calendar of races in Seattle and throughout the Northwest; it's also online at *runningnetwork.com*.

WATER ACTIVITIES

Watching the boats sail in and out of the Ballard Locks is a popular spectator sport, and there are several inexpensive **water activities** centers that enable you to get in on the action on a smaller scale. Foremost among these is the *Waterfront Activities Center* (Map 6, D7; Feb–Oct 10am–dusk; &543-9433), which rents rowboats or canoes for $5 an hour with a valid ID; on weekdays there's rarely a wait, and the marshes of Foster Island are just a few minutes' row away. *The Northwest Outdoor Center*, at 2100 Westlake Ave N (&281-9694), rents sea kayaks by hour ($8–12) and day ($40–60); the same rates are offered by the *Agua Verde Paddle Club*, on Lake Union's Portage Bay at 1303 NE Boat St (Map 6, B6; &545-8570). Cruising around enclosed Green Lake is a tamer option; for that, *Green Lake Rentals* (April–Sept; call &527-0171 for information) rents paddleboats, rowboats, canoes, and kayaks for $8 an hour; sailboats for

$12 an hour. Expect crowds of boaters and swimmers on warm summer days.

More boating tours are detailed on p.17.

For saltwater **fishing**, *Sport Fishing of Seattle* (©623-6364) runs seven-hour trips from Pier 55 into Puget Sound (May–Sept daily; rest of year varies; $65 plus tax and license, with fishing gear and bait included).

Urban Surf, 2100 N Northlake Way (Map 7, G8; ©545-9463), rents board and sail for **windsurfing** at $35/day, plus skates and pads for **rollerblading** for $5/hr and $16/day, and is conveniently located near the Burke-Gilman Trail, where you can put the gear to use right away.

Outdoor swimming is usually not a comfortable proposition in Seattle without a wetsuit, but the hardy do take to the waves at the city's two most popular beaches, **Alki Beach** (p.100) and **Golden Gardens** (p.84) – although the water temperatures are actually warmer, and the crowds thinner, in **Lake Washington** (p.94). The city runs about ten **indoor swimming pools** where you can take a dip for a modest fee, the most conveniently located of these being *Queen Anne Pool* at 1920 1st Ave W (©386-4282) and *Evans Pool* on the edge of Green Lake at 7201 E Green Lake Drive N (Map 7, G1; ©684-4961). There's also the heated outdoor *Colman Pool*, in West Seattle's Lincoln Park (©684-7494), only open from late June through the end of August.

HIKING

Hiking is integral to the Northwest lifestyle, although the best places are a few hours outside of town on Mt. Rainier, the Cascade Mountains, and the Olympic Peninsula. **Mt.**

Si, however, is only about a half-hour's drive east of Seattle, near Snoqualmie Falls. A four-mile climb ascends about 4000 feet to take in glorious panoramas of the surrounding mountains (see p.114 for details). In the San Juan Islands, **Mt. Constitution** on Orcas Island rises nearly 2500 feet; its mountaintop also commands stunning surveys of the area.

Trail maps are found in all good bookstores and outdoors shops, although in Seattle, **travel bookstores** *Metzker Maps*, 702 1st Ave (Map 3; D6; ✆623-8747), *Wide World Books & Maps*, 1911 N 45th St (Map 7, G5; ✆634-3453), and *The Mountaineers*, 300 3rd Ave W (✆284-6310), are particularly good sources – as is the outdoors superstore *REI*, 222 Yale Ave N (Map 5, A6; ✆223-1944). *REI* is also a good place to get kitted out for hiking and camping if you need any gear, or to practice your **climbing** on their 65ft indoor rock, which you can ascend for free with guidance from the store staff. More serious, and more expensive, climbs are offered by *Vertical World* at 2123 W Elmore St in Fishermen's Terminal (Map 8, F7; ✆283-4497), which has almost 15,000 square feet of space and more than a hundred routes of various degrees of difficulty; the entrance fee is $11 ($16 on weekends).

KIDS' SEATTLE

Seattle is very **kid**-friendly: the presence of children in public places and attractions is not just tolerated, but encouraged. In Seattle Center, for instance, there's not only a children's museum and a children's theater, but also kid-sized eating tables at Center House's food court, as well as a section on the same floor for little ones to zoom around in toy cars. Seattle's appeal as a family destination is further enhanced by an above-average number of activities that will be of roughly equal interest to both children and their parents, as well as a wealth of fine public parks in which to burn off excess energy.

There are youth discounts at most museums, sights, and on the Metro and Washington State Ferries.

MUSEUMS

At some of Seattle's top museums – particularly the **Pacific Science Center** in Seattle Center (see p.53) and the **Museum of Flight** (see p.102) – the constant parade of boisterous kids and school groups makes these institutions feel like children's playgrounds being invaded by adults, rather than the other way around. Good fare is also offered at the **Seattle Aquarium** at Pier 59 (see p.25) and the **Woodland Park Zoo** (see p.90), both of which balance creature-gawking with frequent, well-planned programs and talks. The **Seattle Children's Museum** (p.55) caters to kids' interests above all else, with participatory exhibits like an artificial mountain, where youngsters can climb rocks and logs.

PARKS, BEACHES, WATER

Seattle is blessed with a lot of **parks** and plenty of playground space for toddlers; **Green Lake** (see p.92) is the best multipurpose choice of the lot, with a lake, bike path, public pool, and nearby boating/cycling rentals available. The most creative option is **Gas Works Park** (see p.89), whose "playbarn" is a riot of multicolored pipes and engines; the park's windy hill is the most popular place in the city to fly **kites**. The much larger **Discovery Park** (see p.77) has spacious fields that are also well-suited for the sport. For a less well-trod park that still offers grassy space, lakeside views, and a large playground for kids, head for **Seward Park** (p.98), near the southern end of Lake Washington. Further away, and usually overlooked by visitors, is pleasant **Mercer Slough Nature Park** (p.100), with trails through more than three hundred acres of wetlands. The **Seattle Parks and Recreation Department** (©684-4075) often holds kids' activities, especially in summer, from arts-and-crafts to nature walks.

Seattle does have a few **beaches** (p.243), but these are narrow and the water is usually too cold for bathing; the best place for family **swimming** is the outdoor saltwater Colman Pool, open summers-only (p.101).

For cheap family thrills, nothing beats aimless cruising around the Puget Sound on the public transit **ferries** (see p.15), especially if weather permits open-air seating on the top deck. The Seattle-Bainbridge route is the best option, as it's quick (about a half-hour each way) and scenic. Watching the boats bob up and down at the **Hiram M. Chittenden Locks** in Ballard is a crowd-pleaser (see p.81), although children may get bored if the ship traffic is slow. If that's the case, take them to the **fish ladder** a short walk away, where they can watch salmon squirm their way into the Puget Sound, although you should check the migration schedule beforehand to make sure the ladder won't be empty.

THEATER, PUPPETS, FESTIVALS

The **Seattle Children's Theatre**, in the Seattle Center (Map 4, C2; Sept–June; ✆441-3322), offers half a dozen mainstage productions each year. For something more unusual, there's the **Northwest Puppet Center**, north of the U District at 9123 15th Ave NE (✆523-2579; $7.50, children $5.50). Their half-dozen or so shows each season have a multicultural slant that can cover Hindu epics and African-American folktales in addition to the usual Christmas season production. The **Seattle International Children's Festival** (✆684-7338) in May has live music, dance, and theater performances at the Seattle Center; more festivals are detailed on pp.228–235.

SHOPS

For **shopping**, *Science, Art & More*, 6417 Roosevelt Way NE (✆524-3795), just north of the U District, has a quality

THEATER, PUPPETS, FESTIVALS, AND SHOPS

stock of educationally oriented toys. *Teri's Toybox*, in University Village (Map 6, D4; ✆526-7147), eschews the usual mass-market products for puzzles, creative games, and well-designed dress-up clothes. Seattle museums usually have good kids' sections, particularly the zoo, which has a lot of wildlife/ecology-oriented books, games, and toys, and the Pacific Science Center.

Finally **Pike Place Market** (p.20) is a good fail-safe alternative when the kids are restless and you're running short on ideas; there's plenty of fast food and snacks to replenish the blood sugar level, plus unpredictable live entertainment from magicians, mimes, and the like.

SHOPS AND GALLERIES

Seattle is not a city that you come to for **shopping**. There's an increasing glut of showy shopping centers downtown, but you've probably seen them all before, and the prices here are no bargains. Seattle is, on the other hand, a good place for finding thriftwear, with plenty of used clothing stores and the like. The streets of **Belltown**, **Capitol Hill**, and particularly **Fremont** – with its strange junk shops and antique stores – offer the best array.

Seattle has acquired the reputation of a musical capital of sorts in the last few years, but its **record stores** are actually quite ordinary. **Bookstores** are significantly better, although many of the used outlets are pretty humdrum. The best book and record stores are generally found in the **U District**.

Most **gallery** prices are beyond the reach of mere wage-earners, but they do form an important adjunct to the Northwest modern art scene. Their appeal is not limited to collectors, either: anyone with a strong interest in art, particularly glasswork, is urged to check them out, and due to their concentration in the downtown area, a dozen or more can easily be covered in the same day.

BOOKS

Amid the large **bookstore** chains in Seattle are abundant small neighborhood outlets and established specialty shops; most of the used bookstores are comfortably funky, if a bit poorly organized. As a complement to the many stores, Seattle excels in author readings, especially at *Elliott Bay Book Company* (see opposite), which has one of the busiest event schedules of any bookstore in the nation; check the local papers and weeklies for listings there and elsewhere. The **Seattle Arts and Lectures** series (☏621-2230) often features lectures from major authors from everywhere; speakers have included Toni Morrison and Philip Roth. In October, the **Northwest Bookfest** on Pier 48 (☏378-1883; *www.speakeasy.org/nwbookfest*) holds free panels, readings, and workshops, with lots of books for sale.

GENERAL

Bailey-Coy Books

Map 5, C5. 414 Broadway E ☏323-8842.
Capitol Hill's top general bookstore, with strong gay and lesbian sections.

Barnes & Noble

Map 6, D4–E4. University Village Mall, 25th Ave NE & NE 45th St ☏517-4107.
The main Seattle branch of the country's biggest chain

bookseller – as copiously stocked as you might imagine. If you can't find what you want anywhere else, there's a good chance you'll find it here.

Borders

Map 3, C3. 1501 4th Ave *©*622-4599.
The top chain bookstore in downtown has a large selection in all subjects, and eases the corporate atmosphere with an upstairs café, readings, and occasional low-volume live music.

Elliott Bay Book Company

Map 3, D7. 1st Avenue S and S Main Street *©*624-6600;
www.elliottbaybook.com/ebbco.
The best general bookstore in Seattle, with a huge, alternative-leaning selection, a large "bargain balcony" of discounted books with import volumes and titles you won't see at other remainder outlets, author readings on a near-daily basis, and a fine downstairs café.

Tower Books

Map 4, B1. 20 Mercer *©*283-6333.
A sterile supermarket atmosphere, but the selection is pretty good, with strong sections on music, area history and guidebooks, and graphic novels and comics. Open every day 9am–midnight.

University Book Store

Map 6, B4. 4326 University Way NE *©*634-3400.
An institutional, department-store ambience, but the stock is superb in all categories at this massive multifloor outlet. It also presents a top-flight schedule of author readings.

BOOKS

Beauty & the Books

Map 6, B5. 4213 University Way NE ☎632-8510.

The most spacious of the U District's used stores, with nice touches of worn sofas and live cats, but the selection is disappointing in relation to the agreeable setting.

Bowie & Company

Map 3, D7. 314 1st Ave S ☎624-4100.

The best vendor of rare and collectible titles in Pioneer Square, also with old maps, prints, and a search service.

Magus Books

Map, A4. 1408 NE 42nd St ☎633-1800.

The decor is austere and functional, but this store has the best used selection in the U District, especially strong in fiction, art, and history, and with a friendly staff that is more often than not invisible behind mountains of unprocessed arrivals.

Recollection Books

Map 6, B5. 4159 University Way NE ☎548-1346, *www.eskimo.com/~recall*.

A patchy but worthwhile store, especially for its history section, and a cozy second-floor browsing area with a chessboard table, sofa, and dolls to occupy young kids.

Twice Sold Tales

Map 5, C6. 905 E John St ☎324-2421.

Seattle's best used bookstore has deep shelves in all subjects and a comfortable live-and-let-live ambience, in spite of its smart-

aleck window signs. Open until 2am Mon–Thurs, and round
the clock from Friday 10am until Sunday at midnight. There
are also less well-stocked locations (with shorter hours)
downtown (815 1st Ave, ✆625-1611), in Fremont (3504
Fremont Ave N, ✆632-3759), and in the U District (1309 NE
45th Ave, ✆545-4226).

SPECIALIST

67 Books

Map 3, E7. 322 2nd Ave S ✆447-9229.
A one-of-a-kind bookstore-as-art-statement, *67 Books* carries
only 67 titles at any given time (though there are multiple
copies of most selections), emphasizing obscure, unusual, and
lavishly illustrated art books, cookbooks, and children's pop-
up volumes.

Beyond the Closet

Map 5, B7. 518 E Pike St ✆322-4609.
A large, exclusively gay and lesbian bookstore.

East West Bookshop

1032 NE 65th St ✆523-3726; *www.ewbookshop.com*.
New age bookstore that also vends crystals, meditation
supplies, and incense, as well as running programs and classes.

Fallout Records Books & Comics

Map 5, B6. 1506 E Olive Way ✆323-2662.
Half of their space is devoted to punk-oriented records; the
other has a good selection of comics, graphic novels, and
fanzines.

BOOKS

Left Bank Books

Map 3, B4. 92 Pike St ℘622-1095;
www.eskimo.com/~jonkonnu.
The best left-wing bookstore in town, this nonprofit Pike
Place collective has especially strong political, historical,
feminist, gay, and literature sections, and a good rack of
underground 'zines; they also have a mail-order catalog of
radical books.

Metzker Maps

Map 3, D6. 702 1st Ave ℘623-8747.
The place to go for maps of the region or the world
(including hiking and nature trails throughout the Puget
Sound), with a small but quality selection of travel books
as well.

The Mountaineers

300 3rd Ave W ℘284-6310.
The shop of the Seattle publishers of nature-oriented travel
books, specializing in mountaineering literature and outdoor
guides and maps.

Revolution Books

Map 5, C6. 1833 Nagle Place ℘325-7415.
Small store a block from Broadway on Capitol Hill that has the
most uncompromisingly radical focus of any Seattle bookseller.

Seattle Art Museum Store

Map 3, C5. 100 University St ℘654-3120.
Small, but stacked with interesting art books of all types, many
difficult to find elsewhere in the city, as well as a few popular
culture and Northwest regional interest titles.

BOOKS

Newsstands

Seattle has many excellent – and huge – **newsstands**, the best of which may be *Bulldog News*, with locations at 4208 University Way NE (✆632-NEWS) and 401 Broadway E (✆322-NEWS); it also serves coffee and baked goods. *Read All About It*, 93 Pike St in Pike Place Market (✆624-0140), is a great source for international and out-of-town papers, while *Steve's News*, 204 Broadway E (✆324-7323) and 416 Fremont Ave N (✆633-0731), vends thousands of magazines and papers, both mainstream and way-alternative.

Seattle Mystery Bookshop

Map 3, D6. 117 Cherry St ✆587-5737.
Well-stocked with new and used selection of mysteries, hardback and softcover.

Wide World Books & Maps

Map 7, G5. 1911 N 45th St ✆634-3453.
This excellent travel bookstore carries extensive selections of travel guides and travel literature, maps, and travel accessories, with a threshold leading into the adjoining *Teahouse Kuan Yin* café.

CLOTHES

Seattle's not much for designer boutiques, but it's a good place for **secondhand** and **thrift** clothes shopping, with all the youthful hipsters to keep used outlets in business. Pike Place Market is the place for crafts like jewelry and tie-dye shirts, apt to be cheaper and more individualistic there than anywhere else in town.

CLOTHES

Betsey Johnson Clothing

Map 3, D4. 1429 5th Ave ℰ624-2887.

Seattle branch of the chain of designer women's clothing shops, noted for their stylishness and (relatively) good prices.

John Fluevog Shoes

Map 3, B3. 1611 1st Ave ℰ441-1065.

On the outskirts of Pike Place Market, one of the premier stops for footwear with a hip, youthful bent. No bandwagon-jumper, it was advertising in indie rock magazines back in the mid-1980s.

Pendleton Northwest

Map 3, D4. 1313 4th Ave ℰ682-4430.

All kinds of wool clothing and blankets, all made in the Northwest.

Uno Duo

Map 3, D4. 1335 5th Ave #513 ℰ622-9020.

Both menswear and womenswear under the same roof, at a store with more reasonable prices and creative stock than the norm.

WE Hats

Map 3, D6. 105 1st Ave S ℰ623-3409.

Hats of all kinds, spanning fur beanies to "squashy Australian" models. Their catalog, and photos of some of their more striking stock, are online at *www.speakeasy.org/wehats*.

Buffalo Exchange

Map 5, C6. 216 Broadway E ℰ860-4133.

Seattle branch of the long-established vintage clothing chain, which has stores throughout the western states. There's also an outlet in the U District, at 4546 University Way.

Fritzi Ritz

Map 7, D7. 3425 Fremont Place N ℘633-0929.
The most flamboyant of the Fremont used clothing outlets.

Guess Where

Map 7, D7. 615 N 35th St ℘547-3793.
Specializing in men's clothing and accessories, and with a whimsical decor that fits in well with the tenor of its Fremont neighborhood.

The Red Light

Map 6, B4. 4560 University Way NE ℘633-5075.
The biggest vintage clothing store in Seattle, though not the most discriminate, selling everything from bell bottoms and skatewear to old *Nike* shoes.

Time Tunnel

Map 4, F6. 1914 2nd Ave ℘448-1030.
In the middle of Belltown's hippest street, specializing in fashions from the 1960s and earlier.

DEPARTMENT STORES AND MALLS

Downtown Seattle's compact cluster of **department stores and malls** seems unremarkable to everyone but longtime residents, who remember a time not so long ago when there were few such beasts in the business district.

Bon Marché

Map 3, C3. 3rd Avenue and Pine Street ℂ506-6000.
More renowned for versatility than originality, this is nonetheless one of the better department stores in the city center.

Eddie Bauer

Map 3, D4. 5th Avenue and Union Street ℂ622-2766.
The original store of this outdoor clothing and equipment specialist, established in the 1920s, and still focusing to a large degree on outdoor gear, but with plenty of other kinds of clothes as well.

Nordstrom

Map 3, D3. 1501 5th Ave ℂ628-2111.
Multifloor giant with extensive women's clothing and shoe sections, and a reputation for good customer service. It plans to move into an even bigger space a block away, on Pine Street between 5th and 6th avenues, in 1998.

Bellevue Square

Bellevue Way between NE 4th and NE 8th aves, Bellevue ℂ425/454-2431.
More than two hundred shops on two levels, including branches of the *Nordstrom* and *Bon Marché* department stores, restaurants, toy stores, men and women's clothes, and much more. Little to distinguish it from any other supermall, though.

Broadway Market

Map 5, C5. 401 Broadway E ℂ322-1610.
Hipper and more neighborhood-conscious than the downtown

malls, with a mix of boutique fashion stores, beauty/fitness centers, fast-food and sit-down restaurants, a discount bookstore, a cinema, and a half-price ticket outlet.

City Centre

Map 3, D4. 1420 5th Ave ⓒ223-8999.
One of the smaller and more dignified of the downtown shopping centers, and worth a visit for its Pilchuck School glass sculptures.

Uwajimaya

Map 3, F8. 519 6th Ave S ⓒ624-6248.
Most of the first floor of this mall is given over to Asian foods, while most of the second floor is occupied by *Kinokuniya Books*, one of Japan's largest book chains. Mixed in are miscellaneous electrical appliances, dishes, and five-and-dime-type knick-knacks. Definitely worth a browse.

Westlake Center

Map 3, C3. Pine Street between 4th and 5th aves ⓒ467-1600.
Even if you avoid malls religiously, you'll have a hard time missing this one, smack in the center of downtown and in the middle of the *Metro Tunnel* route. It's also where the Seattle Center monorail drops you off. The mall itself is big and crowded, with more than eighty shops, but none too special.

FOOD AND DRINK

Pike Place Market is the biggest and most central spot for fruit, vegetables, seafood, juices, and suchlike. It also holds *DeLaurenti's*, the city's best specialty food store, with a luscious array of Mediterranean foods, baked and deli goods, and wines. Smaller open-air markets are held in the warmer months, including the **Fremont Sunday Market**, in the N 34th Street parking lot just west of the Fremont Bridge (late April–Nov Sun 10am–5pm), and the **farmers' market** in the U District, at the corner of 50th and University (Oct–May Sat 9am–2pm). *Uwajimaya*, at 519 6th Ave S, is the largest Asian supermarket, though it's more like a variety store with a large food section.

For more standard fare, the most omnipresent chain **supermarket** – and a cut above most in quality – is *QFC*, with central locations at 523 Broadway Ave E and 416 15th Ave E (both in Capitol Hill), and 100 Republican St (near Seattle Center). **Health** and **whole-food** stores are well represented, especially by the half-dozen supermarket-sized branches of *PCC Natural Markets*, administered by the Puget Consumers Co-op; you don't have to be a co-op member to shop here, although the prices are lower if you are. The closest branch to downtown is in Fremont, at 716 N 34th St (Map 7, E8; daily 8am–11pm; ✆632-6811).

If you want to take some of Seattle's most famous delicacy home with you, the *Caffè Appassionato* specialty gourmet coffee company, 4001 21st Ave W (Map 8, F7; ✆281-8040), sells about thirty varieties of **coffee** from different regions of the world. *Teacup*, 2207 Queen Anne Ave N (✆283-5931), aside from stocking more than a hundred varieties of **tea** in bulk, is packed with all sorts of tea-serving paraphernalia. *Champion Wine Cellars*, 108 Denny Way (Map 4, B4; ✆284-8306; *www.seattle.2000.com/championwine*), sells a good variety of **wines** from Washington State and around the world.

MUSIC

You'll have no trouble finding current major label **music** releases and most prominent indie ones, but the range of imports, reissues, out-of-print LPs, and non-rock music in Seattle's **record stores** is thin. In fact, many of the city's serious music fans go to Portland, three hours south, for their shopping. Still, there are some unusual items to be found if you've got the time to browse, particularly if you're into old-school punk on vinyl.

Anomalous Records

Map 5, D7. 1402 E Pike St ℗328-9339.
Tucked into the back of a performance/gallery loft space, this closet-sized store offers the sort of hard-to-find experimental music that you would expect to see in New York, from John Cage and Diamanda Galas to all sorts of avant-garde noise artists.

Bedazzled Discs

Map 5, C7. 911 E Pine St ℗329-6500.
One of Capitol Hill's better record stores, with a fair array of used CDs, vinyl, and music books; the low-key ambience is good for lengthy browsing.

Bud's Jazz Records

Map 3, D7. 102 S Jackson St ℗628-0445.
In the heart of Pioneer Square near downtown, this basement store is a bit disorganized, but it's probably the best place to buy jazz in Seattle, with a decent blues selection as well.

MUSIC

Cellophane Square

Map 6, B4. 4538 University Way NE ☏634-2280.
The city's best all-around rock store, with lots of new and used CDs and a friendly staff. Low on truly exotic items, but bountifully stocked with current-day indies. Also carries some soul, hip-hop, folk, blues, reggae, and world music.

Cherry Records

Map 7, D8. 706 N 34th St ☏632-0525.
This tiny Fremont store has a small but almost universally high-caliber selection of jazz and blues, much of it on vinyl. Only open Thurs–Sat 11am–7pm, Sun noon–6pm.

Retrospect Records

Map 5, B6. 1524 E Olive Way ☏329-1077.
It doesn't get much attention from Seattle hipsters, but this is a relatively well-stocked, rock-focused store, with large CD and vinyl sections that offer some pleasant surprises in the used bins.

Singles Going Steady

Map 4, E5. 2219 2nd Ave ☏441-7396.
Extensive collection of vintage and current punk-oriented indie rock, mostly (though not exclusively) on vinyl. Especially strong on out-of-print/limited edition seven-inches, and punk collectibles; it also does mail order.

Sub Pop Mega Mart

Map 4, F6. 1928 2nd Ave ☏443-0322.
Tiny store dedicated almost exclusively to CDs and vinyl on the Sub Pop label, as well as the few indies it distributes, and some random odds and ends. Best for current or vintage Sub

Pop releases that are getting harder to find these days, or for the Sub Pop merchandise of posters and t-shirts.

Tower Records

Map 4, D1. 500 Mercer ℗283-4456;
Map 6, B4. 4321 University Way NE ℗632-1187.
If you've gotta have that new Pearl Jam side project record as soon as it's out, this chain will have it, along with just about every major label release. Otherwise, it's only recommended for its wide range of music magazines.

Wall of Sound

Map 4, E5. 2237 2nd Ave ℗441-9880.
Small selection of new and used underground CDs and LPs, encompassing world music, experimental, noise/ambient, electronic, dub, jazz, and more, with lots of indies and imports that you can listen to before deciding whether to buy.

SPECIALTY STORES

Ah Nuts

Map 7, D7. 601 N 35th St ℗633-0664.
The most amusing of Fremont's many thrift shops demands a wander even if you have no intention of buying anything, with its museum-quality collection of ancient lamps, furniture, and miscellaneous kitsch knick-knacks in a dark, casbah-type space.

Glass Eye Gallery

Map 3, B4. 1902 Post Alley, Pike Place Market ℗441-3221.
Unlike the glassworks that you'll see in numerous Seattle

galleries, much of what's on sale here is actually affordable, though you'll have to scale down to goldfish-size pieces for the truly cheap items. Famous for incorporating ash from the eruption of Mt. St Helens into every piece.

John's Music

Map 7, F5. N 46th St and Interlake Ave N ℡548-0916.
The "Conga Capital of the Northwest" specializes in exotic drums from all over the globe, as well as ethnic wind and string instruments.

REI

Map 5, A6. 222 Yale Ave N ℡223-1944.
The outdoors equipment company's new flagship store has become something of a tourist attraction in its own right, complete with outdoor test trails of mountain bikes, simulated rain room for testing rain gear, and a waterfall by the entrance. The big draw is the glass-enclosed 65ft climbing rock, which can be ascended for free (under guidance from *REI* staff).

Rubber Rainbow Condom Co.

Map 3, B4. 1515 1st Ave ℡233-9502.
Condoms in all shapes and colors, assembled with enough discretion to be mistaken for a kid's store when spied from afar.

Traditions & Beyond

Map 3, D6. 113 Cherry St ℡621-0655.
Sizable Pioneer Square shop specializing in both traditional and contemporary Native American arts and crafts; all profits go to scholarships for Native American students.

GALLERIES

Seattle's **galleries** may be far from cutting edge, but they're refreshingly unpretentious. Glasswork is especially distinctive here, much coming from Dale Chihuly and the Pilchuck Glass School he helped found (see box p.268). The first Thursday evening of every month is **Gallery Walk** – when dozens of galleries in Pioneer Square hold openings between 6pm and 8pm.

....

Normal gallery hours are Tues–Sat 11am–5pm, with shorter hours on Sunday; check the listings in the local paper for exact times.

....

Art/Not Terminal Gallery

Map 3, C2. 2045 Westlake Ave ℂ233-0680.
Artist-run gallery on the edge of downtown, where several dozen artists show their pieces in exchange for $15 per month and six hours of volunteer work in the gallery. This makes for erratic displays, but it is one of the few spots in town where you can buy good art for low(ish) prices.

Donald Young Gallery

Map 5, C7. 1103 E Pike St ℂ860-1651.
Capitol Hill's best gallery, dominated by a huge floor that's well-suited for ambitious displays. Specializes in both contemporary work and major artists of the 1960s.

Foster/White Gallery

Map 3, D7. 311 1/2 Occidental Ave ℂ622-2833.
Half a dozen lofty rooms offer eclectic, sometimes superb, work by Northwest artists that often outclasses what's on at the

GALLERIES

Seattle Art Museum or the Henry. Frequently exhibits glass pieces by Pilchuck staff and alumni. Another branch at 1420 5th Ave, second floor (©340-8025).

Fremont Fine Arts Foundry

Map 7, C7. 154 N 35th St ©632-4880.
www.uspan.com/art/studio/foundry.html.
Elegantly designed two-story, modern building housing studios for several artists, a stone carving yard, a sculpture garden, the *Take 2* photo gallery, and a good exhibition space.

Galeria Coqui

Map 3, D7. 303 Occidental Ave S ©521-8693.
Devoted to contemporary art of Latin America, and one of the most worthwhile recent additions to Seattle's gallery scene.

Glasshouse Studio

Map 3, D7. 311 Occidental Ave S ©682-9939.
Small space displaying pieces by renowned glass artists, particularly Eric Brakken, who founded the studio in 1972 and has continually shown his work here since. Some of the items even get within shouting distance of the $100 price range.

Greg Kucera Gallery

Map 3, D6. 608 2nd Ave ©624-0770.
Small exhibits of major international names in a 3000-square-foot space. Seattle's major-name gallery.

Linda Cannon Gallery

Map 3, D6. 617 Western Ave ©233-0404.
One of the riskier, more whimsical Seattle galleries, run by a woman dedicated to showing work by non-mainstream and

younger artists. Cannon was also, reportedly, the first art dealer in the country to have a Web site (*www.cyberspace.com/lindalu*).

Meyerson & Nowinski

Map 3, D7. 123 S Jackson St ℂ223-1700.
Along with Foster/White, the best of the Occidental Street venues, with five rooms showcasing contemporary artists from the Northwest, among others.

Mwoyo Arts

Map 5, B7. 421 E Pine St ℂ322-9434.
Store selling contemporary art and traditional crafts from southern Africa which also has exhibits of painting and sculpture from the region.

Soil Gallery

Map 3, C5. 82 University St ℂ623-5950.
Artist-run cooperative in warehouse-like rooms, dedicated to work too diverse and experimental for commercial galleries. Highly recommended.

Streetlife Art Gallery

Map 4, D5. 2301 2nd Ave ℂ443-1546.
Not so much a gallery as a workspace and center for social activism, as all of the artwork on display here was produced by women and men who are (or have been) homeless.

Washington State Convention & Trade Center

Map 3, D3. 8th Ave and Pike St ℂ447-5000.
Don't pass this by just because of its corporate look. In addition to work by major artists on loan from museums, the center exhibits numerous pieces by relative unknowns from the Northwest, much of it quite good.

GALLERIES

Dale Chihuly and the Pilchuck School

In the museums and galleries of Seattle and its surrounding area, you're bound to encounter numerous references to the **Pilchuck Glass School** and its co-founder, **Dale Chihuly**. Chihuly, the most renowned glass artist in the world, helped establish the school with other kindred spirits in the early 1970s. Located in the Cascade foothills, about fifty miles north of Seattle, it's a leading generator of glass art talent. Prototypical works are displayed in the lobbies of the City Centre shopping mall at 5th Avenue and Union Street in downtown Seattle, providing an easy (and free) way to take in some of the more astonishing colors and contortions that the artists have blown and otherwise crafted.

The best place to view Chihuly's work is in Tacoma – his hometown – at the city's downtown art museum and the lobby of the federal courthouse at nearby Union Station. Interestingly, in 1996 he also installed a dozen 1200-pound chandeliers around the canals, archways, and plazas of Venice, and the following year gave a glassblowing demonstration at a private party for Bill Gates and influential political/business leaders from around the world.

This mainstream media attention has led to a backlash among the more irreverent sectors of the local arts community; the *Lava Lounge* held a "smash a Chihuly" raffle in 1997 that gave the public a chance to bash an actual Chihuly glasswork to bits in front of an audience. The Pilchuck Glass School is not open for public visits, but the institution does hold an annual **Open House** on a Sunday in July; call ©517-1351 for details and reservation information.

CITY DIRECTORY

AIRLINES Alaska Airlines, 1301 4th Ave (☏433-3100); American Airlines, *Sheraton Hotel*, 6th and Pike sts (☏1-800/433-7300); British Airways, 1304 4th Ave (☏1-800/247-9297); Delta, 410 University St (☏1-800/221-1212); Northwest Airlines, 402 University Ave (☏1-800/225-2525); TWA, 1001 4th Ave (☏447-4900 or 1-800/221-2000); United, 1303 4th Ave (☏441-3700 or 1-800/241-6522).

ATMS Automated teller machines are everywhere. Out-of-state and many overseas visitors can use their ATM cards at many of them if they're linked to the Cirrus or Plus systems – which will be clearly displayed on the machines.

BANKS Keybank, 1329 4th Ave (☏447-5767); Seafirst, 408 Pike St (☏358-0529); Union Bank of California, 910 4th Ave (☏587-6100); US Bank, 723 1st Ave (☏344-4690); and Wells Fargo, Westlake Center, 1620 4th Ave (☏1-800/869-3557). Hours vary, but they're Mon–Fri 10am–3pm at the minimum.

CONSULATES Britain, eighth floor of the First Interstate Center at 3rd and Madison (☏622-9255); Canada, Plaza 600, Suite 412 (☏443-1777); Denmark, 6204 E Mercer Way, Mercer Island (☏230-0888); Germany, 600 University St

(✆682-4312); Norway, Joseph Vance Building, 3rd Ave and Union St (✆623-3957); Sweden, 1215 4th Ave (✆622-5640).

CURRENCY EXCHANGE Most large downtown banks will change foreign currency and traveler's checks. American Express checks should be cashed at their downtown office, 600 Stewart St (Mon–Fri 9am–5pm; ✆441-8622). Thomas Cook (✆1-800/287-7362) changes money at Sea-Tac Airport (daily 6am–10pm), downtown in Westlake Center, Level One (Mon–Sat 10am–6pm, Sun noon–5pm), and 906 3rd Ave (Mon–Fri 9am–5pm).

DENTIST Yesler Terrace Medical Dental Clinic, 102 Broadway (✆625-9260).

DISABILITY About eighty percent of *Metro's* buses and routes are wheelchair-accessible, and their free pamphlet, *Accessible Metro*, includes a map detailing both the accessible and non-accessible routes throughout downtown. Disabled passengers can travel on *Washington State Ferries* for half the regular fare by presenting a Regional Reduced Fare Permit or other proof of disability. Free copies of *Access Seattle*, a guidebook for disabled persons covering accommodations, restaurants, public transportation, and such in the city, can be ordered from 521 2nd Ave West, Seattle, WA 98119 (✆281-5700). *The Washington Coalition of Citizens with Disabilities*, 4649 Sunnyside Ave N, Suite 100 (✆461-4550), is another prominent organization for information and services.

EMERGENCIES ✆911 for police, fire, and ambulance.

HOSPITAL Northwest Hospital, 1550 N 115th St (✆364-0500); for minor injuries, Country Doctor Community Clinic, 500 19th Ave E (✆461-4503). Women can also use the Aradia Women's Health Center, 1300 Spring St (✆323-9388).

LAUNDROMATS *12th Ave Laundry* in Capitol Hill at 1807 12th Ave (℗328-4610); *Fremont Avenue Laundromat* in Fremont at 4237 Fremont Ave N (℗632-8924); and the most enjoyable option, Belltown's *Sit & Spin*, 2219 4th Ave (℗441-9484) – also a café and performance space.

LEFT LUGGAGE You can dump your stuff at Sea-Tac Airport under the escalator between baggage claim carousels 9 and 12; the department is open 5.30am to 12.30am. There are also storage lockers in *Greyhound* for up to six hours for $2.

LEGAL ADVICE Seattle King County Bar Association Lawyer Referral & Information Service ℗623-2551.

LIBRARY The main branch of the Seattle Public Library is downtown at 1000 4th Ave (Sept–May Mon–Thurs 9am–9pm, Fri–Sat 9am–6pm, Sun 1–5pm; June–Aug closed Sun; ℗386-4636). The same phone number is also a cool information line that answers (reasonable) questions on all subjects.

PHARMACIES The prescription department is open 24 hours a day at *Bartell Drugs*, 600 First Ave N (℗284-1354).

POLICE STATIONS West Precinct, 610 3rd Ave (℗684-8917); East Precinct, 1519 12th Ave (℗684-4300); North Precinct, 10049 College Way N (℗684-0850); South Precinct, 3001 S Myrtle St (℗386-1850).

POST OFFICES Generally open Mon–Fri 9am–5pm and Saturday mornings. The main post office is downtown at 301 Union St (Mon–Fri 8am–5.30pm; ℗1-800/275-8777). Other branches (all of which share the ℗1-800/275-8777 number) include Columbia Center Station (701 5th Ave),

Old Federal Station (909 1st Ave), and Pioneer Square Station (91 S Jackson St), all of which are downtown; Broadway Station (101 Broadway E) in Capitol Hill; Queen Anne Station (415 1st Ave N) near Seattle Center; and University Station (4244 University Way NE), near the University of Washington campus.

PUBLIC HOLIDAYS New Year's Day (January 1), Presidents' Day (third Monday in February), Memorial Day (last Monday in May), Independence Day (July 4), Labor Day (first Monday in September), Thanksgiving (fourth Thursday in November), Christmas (December 25). All government offices, and some other offices and stores, are closed on Martin Luther King Jr's Birthday (Jan 15), Columbus Day (second Monday in October), and Veterans' Day (November 11).

PUBLIC RESTROOMS Try the lobbies of downtown hotels, any shopping center, or campus buildings in the university; public park restrooms are usually open during the day.

RADIO KUOW (94.9 FM) is the local NPR affiliate, with excellent public affairs/news programming. KCMU (90.3 FM) is also noncommercial and broadcasts all sorts of rarely heard music. KBCS (91.3 FM) programs lots of jazz, as well as some blues, world music, and such. KPLU (88.5 FM) concentrates on jazz and news/public affairs, with blues on weekends.

RAPE CRISIS LINE ✆632-7273 (24 hours).

TAX Sales tax in Seattle is 8.6 percent, applied to everything except groceries; it's closer to 8 percent throughout the rest of the Puget Sound. There's also a steep hotel tax of 15.6 percent in Seattle, much less in surrounding areas and the Puget Sound.

TELEPHONES Public phones are plentiful throughout the city; if you need more privacy, duck into a shopping center or big hotel. Remarkably, phone books generally remain attached to the phones, even in crowded areas. Local calls cost 25¢.

TELEVISION KOMO (ABC, channel 4); KING (NBC, channel 5); KIRO (CBS, channel 7); KCTS (PBS; channel 9); KCPQ (Fox, channel 13).

TICKETS Most big-name entertainment and sporting events go through Ticketmaster (℡628-0888), which charges a service of $1–5. They have a discount ticket booth at Westlake Center (Mon–Fri 10am–9pm, Sat 10am–7pm, Sun 11am–6pm; ℡233-1111) for same-day tickets, cash only. Half-price, day-of-show theater and concert tickets are sold by Ticket/Ticket, at Pike Place Market information booth, First Ave and Pike (Tues–Sun noon–6pm; ℡324-2744) and Broadway Market, Second Level, 401 Broadway E (Tues–Sun 10am–7pm, ℡324-2744); you have to show up to find out what's available.

TIME Seattle is on Pacific Standard Time (PST), three hours behind east coast US time, and eight hours behind Greenwich Mean Time. Daylight Savings Time runs from the first Sunday in April to the last Sunday in October.

TRAVEL AGENTS Council Travel at 219 Broadway E (℡329-4567) and 4311 1/2 University Way NE (℡632-2448), is a good general source of discount flights, etc.

TRAVELER'S AID 909 4th Ave, Suite 630 (Mon–Tues & Thurs–Fri 9am–4pm, Wed 9am–3pm, Sat 9am–1pm; ✆461-3888).

WOMEN'S RESOURCES The Women's Information Center at University of Washington, Imogen Cunningham Hall AJ50 (✆685-1090), has information and referral services for everything you could think of. The Seattle Office for Women's Rights (✆684-0390; *www.pan.ci.seattle.wa.us/seattle/owr/home.htm*) maintains a large online list of women-oriented social and civic organizations. Planned Parenthood of Seattle/King County, 2211 E Madison (✆328-7713), has clinical services and reproductive health education.

CONTEXTS

A brief history of Seattle

Seattle was settled by white pioneers at roughly the same time that the other major American west coast cities were established, yet it's only been in the last quarter of the twentieth century that the city has begun to wield notable influence in international business and the arts, or to project a truly distinct identity. Its 150-year history, however, is hardly short on local color.

Early native peoples

Before European explorers and white settlers arrived, the Pacific Northwest was occupied by **native peoples**, and had been for thousands of years. Those in the Seattle area were of the **Coast Salish** group, Native Americans who depended on fishing and gathering for their essentials, and who frequently lived in **longhouses** – structures, sometimes several hundred feet in length, in which entire Indian groups lived in a communal fashion. Few records remain today of their culture, which was mostly wiped out by the arrival of white settlers.

European exploration

The search for the mythical **Northwest Passage** – a body of water that supposedly connected the Pacific and Atlantic – fired the imagination of explorers in the 1500s and 1600s, one of whom, **Juan de Fuca** (actually Greek, but sailing for the Spanish), claimed at the end of the sixteenth century to have found an inlet at the latitude of 47 degrees in the Pacific Northwest. His discovery was not officially recognized, and it wasn't until 1787 that English captain **Charles Barkley** found and named the **Strait of Juan de Fuca** in the San Juan Islands, approximately in the same location as the waters de Fuca purportedly visited. The Spaniard **Manuel Quimper** explored the San Juan Islands in 1790, but the Puget Sound wasn't charted until a couple of years later by Captain **George Vancouver**, whose real mission was to settle territorial disputes with Spain; by 1795 the British were in control of the region.

The American presence in the sound was initiated by the **Pacific Fur Company** in the early nineteenth century, and soon countered by the British-held **North West Fur Company**. Several decades of uneasy joint occupation ensued, largely ending in 1846, when the territory known as Oregon country was divided on the 49th parallel in the middle of the channel separating the continent from Vancouver Island. The British received the portion north of the parallel; ownership of San Juan Island remained in dispute. **The Pig War** of 1859, in which British and American camps on San Juan Island nearly came to armed conflict over the shooting of a pig by an American soldier (see p.136), was finally resolved by arbitration in the USA's favor in 1872.

The founding of Seattle

In 1850, there were no white settlements in the Puget Sound except for a small community in **Tumwater-Olympia**, and Olympia was named capital of the territory of Washington in 1853. In 1851, however, a small group of pioneers from Illinois, led by Seattle founding father **David Denny**, were advised to settle in the Puget Sound by a traveler they met during their journey west, and on November 13, most of them landed on **Alki Beach** in West Seattle, where they were greeted by Chief Seattle of the Duwamish-Suquamish tribes.

It was not a promising start for what would become the most important city in the Pacific Northwest: many in the landing party were sick; they arrived in the midst of a driving rainstorm; and Denny, who had arrived a few weeks ahead, had yet to finish building shelter for the community. The settlement of about two dozen people, half of them children, was named New York by one of the men, Charles Terry, and soon derisively called "New York-Alki" – or, in Chinook slang, "New York by and by."

In early 1852, settlement members **Arthur Denny**, **Carson Boren**, and **William Bell** claimed land nearer to the deep-water harbor of **Elliott Bay** to the north. Help soon arrived with **Henry Yesler**, who came in 1852 and chose Seattle as the location for Puget Sound's first **steam sawmill**. The area around Seattle, **King County**, was recognized by the federal government, and Seattle became its county seat. By 1853 there were 170 Seattle residents, many working at Yesler's mill.

Washington territory governor **Isaac Stevens** negotiated land treaties with the Indians in the mid-1850s, designed to cordon Native Americans onto small reservations that would not impinge upon the most desirable land; he was aided by Chief Seattle, who helped arrange treaties in lieu of armed conflict. Still, there were several skirmishes, culminating in an Indian attack on Seattle in January 1856 that resulted in few casualties but the burning of many homes. The so-called **Indian War** also slowed population growth in the area, with some settlers leaving for less risky territory to the south.

In the 1860s, **Asa Mercer** tried to boost the city's population and morale by arranging for the passage of unmarried women from the east to Seattle, where men outnumbered women by about ten to one. An initial scheme brought about a dozen women to Seattle from Massachusetts, but his attempt on a much larger scale largely failed. Contracting a ship for 500 passengers, he secured fewer than 100, only a few dozen of these potential brides; the ship's captain wouldn't take them any further than San Francisco. Mercer finally got a few of his charges to Seattle, but stiffed a number of local bachelors who had paid for their wives in advance – though he did manage to marry one of the women himself.

The coming of the railroads and the Great Seattle Fire

Seattle became an incorporated city in 1869. However, four years later **Northern Pacific Railroad** chose Tacoma's Commencement Bay as the western terminus of its transcontinental line. Undaunted, some Seattle citizens raised money for their own railroad through Snoqualmie Pass to Walla Walla. Indeed, the first few miles of tracks were built with their own hands, but the impetus soon waned. Indirectly, though, their goal was accomplished: Henry Villard of Northern Pacific bought the Seattle-Walla Walla railroad line and built a track in the 1880s that made connections between Seattle and the transcontinental line possible. In 1893, the **Great Northern Railroad** made Seattle its Pacific terminus.

Seattle's growth as a business center was halted only slightly by the **Great Seattle Fire of 1889** (see p.29), which destroyed much of downtown, mostly in today's Pioneer Square. The fire caused $15 million of damage, but the city quickly rebuilt its commercial district, this time using much safer materials. Between 1880 and 1890, the population of Seattle increased by about ten times, to a little over 40,000. Still, it wasn't without its major problems during this time: rampant civic corruption, anti-Chinese rioting, an upsurge in prostitution, and an erratic infrastructure that at one time included a sewer trench on 1st Avenue that ran *uphill*. Soon, however, Seattle would receive the boost to make its dominance of the region unchallenged.

The Klondike Gold Rush

In July 1897, the discovery of **gold** in the Klondike region of northwestern Canada inspired a wave of prospecting fever, and Seattle was in the fortunate position of being the closest American port of appreciable size. The town was inundated with fortune-seekers, their dreams fired by tales – some true – of those who had found unimaginable wealth up north. The Seattle Chamber of Commerce created a committee for drawing gold diggers to Seattle; its chairman, **Erastus Brainerd**, placed numerous ads in papers and magazines across the nation extolling the Seattle-Klondike connection.

Few of the fortune hunters who set off from Seattle returned with their pots of gold, but with the massive influx of traffic, business boomed in banks, shops, ship-building, and real estate. The most far-reaching effect of the gold rush, however, was a dramatic rise in Seattle's population, as many a would-be prospector settled in the city. By 1900, there were 80,000 residents; by 1910, that number had tripled.

The Olmsted brothers and the 1909 Exposition

Seattle's position as an emerging major American city was solidified by the **Alaska-Yukon-Pacific Exposition** in 1909, which drew nearly four million visitors over a five-month period. Much of the **University of Washington** was created by buildings left over from the Expo, and cultural entertainment, led by **theater and vaudeville**, began to prosper.

The UW campus was planned by the **Olmsted brothers**, John Charles and Frederick Law, Jr, who were sons of landscape architect Frederick Law Olmsted, designer of New York's Central Park. The two were also renowned park planners, and were hired in 1903 to design a system of parks and boulevards for Seattle. The result was a city where you could travel from Green Lake through the arboretum down to Seward Park without ever leaving green environs. In 1910, Seattle citizens approved $2 million worth of **parkbonds**, fueled not just by a desire for more green space, but also a need to plan new neighborhoods that had recently been annexed: Ballard, West Seattle, and South Seattle.

Alongside the growth and good times, houses of **gambling** and **prostitution**, which adjoined many entertainment establishments, were flourishing on downtown's **Skid Road** (p.34). In 1915 the state of Washington voted for liquor **prohibition**, and Mayor **Hiram Gill** personally led raids on places that sold liquor; the bootleggers got back at him by providing testimony in a federal grand jury indictment of Gill and others for conspiracy to violate interstate commerce law. Though found not guilty, Gill was impeached, yet the city council refused to remove him. This was very much in character with Gill, who in the 1910s was elected three times, recalled twice, and defeated twice.

More level-headed reform was championed in the subsequent decade by **Bertha Knight Landes**, who in 1926 became the first woman mayor of a major US city. She balanced her desire for greater law enforcement and vice control with a dedication to improved public parks and health programs – but still was ousted after one term.

The growth of industry and the general strike of 1919

Important to local trade was the creation of the **Lake Washington Canal** in Ballard, which opened in 1917 to allow passage from Lake Washington and Lake Union to the Puget Sound. The canal's **Hiram M. Chittenden Locks** insured that the lakes would remain freshwater, crucial for salmon to spawn there; meanwhile, the docks and wharves created employment for many locals, notably the Scandinavians who had settled in Ballard.

With large numbers of its residents employed in **shipping** and **manufacturing** (particularly timber), it's unsurprising that **unions** gained strength in Seattle in the early twentieth century, including the left-leaning **Industrial Workers of the World** (**IWW**). In early 1919, a shipyard strike in Seattle set off a wave of sympathy strikes by other unions, and on February 6, a **general strike** – the first ever called in a US city – began that lasted for five days. Fifteen hundred soldiers were called in from nearby Fort Lewis, but no violence occurred before the largely unsuccessful strike quietly ended. Some of the strike's advocates, such as the leftist newspaper reporter **Anna Louise Strong**, had hoped that the strike would bring the management of industry into the hands of workers. She was thus viewed as a socialist agitator, and, along with other staff on the *Union Record* paper, was indicted for sedition – although the charges were eventually dropped. The IWW had come through with labor-run cafeterias and emergency services for striking workers during the general strike, but it was torn by internal policy disputes in the 1920s and never regained the stature it had enjoyed during World War I.

The most influential labor organizer in Seattle from the 1930s through the 1950s was **Dave Beck**, who eventually became president of the Teamsters. An effective organizer – by the end of World War II, Seattle was 95 percent unionized – Beck was no radical, seeking any solution other than a strike, and was seen by some as too chummy with local business. His influence was greatly eroded when he was found guilty of income tax evasion, for which he served jail time in the early 1960s.

THE GROWTH OF INDUSTRY AND THE GENERAL STRIKE OF 1919

World War II, Boeing, and the 1962 World's Fair

Seattle's shipping and timber industries were hit hard by the **Great Depression**, but **World War II** reinvigorated the port. The war also boosted the city's small black population, as African-Americans moved to Seattle (and other west coast areas) to work in war-related industries. Simultaneously, the Japanese-American population, previously Seattle's largest minority community, was depleted as a result of President Roosevelt's **Executive Order 9066**, which interned them in detention camps – although thousands were eventually allowed to enlist.

These were boom times for the aviation industry, particularly **Boeing**, a company that had been founded in Seattle in the 1910s. The early 1940s saw such great demand for military planes that Boeing was employing 50,000 workers by 1944, though the end of the war nearly killed the operation. However, the company's diversification, particularly into **commercial jetliners**, started its road toward phenomenal success. In 1947, Boeing employed about one in five of Seattle's manufacturing workers; by 1957, the ratio was one in *two*. The talent needed to run Boeing – particularly its engineers and technicians – also gave rise to a significant technological culture in the area.

The marriage of good times and technology was celebrated by the **Century 21 Exposition** (also known as the **World's Fair**) in 1962, for which Seattle's most recognizable symbol, the **Space Needle**, was built.

The political movements sweeping much of America in the 1960s were mirrored here on a fairly small scale. In 1962, City Councilman **Wing Luke** became the first elected Asian-American official in the Northwest. Sit-ins by blacks at the City Council a few years later led to the approval of a fair housing ordinance. There were the requisite Vietnam War protests on the UW campus, including one that blocked rush-hour traffic on I-5 to protest the US invasion of Cambodia, and continued downtown, where paint bombs were thrown and windows broken at Seattle's Federal Courthouse. This resulted in the so-called **Seattle Seven** being charged with conspiracy to damage federal property, though a mistrial was declared.

The 1970s and 1980s

In the 1970s Seattle began to establish itself as one of the most desirable places to live in the US. Both **Pike Place Market** and **Pioneer Square** – the city's two most historic areas – were rescued from the brink of extinction and renovated into the thriving spots they are today. The **Forward Thrust** plan, devised by attorney and activist James Ellis, pushed through bonds approving funding for community centers, parks, and a domed sports stadium, the **Kingdome**, completed in the mid-1970s. The city was still extremely dependent, however, on the fortunes of the area's biggest employers, and sharp cutbacks at Boeing in the early 1970s resulted in a deep **recession** that saw unemployment rise to 12 percent – double the national average.

One thing Seattle still lacked was an international image, though this would change for good in the 1980s, with the rise of software giant **Microsoft**, **grunge rock**, and the **Starbucks Coffee** empire. Microsoft, which actually started up in the 1970s, has been one of the great business success stories of the late twentieth century, yielding the world's richest man, **Bill Gates**, and inspiring literally hundreds of **computer- and software-focused companies** to choose the Puget Sound as their base (many, indeed, founded by ex-Microsoft employees).

A thriving **alternative rock scene**, largely developed on the **Sub Pop** label in the mid-to-late 1980s, burst into

THE 1970S AND 1980S

285

international prominence with the chart-topping success of grunge bands like **Nirvana**, **Pearl Jam**, and **Soundgarden**. The other arts began to thrive as well, including numerous offbeat **theater companies** and **galleries**, as well as dramatically expanded **art museums**. Jane Alexander, chair of the National Endowment for the Arts, was moved to call Seattle the "Athens of the West" in 1997. It's certainly a far cry from 1943, when the then-conductor of the Seattle Symphony, Sir Thomas Beecham, dismissed the city as an "aesthetic dustbin."

Contemporary Seattle

People moved to the Seattle metropolitan area in force in the **1980s and 1990s**, and although the population within the city limits has actually stayed stable at around half a million (the suburbs, especially Bellevue and Redmond, have taken on most of the growth), the city's infrastructure has felt the strain. **Housing prices** have risen sharply; the city's **mass transit** system, though fairly efficient, is due for significant overhauls; and **traffic** is terribly congested for a city this size.

Meanwhile, the explosion of the arts and popular culture in Seattle has been a mixed blessing. The **Seattle Art Museum**, the expanded **Henry Art Gallery**, and the **Experience Music Project** rock and pop museum (due to open in Seattle Center in 1999) have all elevated the city's profile. But with space at a premium, uncomfortable political tempests have occurred, most notoriously in the battle over the construction of new **sports stadiums** to replace the **Kingdome**.

Still, some of the developments have served the city quite well. Seattle re-established itself as a top port in the 1960s, and is now the US leader in container tonnage exports to

Asia. **Fishermen's Terminal**, redeveloped in 1993 at the cost of $13 million, is key to Washington State's $1.5 billion-per-year fishing industry. And tourism is now the state's fourth largest industry.

The big challenge facing Seattle's politicians, power brokers, and citizens' groups as the city enters the twenty-first century lies in balancing its explosive growth with its much-vaunted quality of life. An overriding ambition to become one of the great cities of America has been met. Now Seattle must wonder if the price was too high.

Micromania: Seattle's computer subculture

There's this eerie, science-fiction lack of anyone who doesn't look exactly 31.2 on the Campus. It's oppressive. It seems like only last week the entire Campus went through Gap ribbed-T mania together – and now they're all shopping for the same 3bdr/2bth dove-gray condo in Kirkland.

from *Microserfs*, Douglas Coupland

There are thousands of would-be multimedia moguls in Seattle today, spurred on by a collective dream of unlimited bandwith, the killer "app" (application), and, perhaps most important, stock options. This dream, whether tracked by trend-savvy novelist Coupland or lampooned in Garry Trudeau's *Doonesbury* cartoon strip, has at its roots the real-life success story of **Microsoft**, whose phenomenally successful operations have made its founders, **Bill Gates** and **Paul Allen**, into huge public figures and two of the wealthiest men on the planet, and has manufactured a digital culture in Seattle to rival that of even Silicon Valley.

The breakthrough

The Seattle region was already a technologically innovative place, largely due to the presence of Boeing, when Gates and Allen met each other as adolescents in the early 1970s. They saw themselves more as visionaries than cogs in the machine, however, and made their initial splash in 1975, with the licensing of **BASIC** (the first computer language written for a personal computer), although at the time, the two were actually based in Albuquerque, New Mexico.

In 1979, their increasingly profitable software company, now called Microsoft, moved to the affluent Seattle suburb Bellevue. A string of hit products ensued, most importantly **DOS**, a computer operating system that Gates and Allen shrewdly leased to IBM while holding onto the rights. Others followed: **Microsoft Word**, a word-processing program that is still among the most popular software in the world; and, later, **Microsoft Windows**, a more user-friendly graphical operating system that allowed users to view different application programs simultaneously. In 1986, Microsoft moved to its current "campus" in the Eastside suburb of Redmond and went public with its stock; by 1990 it had become the first personal computer software company to clear $1 billion of sales in a year. Though Allen had left in 1983 to work on his own investments – including Ticketmaster, the Portland Trailblazers basketball team, and various new technology startups – the company hardly skipped a beat.

The principals

Meanwhile, Gates was fast becoming the best-known geek in the world, more powerful than many heads of state. He's golfed with Bill Clinton, met political leaders in areas from India to South Africa to Brazil, and convened a summit meeting of one hundred of the world's chief executives in Seattle in 1997, attended by everyone from the big bananas at Wells Fargo Bank and United Airlines to Vice President Albert Gore. He's taken his fair share of hits during this time, including endless analysis of his every business venture as well as gossip about his personal life, not least the debate over the building of his mansion in the Eastside suburb of Medina – a $50 million structure with 40,000 square feet, a thirty-car underground garage, a sixty-foot indoor pool with an underwater music system, a movie theater, and a golf course.

The more reclusive Allen has not been able to avoid the spotlight either: there was a minor to-do about the unveiling of his personal Web page, on which he lists Jimi Hendrix's *Electric Ladyland*, Kate Bush's *The Kick Inside*, and the Eurythmics' *Greatest Hits* as some of his favorite albums; and despite his philanthropic efforts, including funding the University of Washington's Allen Library, he also caught flak when he offered to buy the troubled Seattle football franchise on the condition that a new stadium for the team be built with taxpayers' money. He privately financed a referendum on this issue, and it didn't help his public image when it was revealed that Allen himself had not voted in at least four years.

The supporting cast

Microsoft is not as large as many visitors imagine. Today it employs a little over 20,000 workers, only about 11,000 of whom live in Washington State. Its influence upon Seattle social life, too, is not as great as you might think, since nearly two-thirds of the Washington-based employees live in the Eastside. Its economic impact, however, is considerable: according to a study by economist Richard Conway Jr (commissioned by Microsoft), for every worker Microsoft employs, another 3.4 jobs are created.

Microsoft's impact on local business and culture is most dramatically reflected in the concentration of other hi-tech companies based in the region, which is now second only to California's Silicon Valley in the US as a hub of technological expertise. Part of this is due to the inordinate number of millionaires the company spawned when it went public with its stock – some estimate as many as 10,000 – many of whom have started their own technical businesses. There are now 2300 software companies in Washington State, including such high-profile outfits as **Adobe**, **Assymetric**, **Wall Data**, **Attachmate**, **RealNetworks**, and the online book retail site **amazon.com** – although for each of these, there are plenty of businesses that fail within weeks of starting up.

The future

The race to catch Microsoft will not be easy. The number of licensed users of Windows in 1993 exceeded 25 million, and today the software performs the basic functions of more than 80 percent of the personal computers in the world. More than 30 million people use the Microsoft Excel spreadsheet program. The company is also challenging **Netscape** in the Internet browser market with its **Explorer** browser, though this hit a snag in late 1997, when US Attorney General Janet Reno declared that by requiring computer manufacturers to include Internet Explorer on computers with the Windows 95 operating system, Microsoft was in violation of a court order agreement curbing monopolistic practices. The Justice Department announced it would impose a $1 million-a-day fine if Microsoft failed to comply with the court ruling – an announcement that no doubt occasioned the popping of numerous champagne corks at Netscape.

Still, Microsoft continues to move into other areas, sometimes buying up its would-be competitors in the process. Indeed, it has forged some 200 alliances, joint ventures, and the like in the past decade alone, while retaining its peculiar place in the public's imagination. The future, it would appear, continues to belong to Bill Gates.

Books

Most of the following books should be readily available in the US, UK, and Canada. Publishers are listed US/UK, unless there is only one, in which case this is indicated.

History and society

Pierre Berton *The Klondike Fever* (Carroll & Graf, US). Thorough and readable account of the characters and events of the 1890s gold rush, by a fine Canadian writer.

Paul Dorpat *Seattle, Now & Then* (Tartu, US). Excellent photo book cogently illustrating the development of Seattle neighborhoods over the last century.

Robert L. Friedheim *The Seattle General Strike* (University of Washington Press, US). The most complete documentation of this 1919 event, though perhaps a bit dry and detailed for the casual reader.

Randy Hodgins & Steve McLellan *Seattle on Film* (Punchline Productions, US). Entertaining reviews of nearly every film in which Seattle locations have played a role (though *Streetwise*, the documentary about Seattle runaways, is strangely missing), with a commentary on Seattle's slim cinematic history.

Clark Humphrey *Loser* (Feral House, US & UK). The definitive account to date of Seattle rock, starting from its pre-rock origins in jazz/R&B, but focusing mainly on the punk and post-punk periods of the last twenty years.

Dave Marsh *Louie Louie* (Hyperion, US). This unusual biography of a song traces the way the garage rock anthem, "Louie Louie," went from an obscure R&B tune to the signature song of many Pacific Northwest bands, in often hilarious detail.

Murray Morgan *Skid Road* (University of Washington Press, US). This often anecdotal history of the city focuses on key people and incidents, to good effect.

Tina Oldknow *Pilchuck: A Glass School* (University of Washington Press, US). An illustrated history of the founding and evolution of the art institution that has had the most profound effect on art in Washington State over the last 25 years.

Roger Sale *Seattle: Past to Present* (University of Washington Press, US). A well-rounded history of the city, by the author of one of the specialist guides listed opposite.

William Speidel *Sons of the Profits* (Nettle Creek, US). Full of rich, humorous, bite-size facts and stories about the corruption rife among Seattle's founders between 1850 and 1900.

James R. Warren *Seattle: An Illustrated History* (American Historical Press, US). A coffee table hardback that mixes concise historical text with superb vintage photos and diverting sidebars on women's suffrage, black pioneers, and the like.

Biography and oral history

Walt Crowley *Rites of Passage* (University of Washington, US). Memoir of left-wing activism and counterculture in 1960s Seattle by the editor of an underground newspaper of the time, who went on to become one of the city's most renowned journalists. It's best when focusing on local historical events.

Paul de Barros *Jackson Street After Hours: The Roots of Jazz in Seattle* (Sasquatch, US). Initially a government-funded oral history project, this covers well the Seattle jazz scene from the 1930s through the 1950s, with great photos and illustrations.

Sandra Haarsager *Bertha Knight Landes of Seattle: Big-City Mayor* (University of Oklahoma Press, US). A straightforward, rigorously researched biography of the Seattle politician who in 1926 became the first woman mayor of a large US city.

Stephen Manes & Paul Andrews *Gates* (Touchstone, US). The most comprehensive biography to date of the Microsoft co-founder and richest man on the planet.

Travel and specialist guides

Theresa Morrow *Seattle Survival Guide* (Sasquatch, US). Entertainingly written resource guide to everything in Seattle, from neighborhoods to schools to entertainment – a cross between a phone book and travel guide.

Marge & Ted Mueller, *The San Juan Islands Afoot & Afloat* (The Mountaineers, US). Trails, parks, campgrounds, and water activities in the San Juans, by authors who have done similar guides to the North, Middle, and South Puget Sound areas.

Roger Sale *Seeing Seattle* (University of Washington Press, US). More than two hundred pages of suggested walking tours of the city by one of Seattle's leading historians, with some off-the-beaten-track routes and opinionated background.

Stephen R. Whitney *Nature Walks in and Around Seattle* (The Mountaineers, US). Guides to several dozen walks in parks, forests, and wetlands in Seattle and environs, from favorites like the Discovery Park loop trail to obscurities like West Hylebos Wetlands State Park.

Literature

Douglas Coupland *Microserfs* (HarperCollins/Flamingo).
Novel-as-journal that focuses on six Microsoft workers, who
also all live together, trying to make it in the shadow of Bill.

David Guterson *Snow Falling on Cedars* (Random
House/Bloomsbury). Well-regarded but sometimes long-
winded and repetitive tale of life (and death) on a rural Puget
Sound island.

Seattle on film

The first major movie shot on location in Seattle was *Tugboat
Annie* in 1933, but it was thirty years before the next, the
Elvis Presley vehicle *It Happened at the World's Fair*. With
Seattle's increased cachet and profile, shoots are commonplace
today, although the area is still probably better known for
hosting television series: *Twin Peaks* was set in Snoqualmie
Falls, 25 minutes away; *Northern Exposure* is shot in Roslyn,
seventy miles east; and the current hit *Frasier* is allegedly set in
Seattle, though aside from some cameo exterior shots, the
series is filmed in Los Angeles. The book *Seattle on Film* (see
p.291) is the best guide to the city's film history.

Films

Cinderella Liberty (Mark Rydell 1973). James Caan is a sailor
on leave, and Marsha Mason his love interest, in a film with
many location shots of a pregentrified, seedy 1st Avenue.
Look for the scene in which a real-life panhandler stumbles
onto the set and asks Caan for money; Caan stays in
character and gives him spare change.

Disclosure (Barry Levinson 1994). Hi-tech sexual harassment
thriller that pits Michael Douglas against Demi Moore in a
battle we'd like to see them both lose.

Dogfight (Nancy Savoca 1991). Shot on location in Seattle, which is somehow passed off as 1963 San Francisco in this offbeat film about an unlikely romance between a plain folksinger and a serviceman about to go to Vietnam (played by River Phoenix).

The Fabulous Baker Boys (Steve Kloves 1989). Mainstream hit starring Jeff and Beau Bridges as a fading lounge jazz act, and Michelle Pfeiffer as the new singer who drives a wedge between them.

House of Games (David Mamet 1987). This modern film noir, about a psychologist who gets drawn into a ring of con criminals, makes effective use of dark, gritty Seattle locations.

Hype (Doug Pray 1996). Witty documentary about the explosion of the Seattle alternative rock scene in the late 1980s and early 1990s that has interviews with most of the major musicians and scenesters and live footage of all the knowns and unknowns.

It Happened at the World's Fair (Norman Taurog 1963). Typically dispensable Elvis Presley film – flimsy plot, mediocre music, and a spectacular location, in this case Seattle's World's Fair.

Little Buddha (Bernardo Bertolucci 1994). Critically panned flick (perhaps Keanu Reeves as Siddhartha wasn't the best move) about a Seattle boy thought by local Tibetan monks to be the reincarnation of a lama. Less than half is set in Seattle, but Bertolucci wanted the city as a backdrop for its architecture and overcast light, in marked contrast to the scenes set in India.

The Parallax View (Alan Pakula 1974). Political thriller starring Warren Beatty as an investigative reporter determined to find the real killers of a high-ranking politician. Most of this doesn't take place in Seattle, but the opening sequence, an assassination at the top of the Space Needle, is dazzling.

Singles (Cameron Crowe 1992). Romantic, very early-Nineties look at young Seattleites living in a Capitol Hill apartment building, with cameos by members of Pearl Jam and Soundgarden. Crowe set his 1989 directorial debut, *Say Anything* (a mismatched high school romance between John Cusack and Ione Skye), in Seattle as well.

Sleepless in Seattle (Nora Ephron 1993). This sappy smash has a widowed Tom Hanks falling for reporter Meg Ryan, with help from his son and talk radio. Great location scenes, and a long comic exchange with Rob Reiner in Pike Place Market's *Athenian Inn*.

The Slender Thread (Sydney Pollack 1965). Little-seen drama inspired by the real-life activities of the Seattle Crisis Clinic. Sidney Poitier stars as a University of Washington psychology student dealing with an attempted suicide by Anne Bancroft.

Streetwise (Martin Bell 1985). This gritty documentary examines (some might say exploits) the lot of Seattle's homeless street kids, but it's not without its moments of tenderness and wit.

Trouble in Mind (Alan Rudolph 1985). Odd, arty film of murky crime schemes and romantic tangles that makes good use of the grayest aspects of Seattle (called "Rain City" in the movie).

Twice in a Lifetime (Bud Yorkin 1985). Gene Hackman plays the lead role in this low-key film about the breakup of a marriage in a working-class family, shot mostly in Ballard.

Twin Peaks: Fire Walk with Me (David Lynch 1992). A full-length, theatrically released "prequel" to the television series, *Fire Walk* was a big flop and something of an artistic disappointment as well, considering the director's background.

Wargames (John Badham 1983). Popular, mildly winning nuclear war fantasy set in Seattle, with Matthew Broderick as the teenage whiz-kid who almost starts an atomic holocaust.

SEATTLE ON FILM

INDEX

Stay in touch with us!

ROUGH*NEWS* is Rough Guides' free newsletter.
In three issues a year we give you news, travel issues, music reviews, readers' letters and the latest dispatches from authors on the road.

I would like to receive ROUGH*NEWS*: please put me on your free mailing list.

NAME . . . .

ADDRESS . . . .

Please clip or photocopy and send to: Rough Guides, 1 Mercer Street, London WC2H 9QJ, England

or Rough Guides, 375 Hudson Street, New York, NY 10014, USA.

Backpacking through **Europe**?

Cruising across the **US of A**?

Clubbing in **London**?

Trekking through **Costa Rica**?

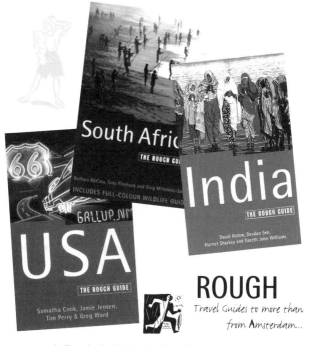

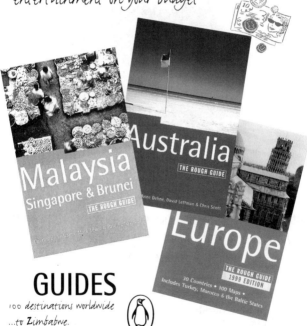

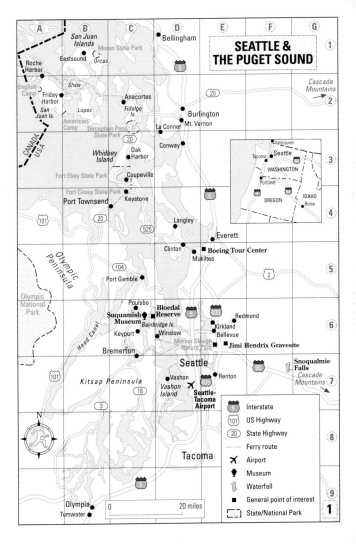

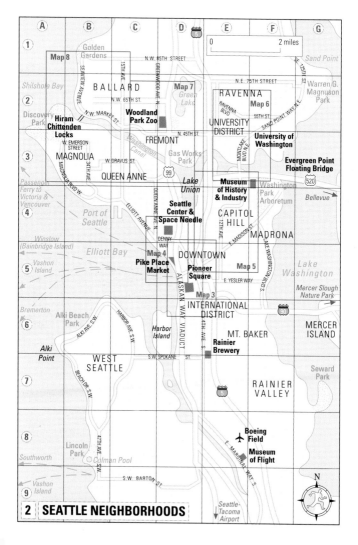

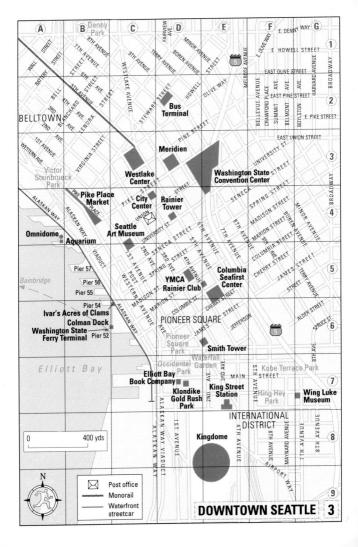

DOWNTOWN SEATTLE 3

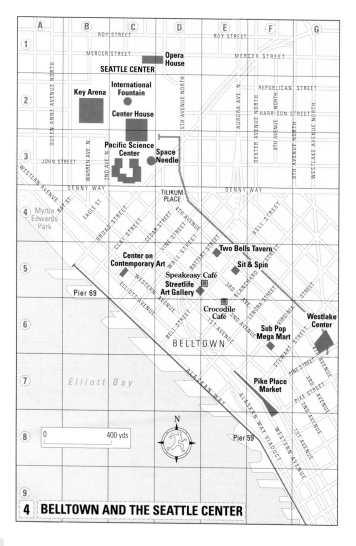

4 BELLTOWN AND THE SEATTLE CENTER

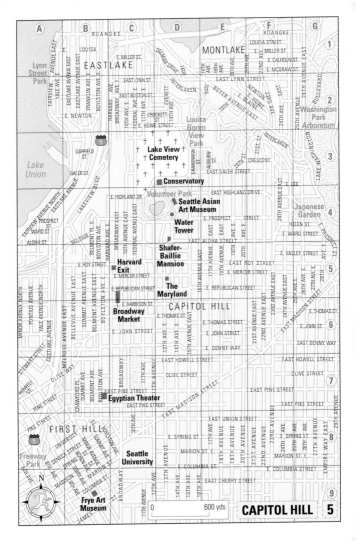

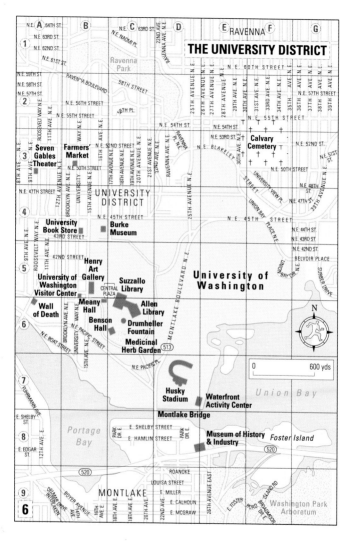

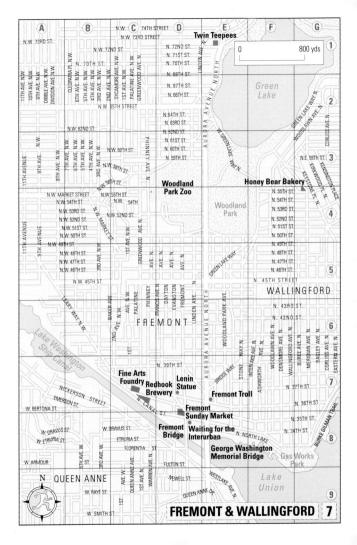

BALLARD & MAGNOLIA

Golden Gardens Park

N.W. 85TH STREET

N.W. 83RD STREET

N.W. 80TH STREET

N.W. 77TH STREET

N.W. 75TH STREET

N.W. 74TH ST.
N.W. 73RD ST.
N.W. 72ND ST.

Shilshole Bay

N

Shilshole Bay Marina

Nordic Heritage Museum

N.W. 73RD ST.

N.W. 70TH ST.

N.W. 67TH ST.

BALLARD

N.W. 66TH ST.

N.W. 65TH STREET
N.W. 64TH ST.
N.W. 63RD ST.
N.W. 62ND ST.
N.W. 61ST ST.
N.W. 60TH ST.
N.W. 59TH ST.
N.W. 58TH ST.
N.W. 57TH ST.
N.W. 58TH ST.

Hiram M. Chittenden Locks

W. CRAMER ST.

N.W. MARKET STREET

N.W. 54TH ST.
N.W. 53RD ST.
N.W. 52ND ST.
N.W. 51ST ST.
N.W. 50TH ST.

W. COMMODORE WAY

Commodore Park

Salmon Bay

N.W. LEARY WAY
N.W. BALLARD WAY
N.W. 46TH ST.

Discovery Park

Fort Lawton Military Cemetery
† †
† †

GILMAN AVE. W.

COMMODORE WAY

BALLARD BRIDGE

W. JAMESON ST.
W. MANSELL ST.
W. ELMORE ST.
W. THURMAN ST.

Visitor Center

Fisherman's Terminal

W. EMERSON ST.

RUFFNER ST.

W. BERTONA ST.

W. PROSPER ST.

MAGNOLIA

W. GROVER ST.

W. DRAVUS ST.

W. BARRETT ST.

PERKINS LANE W.
MAGNOLIA BLVD
44TH AVE. W.
43RD AVE. W.
42ND AVE. W.
VIEWMONT WAY

W. ARMOUR STREET

0   800 yds

8